And Meadows Was the Last: A Vietnam Reader

By David Trout Pomeroy

No lesson seems to be so deeply inculcated by the experience of life, as that you should never trust in experts.
Lord Salisbury

Dedicated to the memory of an American soldier whose name was
Meadows inspired by the bravery of more than three million other members of the military who served their country in Vietnam.

Books from David Trout Pomeroy

Oakland County: Making It Work in Michigan
Southfield: The Center of it All
Auburn Hills: A City is Born
One Brief Run
Swimming Downstream
Facing 50: An Essay on Aging
The (Lost) Art of Listening
Larceny of Letters: Breaking In as a Writer
Days Gone Bill
You Can't Blame the Dog
Addicted to Quack
Fish Out of Water

Table of Contents

Chapter Five – Recollections and Reflections

Introduction
On pragmatism and enlightenment…..

My introduction to this book began with a professional collaboration with the author, Dave Pomeroy. He had poured himself into this work about this event that shaped his generation and American culture. Through a series of exchanges, I discovered Dave's insight, integrity, sense of humor, and dedication to accurately portraying the time: qualities needed in spades when dealing with the Vietnam War. The war snatched 9.7% of the generation for battle and imprinted the rest with defining moments that either built or destroyed their character.

Besides my sister, I was the only kid in elementary school with a Vietnam Vet for a dad. My father married my mother while still in high school before he shipped off to "the service." Dad sometimes gave vague mentions to the service but rarely anything specific. As a kid, he once told me that the intense heat of the jungle made the rain droplets sizzle on his skin. Sizzling rain scurried me away with a great details to tell my politely uninterested third graders. I continued my scurry a few years later when my sister and I discovered a battered box of letters sent between our parents dad's time in the service. As nosy as we were, a "put it back" from my mother was sufficient to push them back into a corner. Still, later, we'd use his Army Service Jacket complete with sharpshooting insignia for dress-up and Halloween. We'd whisper conspiratorially amongst ourselves that our now loudly snoring dad used to be a sniper. Yet, the only things we knew for sure was that slim jacket fit us well, and it was never my turn to wear it.

Over the years the jacket went to the basement, and my dad went into retirement. Occasionally, he sports a Vietnam Veteran cap to block out the South Carolina sun, and gives pragmatic answers to my questions. My father's experience is but one of the many of those at the time. A soldier's perspective both proud of his service and aware of the complexities of the era. Everyone had their role to play in a time that shattered innocence and fostered cynicism. Still, it is an era forty years over our country's shoulder. An era still marked with as many questions and perspectives as people to ask them. Yet, the questions, the reflections, still deserve to examined with clarity and cooling of age.

What of those who did not physically go to Vietnam? The ones who stayed behind waging a fight of their own on American soil. Between the soldiers and the dodgers, the heroes and the heels, another strand existed- the war protestors. They answered a call to consciousness and followed their convictions at home to protest an unjust war. The young people who encountered the draft boards, the events at Kent State, the Pentagon Papers, The Wall, etc. from a place of restlessness and agitation. The protestors loved their country enough to hate its unjust actions and want the soldiers home.

What an undertaking. To approach such project with clarity and grace despite an entrenchment on all sides takes a measured approach that only time can give. This clarity made me not just excited, but profoundly interested in an alternate point of view. While the work may consist of one man's ruminations of a finite time, the implications with the greater context of the lost conflict weave a fascinating tale. As a nation, we will never fail to honor that 9.7% who served, and we will hold our government to task to ensure that future generations will not face similar fate.

Laurin Gracy-Parker

June 2016

Preface

And Meadows was the last.

The last soldier to die fighting under the command of U.S. Army Col. David Hackworth in the American War in Vietnam. Before him countless other Americans met their death under Hackworth's celebrated command—Deboer, Aguda, many others, many dead. Their names resonate poignantly today, more than forty years after the end of The American War in Vietnam. Behind every name was a face, a life a family, a destiny unfulfilled. Their sacrifices occurred randomly, anonymously in a wildly misunderstood country halfway across the world from the United States. Out of sight, out of mind.

Even as we assembled our ferocious might to go off to wage war in Vietnam, no one in America knew a damn thing about the place, its people, its history, its destiny. There may have been 12 people in America who could find it on a map. We were stone ignorant about other countries and proud of our empty-headedness. Americans took pride in being dumber than plankton about the world outside our own, while coloring our provincialism in shades of nationalist conceit.

As bad as that was, it was only the half of it.

Names meant nothing at the time. They mean everything today. As the war was *prosecuted*, the names of the American soldiers who were being killed in the war were seldom noted, certainly not in the media. People called "soldiers" were mere numbers in the larger script. The category "killed-in-action (KIA)" lacked a soldier's name, a soldier's face, defied anything resembling actual identity.

Throughout the mid-to-late 1960s, American casualties were noted strictly in the aggregate on Friday evening network TV newscasts. On a typical week during the middle of the war, we appeared to be maintaining about a ten-for-one advantage against the enemy as measured by alleged battlefield assessments; an announcer might cite 375 American deaths compared to a reported 3,320 enemy dead.

Hypothetical numbers, cited solely as an example.

The numbers are not exact, not now, not then. I made them up for the purpose of demonstrating the general range of enemy dead vs. American dead that was sold to TV viewers throughout the mid-to-late 1960's. Network news ruled during the course of the Vietnam War. Cultural conditioning in that pre-cable era assured the absence of a "buyer beware" mentality among the proletariat. If David Brinkley said it, Joe Six Pack believed it.

I felt my heart being crushed during this protracted period. I became so alienated during the war that I came to feel like an actual alien, a visitor from a different planet, exacerbated by a few hundred acid trips. Certainly I was not the only person to have this experience. There were millions of us.

To escape, we engaged in the kind of space flight that enables astronauts and others to vacate the restrictions of Planet Earth for a few glorious hours, strap on the earphones, put on a Beatles's tape, rise high above the disarray and wonderment, gaze down wistfully and be reminded of the significance of birth, life, death, space, eternity, existence, social progress, and love. After flight, we cooked dinner, got ready for work the next day, called up our parents on the phone, played some music, fed the cats, and tried to ignore the war if only for a minute.

I yearned for the night David Brinkley would say something more like, *"Among the American casualties this week was the following individual, Arthur Wilson, a Methodist boy, a gifted young scientist from Wichita, Kansas, killed by an enemy bullet while walking cautiously, as if not to disturb the plants, through a rice paddy on the edge of the purported enemy's village. Wilson leaves behind a grieving widow who will never-ever in a million years fully emerge from the chilly chasm created by his death; two children who will never know their father or benefit from his love and guidance and implicit goodness; two heartbroken parents, Jim and Pauline Wilson who gave every bit of themselves to raise a son worthy of the promise of his homeland; hundreds of friends left dazed, bewildered, depressed by his senseless death in a senseless war. Arthur possessed a gigantic spirit, heart and soul and an IQ measured in excess of 140. He was studying to be a researcher in the medical field when his country demanded he instead submit to propaganda-based brainwashing, become a solider go off to a distant country to engage in a pointless military adventure and die a painful, protracted death in a distant field, six thousand miles from his wife's side."*

Chet Huntley, David Brinkley, John Chancellor, Walter Cronkite, all the news anchors at the time adopted a different approach. Our losses were cited in statistical block form. It was code for obfuscation. We were lied to, distracted, exploited, slaughtered, ignored, run over, conscripted, and programmed to become killers, invaders, and Nazi caricatures.

Over the long haul, we got over it.

If our country has grown up at all in the last five decades, it would be safe to say that is a good thing. Incalculable perhaps. Would you as a contemporary American buy this premise: the enemy in Vietnam was sub-human, a "gook" in fact? Your forefathers in the 1960's accepted that as a plausible explanation for why we should feel no shame in killing them by the tens of thousands.

Diving deep into our Vietnam War years taught me this: I now know how little I actually knew then, or even know now. I know that in learning more through researching this work I've become less cocksure, more contemplative – a late-in-life gift from me to myself.

We knew very little as young people, when the demands of the war were thrust upon us, forcing us to decide what to do in a basic information vacuum. As older people now, we know the greatest of all life truths, and that is, *the more you know the more you know you don't know.*

It's why old people like me enjoy sitting around reading a good book, of which there are millions.

This book intends to teach … a bit, ideally to expand frame of reference. It is formed from the basis of elements of historic verity, insider accounts, longitudinal thinking and multiple layers of erudite consideration. In any event, what I have for the reader consists of random glimpses that I find to be vivid, revealing and worthy of inclusion. Giving birth to this collection of sentiment has been a singularly cathartic relief.

Enduring our Vietnam War was the epic event of my life. I was branded by my opposition; passions enflamed, bitterness engendered, lasting hostility engrained in the way I see myself, and the world around me. But, then, in 1976 Americans like me were engulfed in the cathartic bliss of The Bicentennial celebration, mere hours after we began to process the awful aftermath of our ambiguous adventure in Southeast Asia.

Our benevolent Bicentennial came just in the nick of time, for me and doubtless for an infinite number of others who had just spent way too many consecutive years categorically despising our government for anyone's good especially our own. You couldn't help but feel good about America in 1976; about being an American as this yearlong happy-fest proceeded through the towns and lives in our country. So much emphasis was placed on identifying the true core of our national spirit, anyone paying attention had to be moved by the auspiciousness of it all. Besides all of that, I think most people were fairly pleased that the long war in Vietnam was over, even as we appeared to have lost it.

Fifty-years later, my anger gone, the uncertainty remains.

For someone who had come to truly hate my country's ass in an unforgiving way, stepping back from that extremism was good for the soul, healthy for the brain, redemptive salvation for the heart. My sense of how it was at the time has been fortified by accounts I've heard or read in the intervening years: the impact of *the perceived disparity* between our losses and theirs was a dominant factor is sustaining the support of the American public.

Skepticism as we know it today had not yet entered our vernacular. America in 1965 was perilously naïve, unfathomably less aware than it is today, not to mention tomorrow. Viewers were not made aware of the names of those who died, from either side. We were pretty much a nation of fools and few if any of the fools had enough intellectual wherewithal to see outside our childish view of the world, featuring the USA as epicenter to all enlightenment and good.

On top of that, we were completely oblivious to the fact the enemy, regardless of the toll of the war on its troops, had zero quit in him. In fact, he was prepared to fight the U.S. to the last woman and child. After all, it was his country he was fighting for. No one told us this. Few bothered to ask. We assumed they would succumb to our superior firepower, technology.

We were wrong.

Meadows, Deboer, Aguda and nearly 56,000 other Americans died fighting for an uncertain cause in a war so controversial its ambiguity nearly tore the U.S. apart; a war whose aura of nagging historic uncertainty continues to kick around in the womb of our national spirit, like an apparition representing the essence of a lost soul, dead in body, but too troubled, not quite ready a spirit to ascend to the Afterlife.

Discord engendered by this less than popular military adventure ripped through our national life, dividing factions and families, pitting young vs. old, educated vs. blue collar, father vs. son. Lives were irrevocably changed mindsets altered forever, tribal alliances formed, marinated and solidified to this day. The average person impacted by the war as it was being fought ended up sticking with their beliefs, as average people are wont to do.

All of us who engaged in this discord are older now-ostensibly more mature, capable of greater diversity of thought, perhaps better equipped now with sufficient humility to admit we were wrong, or, accept we were right, perhaps not altogether right or wrong at the time.

I've traveled from completely convinced of the honor of the positions I adapted during the war to greater ambivalence now. My evolving sense of it all emerges primarily because of what I've learned in the last five decades, all of it influenced by the realization I've gained that what I do know is way less than what I *could* know.

Reading everything I could find in my personal files on the subject enlarged my sphere of awareness, rocked me in my chair a number of times.

Yes, your Honor, I began to question opinions that instructed my views in the past in an effort to provide readers in the future with an objective, comprehensive set of historic interpretation.

Odd to acknowledge, I found slipping into the center to be emotionally comforting, as if I'd been relieved of the burden of having to take a position on a subject I'd never fully understand. The older I become, the less inclined I am to proclaim anything resembling a definitive explanation. This mirrors the adage, the more you know the more you know you *don't* know, you know?

I do know this much: The more anyone learns about what actually happened to us in Vietnam, the more likely it will be that as students of history we'll come to more fully appreciate the controversial nature of that engagement. What once seemed certain can over time in an ever-expanding, dynamic mind be seen as more of a complex, open-ended, unfathomably complicated, Byzantine consideration.

I am proud to have been a war protester.

Yet, at this juncture, I only know all of us from a certain generation of young American men had to confront our obligation to fight in and possibly die in a war we sought to understand. Some went, some stayed home quietly, some stayed home in full protest mode. At certain intervals, reality required us to make a choice: answer the call, dodge the draft, avoid in quiet acquiescence, protest peacefully or take to the streets in full radical reaction, railing against an imperfect system. Little wonder many of us are locked into that timeframe, frozen in history in many respects, permanently obsessed with trying to make sense of what in the final analysis may have been a totally insensible adventure.

That final analysis matters.

It's important because this son of a bitch kicked our ass, as the grizzled G.I. said to the Mama San with the bomb, one kind of bomb or another.

It's important because so many of our brothers and sisters died in the cause. It is now morally perverse to ignore it in any way.

And it matters forever because America killed perhaps three million people we deemed our enemy in the process of pursuing what we regarded as something integral to our God-divined manifest destiny.

American veterans of the American War in Vietnam form bonds now. They wear the colors proudly proclaim their service on the hats they wear, the groups that sustain them, the pride they sustain from believing they served in virtue and honor. The bumper stickers on their vehicles proclaim their status for the rest of us to contemplate, respect, and take seriously.

I once remarked to my wife those of us who resisted the war, men of the exact same generation that served, do not enjoy the benefits of similar support mechanisms. No one issues hats to us that announce the fact we stood up in opposition to a disagreeable war.

"You weren't the type of people then who need to wear hats today," she said.

I believe she got it right.

No offense to those who reveal the lingering importance of their military background through messages on their cars, their hats, shirts, chests, sleeves, wherever. They bonded through their shared experiences in service to our country. They gained pride in their actions. Now they're a part of a large tribe of veterans who feel a deep sense of allegiance to the cause they fought for and the veterans' organizations that provide compassionate support.

As Aunt Jemima told Mother Wattles, "It's all good."

I will never question their character, goodness or heroism, not to begin to mention their adherence to the primacy of military responsibility in the name of retaining our American way of life. People of their ilk did what they felt they had to do.

Perhaps certain people of my ilk took a different path, no less admirable as seen against the intervening period of retrospection.

The greatest lesson of the American War in Vietnam may have been this -- all of us who were so immediately impacted by it gained insight from our experience. We learned the real truth that we all came at this from different angles, different places, different backgrounds, life stories, families, histories, legacies and multi-various other spheres of influence. We learned it was NEVER appropriate for any of us to say to any one else from our generation that they should not have done what they did during the war.

Any expression of judgment was flawed by lack of understanding of where any individual was coming from when the Vietnam War train came roaring down the tracks. None of us came at this thing from the same place. We had vastly dissimilar backgrounds despite being of similar age. I believe once most of us figured this out a great burden was lifted from our shoulders, ancient animosities slowly vanished as we came to first understand then fully embrace the dignified singularity and uniqueness of one another's place of entry into this most confusing historic period.

Chapter I
Thoughts on the American War in Vietnam

Agony has never made a society quit fighting, as far as I know. One wonders now where our leaders got the idea that mass torture would work to our advantage in Indochina. It never worked anywhere else. They got the idea from childish fiction, I think, and from a childish awe of torture ... But children believe that pain is an effective way of controlling people, which it isn't – except in a localized, short term sense. They believe that pain can change minds, which it can't.

As I approached my fiftieth birthday I had become more and more enraged and mystified by the idiot decisions made by my countrymen. And then I had come suddenly to pity them, for I understood how innocent and natural it was for them to behave so abominably, and with such abominable results: They were doing their best to live like people invented in story books.

Kurt Vonnegut

In the years following the certain conclusion of the American War in Vietnam an *uncertain* consensus persisted, clouding the question of whether our actions were justifiable.

Many observers continued to argue we never should have gone to this war. Large numbers of other equally informed parties maintained our policies were rational, correct, fully appropriate, that we should and could have won the war had we stayed the course, or kept the politicians out of the decision-making mix.

The passage of time did little to calm the waters of disagreement. Both versions of history remained central within the vernacular of Vietnam.

Eventually something resembling a centrist interpretation began to manifest.

Decades after we left old Saigon, a semblance of an apparent majority of commenting observers appeared to conclude: the entire military adventure had been ill advised, mismanaged was generally a colossal mistake of horrifying proportion.

Yet "the majority" was only "apparent" to those perceiving it that way. Not everyone concluded "the entire" war was a "colossal mistake."

These words appear on the page in context. They're accessible to me. They strike me as accurate.

But I'm also closing in on Geezer'ville now, enveloped in what I have come to regard as empirical discipline.

According to my current way of thinking, *some semblance of an apparent majority* a minority doth make. Historians worth their salt would condemn such a shaky formulation, choosing instead to conclude there is no conclusion.

So what if – as a hypothetic model – say, 75-percent of board-certified students of the war now agree it was a bad idea?

And if 25-percent say we went for the right reasons and accomplished something positive in the process?

Who among us is sufficiently enlightened, fully endowed in historical verity to be able to say which group has it right and which group has it wrong?

Nope, none among us is equipped to issue a binding verdict on this nasty persistent conundrum of historic consequence.

There is no ultimate authority figure on this chapter.

The arguments can and will go on forever.

In the meantime, reasonable minds have more important work to do.

It's "on us" now to examine those elements of factual history that exist and identify mutually acceptable lessons to draw on going forward.

The time to kick around the "how's" and "why's" of good old *"Veet Nom"* is running out of the hourglass. We've engaged that national conversation long enough. Now comes the instructive part, wherein enlightenment converts into enlightened behavior.

Reasonable minds can disagree on the whole mix of studied opinion regarding whether or not we should have gone to Vietnam beginning with the period immediately following the end of World War II.

Also subject to controversy is the question of *how* we went to war there, how long we should have stayed, how it all played out.

It was dicey then and is equally perilous today, a confounding subject of historic retrospection.

Positing opinion of any kind, as I see it now, is risky behavior, no small gesture of intellectual arrogance really, a foolish fit of pomposity wrapped in pseuto psychobabble. I spent most of my career as a hack writer cranking out papers, poems and random pap, freelancing forever, working for peanuts as a newspaper reporter/columnist, writing books, magazine articles surviving many decades as a creative director in the automotive training industry. By now so much of my prose has been knocked-back at me I'm reluctant to evoke any assertion other than, *"Scuze me."*

A nervous shudder rides up my spine when I break out ostensibly definitive word choices like "accurate," "horrifying" and – most of all – "justifiable."

For the life of me I can no longer justify *justifiable*, I just can't.

What I *can* say without hesitation is this: the question of whether we could or should have prevailed in our war in Vietnam remains solidly unanswered five decades later.

As the years roll by, clarity on the subject continues to elude those seeking to visit evaluation on the matter.

The real truth after the war went pretty much as follows: Any so-called consensus was not only uncertain, it did not exist.

Nor does it today. Such an assertion remains shrouded in subjectivity.

Others have analyzed the same basic data that I've tried to include. Many have come up with entirely opposite interpretations.

Others have written books on The Vietnam War, reaching divergent conclusions, often drawing on their own first-hand participation in the war or what ever other roles they played at the time.

Their thoughts on the subject deserve attention. Even the positions I present are worthy of consideration as they derive from close proximity to the subject, both personal and professional. Like so many others now determined to write about our Vietnam War episode, I was there. But the "there" I inhabited back then was entirely subjective.

My life transpired in an unsophisticated dimension of existence. Not only did I NOT go to Vietnam, I managed to essentially bypass the entire military experience.

In this case, I always felt that you didn't need to go there to be there. Not entirely at least.

It's all ancient history by now. We are talking 50 years ago about a very young man whose grasp of global reality was, expressed charitably, feeble at best.

I not only did not know Jack Shit, I didn't know his wife Mrs. Shit either.

Alas, isn't that how it goes? We do a much better job of figuring out our lives decades after much of that life has occurred than we do in actual context.

Young or old when the gig went down, the American War in Vietnam rocked our world. Not a one of us who lived through the daily nightmare of that 10-year descent into darkness was capable then, or now, of visiting historically valid evaluation. We were like the ice cubes and drink mix in the bartender's mixer, getting constantly *all shook up*.

Even as the weight of historical consensus now suggests our mission in Vietnam was deeply flawed in its entirety, circumspect thinkers continue to step back, ever willing to analyze the evidence.

The subject itself was always too complex to justify a simple assessment, especially from essential nitwits like me who avoided conscription when the deal was going down, let alone everybody else.

Fifty years following the conclusion of our adventure, I now look back on my opposition and see it was youthful, idealistic and mostly borne of the larger reality of my own exposure to the draft, the war, the entire agenda of our government.

I came from a generation that was instructed to go off to fight in this crusade. Ours was to either answer the call or figure out a way to finesse the system and avoid service. I'm still struck by how abjectly this war interceded in our shared ascent. Even more so, I remain in permanent awe of the bravery and character of so many other people of my age, from veterans of the war to veterans of the protest movements here at home.

I'm about to spill my guts on the subject, shine light on what it was like to oppose the war, survive the shattering reality of Kent State, move on from there dedicated to the challenge of imparting lessons learned.

What I offer is merely one man's account. Other men have other stories. If they went off to engage in this war whatever they can now share looms considerably larger than anything I may bring to the table.

They're the real keepers of this tale. They deserve more respect than I'd ever feel entitled to receive. Their voices meet the quality test.

I hear them, visualize their experiences honor them forever.

My Vietnam Experience

Many moons after the last G.I. beat it the hell out of downtown Saigon, diverse interpretations of "what happened to us" in Vietnam continue to permeate the discussion.

In the absence of consensus, disagreement over our role in Vietnam is as rampant today as it was throughout the war. One narrative makes the most sense to me now.

It says our war in Vietnam was cruel folly, an excursion into the depths of pointless horror.

As strongly as I feel today, I'm also significantly more in tune with divergent perspectives than I was during the time of the conflict.

During the years I attended college – 1963-68 – none of this had occurred to me. For most of that time, our war in Vietnam was out of the headlines and deep in the back of most people's minds.

Age-qualified individuals knew we were in the crosshairs of The Draft, that great equalizer. As long as we stayed matriculated at an accredited institution of higher learning, we were able to largely ignore the details of the war and focus instead of earning grades sufficient to remain enrolled at one school or another.

As someone who earned rather dismal grades in classes attended at a number of colleges and universities over a number of years, I was among those whose complete attention was on sustaining winning relationships with as many college registrars as possible.

Millions of us, I suppose, danced in this ballet in order to gain the compliance of key administrators in our less-than-proud scheme to keep the government aware of our status as students in good (?) standing.

Only after I received a bachelor's degree in '68 and entered the work force as a practitioner of political public relations did I begin to engage the topic. Vietnam as a force to be reckoned with edged more closely into the bullseye of emerging perspectives. At the same time, mainstream America was engaged in a similar process. A massive awakening began taking place as average citizens started paying much more attention to the war, sorting out the evidence, many of them concluding the war lacked basic rationale.

Later that summer as I worked as an advanceman on a U.S. Senate campaign in Ohio, television cameras captured dramatic images of student protesters fighting with police in the streets of Chicago as The Democratic Party staged its convention.

I sat on a bed in my motel room watching network news coverage. My entire political orientation changed as I saw beefy Chicago cops wail upon the heads and upper torsos of war protestors, who happened to be people of my age group, young then, old now.

It was a transcendent moment, for the nation, my generation and myself.

I did a complete "180," went from neutral to fully oppositional to the war before the next commercial break began.

Shortly thereafter, concern about the war took over my entire disposition.

I bought fully into the notion that the excursion into Southeast Asia undertaken by our federal military apparatus was, as I believe it is now, generally assessed, a monumental disaster.

As it turns out, even if that thinking prevailed in the minds of many of my ilk in the aftermath of the decade of war, it didn't last forever. It eventually gave way to larger ambiguity.

The mere passage of time began to whittle away at whatever shared historical consensus may have existed about the "why's" and "how's" of the Vietnam War. That erosion was compounded by studied revisionist efforts promulgated by many of the original architects of the war. Evoking "revisionism" requires a level of erudition to which I don't easily aspire. It's a term that amateur analysts break out casually, as if they know what they're talking about, which most of them (us) don't.

Several notches south of brilliant, I see myself as a merchant of rhetoric, conveyer of stories, accounts, fragments of history, all intellectually restricted by limited empirical reach.

I perceive the word "revisionism" for what it is in the context of the chamber of mush that is my now-elderly brain – utter ambiguity.

Many millions of young American men of my generation experienced our war in Vietnam in many millions of different ways.

More than 10 million served in our military during our Vietnam War years, about one-third deployed to Southeast Asia; perhaps ten times that many did not serve. We were and remain the extremely bloated post-World War II generation, by and large. There were a whole lot of us.

My walk through this historic interlude was incidental, largely unnoted and certainly of no consequence as seen within the greater complexity of the period.

All that differentiates me from anyone else my age is the impulse to write about it.

It derives not from obligation to inform the masses but from my own need to rinse the residue of the Vietnam experience from my core.

It needs a bath.

I was so consumed with the enormity of the struggle that I, and so many others engaged in trying to stop the war should probably take our soiled impulses to the dry cleaners.

Studied revisionism. The brain warns: tread carefully when stringing those words together.

I long believed it was predictable that the patriot-militarists who took us to this God-awful war would cling to their initial mindset. It was fairly predictable they would adhere to their core reasoning for as long as any of their voices could be heard.

It wasn't hard to figure them out, especially because so much of what they believed in made almost perfect sense. The prevailing rationale for this war – as it was presented -- was to oppose communism. It didn't take a lot of intellect to identify its evils.

Totalitarianism had been defeated in World War II, according to the history books we read. No wonder that most Americans got riled up when anyone suggested that the war in Vietnam was the next inevitable chapter in our eternal struggle with evil.

Communism and totalitarianism were equally bad news in the average American mindset, circa-1965.

As understood both represented pretty much the same diabolical brand of tyranny, similar contempt for our sense of freedom, justice and liberty for all.

Against the backdrop of The Cold War, within the calculus of looming nuclear annihilation and apocalypse, knowing both we, and the Russians could blow one another to smithereens at any second …nimble minds tried to sort all of this out.

If Vietnam were to be the setting of the final showdown between communism and The West, how would that matter be settled?

Was Vietnam to be the end?

We hoped not, "we" being tomorrow's leaders in yesterday's blue jeans.

In doing so, we looked for ways to engage the Soviets without igniting Planet Earth.

Desiring to avoid nuclear holocaust, we became committed to finding pragmatic methods for both ideologies to coexist so as not to fully eviscerate this fine floating rock in space that gives everyone life.

Contemplating truth, half-truth, fragments of truth, ideology, jingoism and multi-cultural ennui we envisioned accommodation, not as some form of compliant capitulation to a greater force, but as our last best sane measure to ensure the perpetuity of our species.

So it was I saw our agents of war as sinister, wrong, borderline diabolical.

These persuasive entities struggled mightily to continually "rewrite" the history books on whether Vietnam was a disaster, or a noble mission to the extent any such commonly endorsed books exist.

In fact, no honest postmortem on our Vietnam War has appeared since the war's end many years ago.

President Ronald Reagan called it "a noble war." The late Army Col. David Hackworth wrote, "The whitewash has flowed fast from Army brushes to cover the more ignoble truth."

Perhaps a larger consideration would be, there is not now, nor will there ever be a conclusive, inarguable "history book" on this subject.

Yet few disagreed the sheer enormity of the Vietnam War throughout the 1960's consumed American society. It took over people's consciousness, occupied every crevice of being, reshuffled the deck of the heart, soul and mind. Interpretation varied in a complicated world, where Conservatives and Liberals ascribe to respective conflicting sources of fact and truth.

The concept of any established centrist based actuality evaporated quickly in the polarization of an oxygen-deprived vacuum wherein true ideologues clash permanently, ever-short of recognizing the core commonality that unites them.

Like all other matters of historic importance, no person, institution or governmental entity of any kind ever proclaimed official judgement. The question of whether or not we won or lost our war in Vietnam remained unanswered, both in the years immediately after its conclusion and into the open-ended vortex of time immemorial.

In spite of the lingering impasse, this to me is certain: it doesn't really matter now, this question of who won or who lost. It's like arguing evolution vs. creationism. What difference does it make?

The only lingering "truthes" to come out of our military experiences in Southeast Asia now have everything to do with edification and guidance. Too much nasty shit went down in 'Nam to ignore whatever lessons or insights we can derive from attempting to study the episode.

Among those of us that were alive and attentive at the time -- there in whatever manner – a prevailing sense of obligation resides in our shared conscience.

A definite moral imperative drives my impulse to forever pick and probe at this topic. Its impact on so many of us remains germane a subject of permanence.

Thus quite certainly it's on us now to continue to search for what seems true, to gain an objective understanding of what we should have taken away from this all-consuming incursion into the culture and environment of a foreign land.

People whose lives were directly impacted by the terms of the adventure owe it to others to share with them what we think we learned, during the war and thereafter.

Actual expertise is not required to pretend to be informed on this topic. Anyone with a word processor and a willingness to park his or her ass in a chair long enough to spill some ink on the subject can become a subject expert, small "s," small "e."

Internet self-publishing has taken this amateur art form into new egalitarian galaxies of possibility.

High school flunkouts like me now have the capacity to posture as valedictorians. Riding the rocket ship that is a personal computer we can flaunt our willingness to spend the days of our lives in front of modern-day typewriters, recasting thoughts of others embellished within our own opinions.

Aware of the relative limitations of my own perspectives, I've co-opted what I regard as relevant words from sources significantly better informed than I am, today, yesterday forever.

I proceed confidently knowing their agendas were pure and accurate in intention.

A Long Shadow

Few would have imagined America in subsequent years quickly forgetting the sheer impact the war had on us. All of the hard-earned wisdom we thought we had acquired seemed sufficient at the time to discourage similarly errant foreign policy decision-making.

The mere idea of America once again venturing into another pointless intervention in some distant misunderstood country was barely remote.

Few would have thought we would soon be foolish enough to entertain the likelihood of us believing we could take up arms and go off to make a positive difference in any conflict.

The very notion seemed entirely unlikely -- well off the probability charts.

Then came September 11, 2001.

Sadly, what we learn from history is that we fail to learn from history.

We also learn history is both science and art, that what you see is ultimately a byproduct of how you see it.

My statement to those who follow in the time continuum is that I believe the war we fought in Vietnam was abjectly evil -- disastrous for all involved.

I'll be satisfied if the thoughts I share play any role in helping to avert similar bull-headedness, even more uplifted if any light shone from my take helps reduce the likelihood of similar dimensions of poor decision-making from driving national policies again.

My Vietnam experience taught me government is perfectly willing to lie to me, leading me to further deduce they will lie to your ass just as easily.

Because being deceived created considerable hurt in my life, I decided to do whatever I could to help eliminate the possibility of that ever happening again.

It was a grandiose proposition, derived from a tumultuous time. I promised myself then to say this to you now:

Beware of government subterfuge.

Stated otherwise, don't let the bastards lie to you.

They will lie to you. We weren't always clear on that. We are now. They will lay waste to truth.

Please be skeptical consumers of platitude. Be wary as a calf in a slaughterhouse of everything you are told. Trust no one, not me for sure.

The world is less than fully reticent to lie to you.

Be aware; people are driven by self-interest. No one cares about you except, if you're lucky, your Mother, on a good day.

We didn't always know this. The Vietnam War taught it to us.

Government – any government – will try to sell you a bill of goods if they see doing so as being within their self-interest, but certainly not within yours.

If they need millions of soldiers to take up arms in a conflict they deem worthy of your potential sacrifice, they will tell you whatever you need to hear to gain your commitment.

If the methodology utilized to determine worthiness of conflict appears blatantly flawed, or less than suffosed in pure moral purity or whatever, hey, what the heck, man? These things will happen, much as they always have.

Weapons need wars. Wars need excuses. There isn't a whole lot else to say about the matter.

The problem as Vietnam War protestors found out is that any policy any government deems worthy of asking you to give your life for may or may not necessarily pass the value test.

Faulty foreign policy has a nasty way of denigrating good intention.

"Good" German soldiers were ordered to turn on the gas in concentration camps during World War II.

You will be hard-pressed to find any historical accounts of any of those prison guards rising up to protest against the instructions they obeyed.

Similarly, you may choose to factor in the Nazi experience to your understanding of how any of our own soldiers could gain the capacity to assault a Vietnamese village and slaughter its women and children.

In the long march of history, these uniformed cadres march shoulder to shoulder.

Weapons need wars. Wars need excuses.

Because they need your body and brain to fulfill their chosen mandate, they'll tell you that invading and occupying someone else's country is virtuous activity.

They will tell you to ignore your instincts and believe their instincts instead.

Please remind them your brain still works.

They won't like that.

But your brain does work and it happens to be your main asset in your quest to survive.

Clarifying Charley

Picture millions of guys named Charley.

This handle worked well as an all-purpose name for anyone representing the North Vietnamese, as opposed to the South Vietnamese. Even protestors stateside knew what it meant.

Those serving in the war knew it even better. They walked the walk. If a Charley showed up in the sites of their rifles, they fired, without hesitation, assumable.

Many of us who chose not to go made decisions based on self awareness, knowing we didn't want to put ourselves in a position where we would have to pull that trigger on the government's premise the person we were about to kill deserved to die, for his country, for what he believed in. We assumed Charlie's theology to be nationalism. It seemed correct to us to let him live, all other things being equal, of course.

Letting the bullet sail was accepting the premise that the target needed to die and you needed to be the one to affect such demise.

Plus, if you didn't shoot him, he'd shoot you.

He might have found himself with you in his sites. Would he have pulled the trigger? Well, it WAS his country and you were an invader from some faraway place called Jersey. You could bank on him doing it.

The great question of whether any American kid was justified in accepting our government's idea that getting on a troop plane for Vietnam to participate in the killing hasn't gone away, even if the conflict did. It has not gone away, nor should it. Ever.

Too many people died in Vietnam for any of us to take it lightly, not in our lifetimes. If we don't probe this thing forever, seeking answers to help clarify what happened, we will do a huge disservice to those who fought, those who died, those who came back, those who are with us now.

Was Charley asking for it?

Was this ever a case of good vs. evil, right vs. wrong, humane ideas vs. inhumane ideas?

We owe it to ourselves, to our veterans in hospitals with their legs blown off, to figure this out, while we still have our senses about us, assuming we ever did.

I met an American Vietnam War vet at a car dealership in California. He told me the North Vietnamese regulars were total riff-raff, bottom-barrel losers from Vietnamese society, unlike the South Vietnamese, whom he said exuded greater sophistication.

This distinction enabled this individual from Pasadena to continue to justify his role in the American military effort.

I found his story incredible less than persuasive.

The propaganda mill in America provided considerable rationale for young recruits who wondered why they should go ahead and do what they were trained to do, and that is, kill the enemy in Vietnam.

The big myth, the myth that overcame most logical skepticism, was that life really didn't mean as much to Asians as it does to us Americans, who are, presumably, farther along the evolutionary trail on this issue.

Because life did not mean as much to them as it does to us, killing them was less onerous than, say, killing someone from Kansas.

Most Americans were as dense as molasses at the time. Which was why the average person bought this rationale. It worked well for millions of American soldiers who took the tour they were asked to take, many with great dignity, all with courage that defies comprehension.

There were other myths to buy into.

The so-called "Domino Theory" swayed millions of myopic minds.

It later proved to be pure mythology but at the time it made compelling sense to the citizens of a country that had no international awareness whatsoever, let alone any appreciation for the specifics of the various cultures and nations of this world.

For anyone who has played dominos, the theory is pretty simple.

You stack a bunch of dominos in a line, and tip the first one over.

If you stack them perfectly, you can create a sequence of singular impacts that ultimately leave every domino flat on its ass.

Got that?

Most Americans did.

They understood that if we didn't stop the North Vietnamese in their own country, creepy, craven American-hating Charley guys would inevitably be streaming on shore in Crescent City.

The dust has supposedly settled on this matter even as many continue to believe the Domino Theory WAS correct, that our intervention in Vietnam did make a positive difference and that even though Charley didn't make it to northern California (yet) he didn't make it to Guam either, because of our military presence in the region, however temporary.

There you have more evidence of the unresolved historical verdict on Vietnam, from the passionate views of those with skin in the game.

The violation meter in my intellect goes aflutter when I approach alleged certainty. Nothing seems firm any more. It's all fluid, suppositional.

Regarding my opposition to the war I am longer sure that what I did was right.

Maybe there was something to the Domino Theory.

Maybe Charley did deserve to die.

The further we get away from that experience, the less certain I am of any of the things I did to protest the war.

Close friends suggested I sought not to go for fear of being killed. They may have been right. If anything, I am a lot more open to all possibilities now than I was then.

I only know any of us of military age from that period were forced by reality to make a stand.

Three basic positions were available. We either went, we stayed home quietly, or we stayed home and protested.

Time didn't wait for any of us. We had to make a choice.

Years later the only thing that matters to me is to thank those who served *and* those who protested for sincere reasons.

I'm A-OK with anyone who showed up spoke up put his ass on the line. Conversely, I really don't have a lot of respect for anyone who stayed home and kept his mouth shut.

I resent a former president for not coming clean to the American people about what he did at the time and why he did it.

His decision to obscure the matter remains a permanent insult to the real people who matter, all these years later.

They are the survivors, family members of men and women who died and veterans who came back, to whatever kind of life they found at home.

If you are the son or daughter of an American or a Vietnamese citizen who died in the war, or a parent, still here with us, know how entirely considerate someone like me is to your emotional and spiritual wellness.

It's easy to say the following: Your loved one did not die or become injured in vain. Rather, their courage and commitment to accept their country's call looms ever larger now for all of us, former soldiers and former protestors alike united now in mutual understanding, alive in a world where opportunities for heroics seem hard to come by, tough to identify, difficult to act upon.

Harder than saying that was accepting the call, boarding the troop ship, taking up arms, stepping forth in battle for the many virtues embodied in our long national narrative putting it all on the line for freedom, liberty and an unquestionably "exceptional" America.

Then and now, people believed in the God-endowed virtues exemplified in the American experience. They willingly endorsed the notion our country among all others is a singular beacon of diversity and cultural wonderment. Verity or myth, I see little wrong with their interpretations. I maintain reasonable expectations of my fellow citizens.

If your father died in the Vietnam War, if your brother didn't come back, if your uncle returned without a leg, if you were among the millions of us who had your hearts broken in infinite ways, you have earned the gratitude of all caring souls.

We perceive a living war, one without end. Because it happened it is still happening.

For us to ever stop talking about the American War in Vietnam is morally reprehensible.

We're still here. We haven't forgotten.

The saddest thing I ever saw – BY FAR -- was a group of about 15 family members saying goodbye to their son, brother, husband at the Pittsburgh airport one entirely unforgettable evening in 1967.

I knew I had never seen such a magnificent stud of a young man.

He was taller than an outdoor totem pole, cast a bold persona, re-defined regal dignity stood in our midst with remarkable poise, grace and physical magnificence. I wondered if I had entered an alternative universe, where larger-than-life presences dominated.

He was a veritable Adonis, magnificent like an all-pro NFL wide receiver, smiling non-stop, striking, serene adorned in uniform, medals and stature.

I watched the solider and his large entourage hovering about from a vantage point of 20-ft. away.

What I saw I still see, a sight that has seared a permanent picture in my mind. It could just as easily happened two seconds ago.

Everyone in our proximity pretty much understood that this brave young man was in the process of putting himself in harm's way, big time. He wasn't going to Disneyland. Implicit in the moment was the near certainty that he was on his way to war and quite likely would not come back, alive or intact. And off he went.

They were all the way to the airport he wasn't going to turn around now. No.

He was going to squeeze his kids for forever, kiss his wife and mother good-bye another 20 times or so and board the jet.

Any of us from that era who are still here need to focus on that moment, or any other that gets the job done. The task requires an open mind, an open heart a soul that works.

We better be damn sure we know what we are doing if and when we as a country ask our young to take on the burden of war and death again.

Our cause better be rock solid so that no one among us will ever again need to question the sacrifice of our young, and that of the alleged enemy.

Hearts were broken that afternoon in Pittsburgh, mine included.

The Class of 1963

Members of The Class of 1963 had been out of high school for several years by the time the protest movement revved up.

Those of us who chose college rather than war, prison or Canada, had milked our deferments as long as possible.

We had entered either grad school or the working world.

No longer could a friendly university registrar protect our civilian status. They helped hide us as long as we maintained passing grades and/or as long as they could extract tuition payments from our wealthy parents.

By 1968 most of us had amassed so many credit hours they had to throw us out of our dormitories before we adapted permanent residence.

College for us, like it or not, was over.

Hence we were fair game for a draft mechanism designed to suck up every young adult male in the country.

We left high school with few choices. A few years later, we left college with one less.

We stared Vietnam straight in its distant geographic self as options diminished, in number and appeal.

By 1969 there was no more margin for dallying around. The war wanted everyone. If you didn't want the war you had to get very creative now.

Millions of us began scrambling defining our positions. Doing so had become imperative. You were either in on this deal or you weren't. Fence sitting had become abjectly perilous.

My draft notice arrived in the mail at my parents' house in early 1969, about half-a-year after I graduated from college.

A year earlier, as a fifth-year senior, I spent three months studying international relations as well as women from California at a university in Mexico. Upon returning from that experience, I became ill with a liver disorder that was attributed to drinking bad water while living and traveling south of the border.

The bug knocked me off my feet for a few months, gave me a chance to catch up on my sleep, read a few hundred interesting magazines and begin to plan my future.

Somehow during this phase I do not recall worrying about getting drafted. For whatever unknown reason, I assumed because I'd been protected during so many years in college that they would forget about me.

This was worse than delusional thinking. Clearly I wasn't counting all the cookies in the jar.

I cannot for the life of me figure out how I swept this matter under the rug and just went about my business as if the draft no longer existed. I must have been crazy.

Half a year had past since I lost my deferment but those bad boys were not about to lose track of me, not for long.

I was in San Diego when the draft notice arrived. I had pulled in there in my MG-B that same day after spending more than a month driving across country from Detroit.

My father dropped the bomb on me on the phone.

"Are you sitting down?" he asked me.

He must have loved that. I was sitting down, soon to lie down.

"Your draft notice arrived in today's mail." At first I hoped he was kidding me. Then I remembered he really didn't have a sense of humor.

Once I learned I hadn't miraculously fallen through the cracks of the conscription process, my attention to the matter became fully focused.

I knew I would never go to war but would always cooperate with the draft board. And that would require turning around, retracing my steps and placing myself in a position where I could deal with the matter in an acceptable way.

After spending a few months hitchhiking around Mexico and the West, I bottomed out on the road, had my possessions taken from me, experimented with ancient Mayan ritualism and lost the outer edge of my rich suburban kid veneer.

I didn't get to stay in California, though, thereby missing out on being at The Troubadour as the folk-rock movement germinated in Los Angeles. Compared with having to go to Vietnam, that was no big deal.

I returned to the fine breezes of the Great Lakes region to resolve my military obligation one way or the other, hoping it would be the other.

As a hedge against the likelihood of being drafted, I agreed to accept a position as a field counselor at my alma mater in West Virginia; implicit in the arrangement was the promise the college would notify my draft board that because the school was located in Appalachia, my position there would qualify as draft deferrable. We never put that to the test.

Back in Michigan, I found out blood test results from that time indicated my health had been somewhat compromised by the hepatitis that laid siege to my once-robust ability to bend over and tie my shoes.

Four months after receiving the notice I took my medical records with me on a visit to the local draft board, in my case in Pontiac, Michigan.

I asked for and was granted a moment with the top official, the infamous Mary Kelly whose name appeared in bold print on all of our draft cards.

Sitting across from Ms. Kelly, armed with the confidence only a fresh haircut can offer, I told her I had come to Michigan from California in order to confront my draft requirement directly.

I was then and remain today immaculately polite.

I knew this woman was the constant recipient of considerable animosity from many of my peers who approached their Selective Service obligation with disdain. My instinct was to proceed with courtesy and respect. I treated her with kindness, deferring to her authority acknowledging her burden.

It seemed to resonate.

When I told her I wanted to ascertain whether my medical history would have any bearing on my draft status, she decided to directly route me to the office of the chief medical examiner for our local draft board.

To the extent I understand any of this, I believe her gesture was unprecedented, uncalled for and of possible religious significance.

She called on the telephone asking him if I could come over immediately and show the esteemed gentleman my paperwork.

The timing was apparently perfect; he had a few open minutes before lunch on his calendar.

I wasted little time walking the three blocks between their respective offices. I did make a point not to step on any lines between the concrete sidewalk sections, hoping to lessen any jinx that would follow such indiscretion.

I found the doctor in the splendor of his personal office adorned with oak paneling, bookshelves and other comfortable dining room furniture.

He was aged and dignified a Col. Sanders look-alike with a friendly smile. His office exuded considerable tastefulness.

Acknowledging the many artifacts on display, I inquired whether a certain framed photograph of a half-dozen young people contained images of his children.

Bingo!

One question led to a dozen or so soliloquies from this erudite physician detailing whom the various people were in all the photos on display.

The man seemed to revel in the pleasure of telling me about his wonderful sons and daughters, their careers, present-day lives, plans for the future – "too much information" as it later became known.

Minutes ticked by as I soaked up his rhetoric with avidity, the skills of a born listener put to the ultimate test, my very draft status completely on the line.

I'd spent several years doing everything imaginable to remain a civilian. And now this one elderly man dressed in doctor's whites had my entire fate in his hands, or, in a file on his desk.

Nearly half-an-hour passed before he stop talking long enough to realize I'd come to his office for a reason other than to learn about his adult children.

He needed to review my blood test results.

First he needed to sit down and put on his glasses.

In a comparative instant, he lifted his head from the documents and shared this weighty summation: "The Army doesn't want you, Dave."

Oh Jesus, no kidding doctor, I was tempted to say.

Instead I sat there in a peaceful state.

I was lucky enough to be the "Dave" he was talking to. Of course it had been more than luck that delivered my white boy ass from a motel room in San Diego all the way back to this man's office in Pontiac.

I'd created that opportunity out of dedication to the proposition of avoiding the draft while also honoring my family's name by not ignoring that draft, only finessing it. I walked out of the building feeling a combination of guilt and relief.

Shortly thereafter I received in the mail a new draft card with a designation that implied I would be called to duty only after women, children, felons, derelicts and people lacking happy trigger fingers were called, certainly not in the following week.

Years of assiduous draft avoidance had finally delivered me to freedom.

I had toughed out several colleges, survived a nasty but not life threatening disease and now I'd gained my reward – all the options I'd never had.

One day in Heaven I hope to meet Dr. Christie.

Until then, I am meeting him again today as I type.

Hi sir. Do you remember me? I remember you.

A Skeptical Inclination

Weapons need wars. Wars need excuses.

Ancient idiom

In the 1960s, young American men had four choices.

1. War
2. College
3. Prison
4. Canada

This particular item strikes me as somewhat remarkable in 2015.

The further away we drift in time from the American War in Vietnam era, the more salient this distant reality becomes.

Generations of young Americans have come of age and matured significantly since the time my age group was by and large conscripted.

In 2015, young men graduating from high school can choose from a variety of early directions in life.

They can do nothing at all, hide in their parents' basements for years at a time, start an Irish folk ensemble or pursue a career in medicine.

They can become tattoo artists, food truck entrepreneurs, lady pleasers, bouncers or high tech *wunderkind.*

Their choices are infinite.

For my friends and I in 1963, war was the binding, prominent, unquestioned option.

It was imposed by a draft system that required all men of a certain age participate, like it or not.

It was born of an accepting culture accustomed to war, conditioned to its controversial nature, lacking any natural imperative to question any prevailing rationale.

It was certified in its rigorous application.

You couldn't slip out if you wanted to.

Many skeptically inclined young men wanted to. Despite that abundant truth, a larger reality defined the era: war was a popular decision for the average young man born during the time period of approximately 1945-1952.

Many of their fathers had served in World War II, generally regarded as a worthwhile exercise. If duty called again, most men took it for granted they'd also feel obliged to participate.

Their acquiescence derived from a larger assumption that if called to join the military it could be assumed the rationale for doing so outweighed whatever disruption it created.

Getting out of high school in America in the mid-to-late-1960's meant hearing clearly the giant sucking sound of a military draft that processed millions of men into an engagement featuring the expenditure of hundreds of thousands of weapons in need of war.

Excuses knew no illogical end-point.

The Vietnam War came down on my generation like a massive tree fallen across our path to the future. We couldn't get there without navigating the massive trunk of reality called military obligation.

Nine-out-of-ten did what they were told to do. One-out-of-ten rejected the rationale, found their way through the storm.

Somewhere in the town or city where you reside does surely exist a chapter of the Veterans of The American War in Vietnam.

Its members are easy to identify. They're not reluctant to wear hats and buttons identifying themselves as survivors of a distinctly valiant crusade.

Many proud members of this mass of Nam veterans use crutches or wheelchairs, others adorn in hats cluttered with symbols of valor. Other Vietnam vets keep their hats under cover, not forgotten but not worn at the super market.

Please excuse this writer for sharing this sentiment: I admire these people.

They share in common many binding experiences and a connective sense of what happened to them in war, as well as after those bitter interludes.

That a war-weary populace welcomed them home with both indifference and absence of meaningful recognition or appreciation was double jeopardy taken to the extreme. It singed already unraveled consciousness within the average returning combatant.

All of this has emerged over subsequent decades as more-or-less accepted narrative regarding this chapter.

Images of returning veterans being spit-upon by effete war protestors at airports across the land entered the lexicon of commonly referenced occurrences, lending some credibility to the notion.

Many veterans I've spoken with evoke memories of similar events leading me to believe these types of unfortunate incidents did surely take place, even though I never witnessed any.

On the other hand, the very notion of some lame brain citizen stateside hurling saliva upon a returning soldier seems counter-intuitive, assumes the soldier would quietly acquiesce to a highly insulting gesture.

In the spirit of trying to make sense of this possible contradiction my instinct is to believe our returning veterans did indeed have the maturity and wisdom to endure the ignobility of any kind of insults that awaited them as they returned home from a deeply unpopular war.

"I was never a big fan of the Vietnam War," Donald Trump said to a crowd of admirers many decades later. He was among the majority, not that it made him right, then or now.

Friends of this writer who went off to war and returned thereafter to civilian life came back to a land ripped apart by division and fatigue.

In my case, they also returned to encounter family members and friends who celebrated their presence, heaped massive appreciation upon them, encouraged their transition back to normality and conveyed sincere respect for their service to country and cause without reservation. Rarely did anyone's survival of one or more terms in the war zone enter into average discussion.

The overall mission had been so rigorously questioned after 1969 that most people I knew suppressed undiluted jingoism.

Half a lifetime after the end of World War II those who fought in that noble epochal event were dubbed "The Greatest Generation."

The distinction was granted by a large consensus of voices, including history-buff apostates and other observers of note.

It was taken for granted they had so much of the right stuff they more than earned their place in the annals of over-statement.

A different fate became many among the Vietnam Crowd. Their mission lacked any perception of nobility in so many respects their service to country and cause was diminished by the commonly perceived unworthy nature of the episode in which they expended themselves in action. Their conduct in conflict was no less heroic or distinctive in any way than their father's valor exhibited in Europe and the Pacific during World War II.

Only in lack of cause did their efforts induce a less-than-hearty response.

Convincing members of my generation to accept the call to go off and fight against Vietnamese peasant farmers in rice paddies many thousands of miles from our shores required rail car loads of what I considered to be an unholy mix of propaganda, misinformation, distortion and pure horseshit. We were sold tons of garbage as part of our government's effort to convince us to give up civilian status and join in the eventual entirely surreal reality of a grim scenario depicting many millions of young Americans showing up in Vietnam as soldiers.

In order to willingly kill the enemy we had to learn to hate the enemy first. Dehumanizing them was a helpful strategy.

Cultivating and sustaining the impression they cared less about living than we did was especially useful. Instead of regarding them as "people" we were led into seeing them as "gooks," a desultory reference to the nature of matter resulting from mucous based eye build-up.

After the war it was estimated America suffered more than 50,000 casualties, Vietnam (both South and North) about 3,000.000.

We killed a lot of them until we began to realize we couldn't kill all of them.

For one thing, they had us outnumbered.

For another thing, the American public back home was growing weary of what was increasingly perceived as a no-win, horrifying military mission that was gobbling up American lives and resources at an unsustainable rate.

Some candid Vietnamese suggested afterwards they were prepared to fight us to the last man, woman and child. It was their country after all. We were mere invaders, not the first they'd fought.

It sounds grotesque in retrospect.

Average Americans were less aware of the ways of the world then than we are today. We lacked both media and curiosity.

Information existed in arcane corners of general awareness. Average people had no idea where Vietnam was, why its future had anything to do with our own who its people were or anything in the realm of what we today might regard as relevant.

Throughout most of the decade of the 1960s mainstream Americans accepted the government's explanation for the war. Without giving it much of a second thought, they participated in its orchestration without question.

They endured the increasing revulsion of its consequences as expressed in regular weekly death toll reports broadcast on dominant network newscasts, as alluded to in the Preface of this book.

On most Friday night shows, the tally had greatest impact. The casualty reports from the distant battlefields conveyed a consistent pattern of statistical "evidence" suggesting we were winning the war.

In a typical Friday evening newscast, it was announced that America had lost a gut wrenching 385 casualties, Vietnam 4,000. The disparity in numbers as reported was mightily convincing.

Viewers did the math. We calculated we could outlast them. I remember thinking at the time those dirty bastards could not last another week given the rate of reported casualties among their ranks.

Like most others, I had no idea we were all being lied to, big-time, week after week after week. Few dared wonder if it was worth it morally or otherwise, until that is the arrival of the year, 1969.

Only by the absolute end of the decade did dissent as a concept or force-to- be-reckoned-with begin to emerge from the core of the center.

By then the focus of attention was shifting from indifference to emerging opposition. America beheld the birth of the skeptical inclination.

Television worked both ways. Propaganda was primary fare in newscasts. The phony body counts sustained average American's support.

But viewers also saw on their TV screens horrible images of death, destruction often depicting American soldiers in compromised situations in which killing the enemy equated to killing the enemy's parents and children as well.

Even as most young people went along with the government's need to engage them in the military, doubts about the overall efficacy of the war began to manifest where once blind allegiance held serve.

If the dreaded draft wanted you – and it did – then you, whoever you were, began to have considerable skin in the game, as in accepting the call, going off to kill or be killed. As ever-increasing waves of hundreds of thousands of teenaged soldiers flew off to fight, the questioning spiked as well.

Events of the prior year set the stage for what followed in 1969.

A year before, anti-war demonstrators confronted the Chicago Police during the Democratic Party Convention, evoking violent response aired on national TV.

The country was deeply divided in its response.

Of equal significance, Richard Nixon was elected President.

In his campaign he evoked a secret strategy to end the war. Clearly its lack of popularity had become a dominant political factor.

'Nam-Mon

The Vietnam War raged in Southeast Asia throughout the decade of the 1960's. During the first four or five years of the conflict, few in America questioned its persecution. Major news sources reported the facts the citizenry generally ate them up.

Prior to 1969, protestors were extreme left-wingers, college intellectuals and an occasional grandmother with a headband. Their pleas for sanity failed to resonate with the masses; they were perceived as fringe elements with positions so esoteric they were inaccessible in their time. After 1969, the tide had turned, the President-elect had gained office on a pledge to end the war and returning veterans began to encounter a country either hostile to them and their designated cause or indifferent, at best. These were dramatic times, a period in which life experiences became persistent memories.

Being a Vietnam War protestor was a total drag a complete bitch. There were quite a few of us, which seemed significant when we were all standing in a pack together. For the most part, though, being a protestor was a lonely pursuit within the context of society at large, where most people treated us like creeps. The safe thing to do at the time was to keep your mouth shut, blend in and make a lot of money.

Going to Vietnam required obedience to government, right or wrong, not to mention a large load of courage, balls and a good upbringing.

Protesting Vietnam required less courage, smaller balls and any background that applied. It also took a fairly aggressive intellect to digest the evidence; wash it around in the saliva pit of limited intellect make sense of what could never be sensible. Existing innocently within these two camps became the most common approach.

Protestors were treated like crap throughout their late-'60's quest for sanity. When the war was finally over in 1975, their place in American society was somewhere between ignored and discredited.

Even though historians began to assess our Vietnam strategy as incorrect and wrong-headed, those of us who exposed those positions when the argument was at-hand were relegated to So What City?

Nearly fifty-years after the end of the war, this former protestor navigates society alone, one man in a world of veterans still in search of the respect and appreciation they were denied after they came back from Southeast Asia. When I can, I seek to mingle among them, inquisitive, supportive, disinclined to evoke my own Vietnam resume as it now seems compartively inglorious to me when measured against the experiences of so many of my contemparies.

One week ago, on a Saturday evening in May, 2016, I hauled my tired old former protestor carcass into a tribute and recognition event for Vietnam War veterans in Pontiac; it was organized by a trio of area politicians to coincide with Armed Forces Day.

During the three-hour marathon about a half-dozen veterans had commemorative pins affixed to the lapels of their sports coats; the wife of one vet appeared in his behalf.

A similar number of community members attended, including this writer; I'd been stirred from lethargy by a newspaper article announcing the event, including this reference: "Any interested Michigander may attend the ceremony ..."

The veterans who attended were not identified by name nor encouraged to do so. They were not asked to share remarks and conveyed no references to themselves that would enable this audience member to better understand who they were, when and where they served or what their lives have been like following the war.

Including their respective aides, the number of politicians in attendance equalled the turnout of veterans. Assessing the overall flavor of the event, I felt as if more attention was drawn to the elected officials than to the guests of honor, although I may have brought a certain bias to eventually gaining that probably meaningless impression. One of the politicians told those in attendance that our military did not lose the war, that it had been our politicians that lost the will to keep on fighting.

Later, I wanted to ask him if he agrees with the supposition that polticians advocate positions consistent with the views of their constituents. I didn't have an opportunity to pose that question which was just as well; this was not a night for cynicism and discord.

For the record, I lost quite a bit of respect for the local pol who made that remark. I felt it failed to factor in the larger context of the question at hand. I thought he could have made the same point while also acknowledging the controversial nature of the war, the fact that many other learned analysts and observers have reached dissimilar conclusions. Again, this was not a night for nuance, nor was it "on me" as a community member attending an event to honor veterans to insert my own surely smug opinions. The evening was not without its highlights. For me the apex moment occurrred as I renewed an acquaintance with a fellow Optimist Club member from the area whom I had not seen in a significiant number of Moons. I did recall he had served in the military in Vietnam, as that aspect of his background remains a central component of his life story, a genuine badge of honor in most everyones estimation. Seated at a table with him that night, I learned he had been a medic in the war – an aristocrat among mortals. Knowing medics defined the upper stratra of wartime pedigree I peppered him with questions, frequently acknowledging my own awareness that our medics served with utmost distinction in Vietnam, defining bravery projecting so much character their wartime heroics loom permanently now, as significant today as they were in their time of action.

He went down with four helicopters he told me, using up almost half of his cat's nine lives before he was 25. During the fourth crash he took schrapnel in his back, earning a Purple Heart which he proudly wore on his perfectly pressed suitcoat the night of the banquet. Others fussed over this adornment, effusing appropriate praise feeding the beem of this noble gentleman's smile.

I gleaned elements of his life story. He spent his adulthood in purposeful pursuit of various altruistic agendas, traded in industrial metals, became "a scrapper," known in some circles as "dumpster divers." He found creative ways to create wealth from others' waste and various effluent jammed in garbage cans, developing an amazing capacity to differentiate among large black plastic garbage sacks filled with refuse and identify items of worth, simply by the feel of the bag. I was mesmorized.

He and his wife eventually beget nearly two-dozen grandchildren, he told me, less than boastfully but abundantly happy to exclaim about the proliferation of offspring around him. The more he shared, the more I found myself in awe of being in the presence of a great American.

I knew on this night, keep in my heart at all times, that the best of my generation chose to go and dive right in balls-out to our Vietnam War. That awareness doesn't suggest I harbor any less admiration for "the tribe" I inhabited during the war. We were no less virtuous in nearly every respect, "nearly" being the operative word in a highly nuanced topic of discussion.

I agree with Vietnam veterans that they deserved a parade. I'd give them one tomorrow and every day after that as long as any of them still wanted a parade. They did what they were asked to do.

Give them all the credit in the world for that. If they didn't get the reception they felt they deserved when they came back from Vietnam, I'd say they got screwed. Again.

What I remember, of course, is they didn't throw tons of confetti on us either, not that any of us felt we had earned a hero's welcome. If you protested the war you got a ton of condemnation from just about everybody alive. You earned the distinction of being called a coward or worse, a draft dodger or a commie.

There were plenty of words for those who stood up and opposed the war.

A couple of meatheads driving by me-as-hitchhiker in Barstow, California one hot afternoon flipped me off, called me "a Berkley Beatnik" and said they would be back to kill me at dusk if I was still there.

I felt honored, and scared.

We were very visible and highly contemptible. Our cause was the opposite of popular. People back home wanted to kill us.

At Kent State University in Ohio in May 1970, they did just that. (See Chapter Two.)

America applauded that atrocity.

Fifty-years later, not much has changed.

America's Vietnam War vets got the memorial they deserve in the nation's capitol. The names of those who died appear on a waving wall of granite and courage.

You can't help but be moved, no matter how you felt about the war when it was waged or how you feel now. You just see valor and heroism in their names and tragedy in the aura surrounding the place, knowing how controversial the war was and how the losses of those military personnel seem so jaded now by the understanding many have gained of the truly controversial nature of the Vietnam engagement.

And that's just my interpretation.

The greatest lesson I learned from Vietnam is that all of us came at this thing from different places different circumstances different places in time.

We need to forgive one another for whatever we did then for we were each dealing with the matter in ways intrinsic to ourselves, not necessarily others. What was hard to imagine then is quite apparent today; others have their own views, all coherent and correct, from the perspective of the varying individuals whose lives were affected by those events.

Deep History By Now

Fifty years is large dollop of time, a gaping hole in the evening mist by anyone's estimation. This is particularly true from the perspective of humans who monitor such things.

Because most anthropoids stick around for only about 70 or 80 years—if we're lucky—most of us bozos on this bus see any sequence of decades for what it is—a long sleep cycle.

Five decades ago in the country called USA a mighty cauldron of cultural storms did wreak powerful havoc upon the body politic and the brain cerebral. Moorings that hitherto bound the multiple essences of North American civilization to a structured foundation gave way between 1968 and 1972 to an inexorable wave of societal upheaval, by God!

Now it's 2016.

Still, some of us can reach back and touch 1968 with the ease of a gifted forklift operator.

Because 1969 was so poignant we can seamlessly revert to that epochal time in history, revved up and ready to recall, wired like garrulous optimists peddling adrenalin supplements to drunken Texan oilmen on R&R in Rio.

Because 1970 vibrated with maelstroms of cultural upheaval, we're still recovering, doctor.

Which is OK with me. For I've made a number of incredibly positive adjustments over the years, including but not limited to getting older.

Because 1971 was overly chronicled, I and half the people I ever knew can gather its essence effortlessly, relying on books, movies, notes and letters we received from other star-struck inhabitants of that crazy passage in time.

Since 1972 stands among all years as the most nauseating 365-day run ever invented, even a child can recall the sound of George McGovern's false teeth moving in his mouth as he denounced the Vietnam War and lost by a landslide.

Sure, it's half-a-lifetime later as I sit here before this Buck Rogers word processor describing a period long past.

But that doesn't mean any of us got over it. Shit, I mean *hardly*.

Because no one made us get over it, some of us still get under it, as in, thinking about it, analyzing it, assessing judgment upon it as objectively as possible and then opening another bottle of beer and thinking about something else.

In November 1969, an anti-war moratorium took place in Washington, D.C. More than half-a-million protestors converged on the nation's Capitol.

Their number included a rather crazed individual, a guitar-pickin' folkie buzzed beyond belief on bodacious Asian marijuana, a pathologically disenfranchised hemp addict who drove in from Charleston, West Virginia.

Getting there was a trip. Being there was transcendent. Remembering it causes his body to convulse.

It was a milestone in the movement. Things really started to change after this event.

Once perceived as obscure and radical fringe, the anti-war presence on this one immortal date in history forever thereafter took on the identity of a larger, more significant force.

No one had dared anticipate 500,000 people attending the event. Because it was unprecedented, no one could predict anything. There could just as easily been 50,000 people there. That would not have surprised anyone.

Instead, ten times that many appeared.

Being a part of that swollen, unlikely mass cemented my convictions.

After surviving a flat tire on an interstate highway, being rescued by a trucker who recognized me as a protestor, said he disagreed with me but still felt obliged to save my ass, my small German car and I limped into D.C. as the sun went down.

I took my cues from full-page counter-culture newspaper ads promoting what was called "the November action." The march on Washington was specifically organized to "bring all the troops home now."

It called for immediate and total withdrawal from Vietnam; self determination for Vietnam and Black America; an end to the repressive incarceration of political prisoners, the draft, all forms of militarism, racism and poverty; free speech for GI's; self government for Washington, D.C.

People with signs were directing visitors onto side streets, where other volunteers awaited to greet us and help us find friendly homes that were accommodating the hordes that had come to protest. I ended up sleeping on the floor of one house along with a dozen of so others.

We awoke to meet our friendly hosts, share juice and bagels then be on our way to The Ellipse. Beginning on relatively obscure side streets and in small numbers, we ventured on to larger roads in greater numbers until great masses of us joined ranks in the shadows of our nation's most stunning monuments and edifices.

The morning was chilly but clear. The empowerment I experienced was conclusive.

For a few pristine hours, it was as if every living person was opposed to the war. We knew that wasn't true even as it seemed that way.

Picture half-a-million mostly young men dressed in blue jeans and T-shirts, standing together, side by side in rows of hundreds, stretched out as far as the eye could see.

Imagine an occasional skinny joint coming at you from left or right. Visualize a parade of speakers, celebrities, singers and politicians bellowing opposition to an increasingly untenable war, exhorting the masses from a very distant stage. Be the change you want to see.

I changed 900 percent that day and so did 900 billion others like me.

By arriving that day, we arrived.

My employer, a small liberal arts college in north central West Virginia, did not like my anti-war posturing.

Word got back to members of the Board of Trustees that I was not pledging allegiance at college day events.

Even though those excruciating ordeals were over, the trustees called me into a special meeting to confront the allegations.

The meeting took place the day after the moratorium, November 16.

I was polite but unyielding, conveyed appreciation for the basis of their rational while also surrendering no ground on my position of opposition to the war.

They were firm and concise: something had to give.

Looking back on this fifty-years later I quiver with shame knowing my unwillingness to "say the pledge" created such a stir. I also recall the special satisfaction I took for having an opportunity to convey to people of real power how entirely ready to rock the boat so many of us had become.

The celebrated "generation gap" was in full reveal. I grasped the theatric potential of the moment dug deep to share the rationale for our protests.

I hope the trustees had other agenda items that day.

Young as I was I understood defending my position to this or any group of adults was an opportunity to explain "our" position, put "our" impulse to protest in perspective.

In my case, it provided a dramatic forum in which to convey depth of passion. Coming hot on the heels of the Moratorium, I was emboldened, felt fortunate to reveal to the trustees the nature of opposition to what many perceived to be a monumental inequity, one that was body-slamming people my age.

I remember thinking as I stood before the board that it was the very quality of education I had earlier received at the college as a student that had by now helped foster the intellectual dexterity required to see within the government's rational for war and reject it as empirical hogwash.

It was more than a touch of self-serving delusion, of course. There was little likelihood anything I would say to them would change their opinions.

I committed to myself to do my best to eliminate the possibility of engaging in future controversial behavior, although I continued to skate near the edge of the pond.

I kept my job by agreeing to at least put my hand over my heart if ever asked to pledge again, knowing the college night programs were over for the year.

That I survived that interlude of mind-numbing appearances in each of West Virginia's counties was more than a miracle. I fit into the traveling group of college reps like Satan at a Bible convention. The more the 12 of us got to know one another, the more the other 11 wanted to skewer my carcass.

Only one rep conveyed an attitude of understanding and respect, Leonard Golembleski from the University of West Virginia. Len was a school superintendent from southwest Pennsylvania who was completing his doctorate by serving as a recruiter. Unlike the others, he was receptive to the winds of change, aware of how an unpopular war was dividing the country and somewhat in-tune with the thinking of young people like me.

We ended up rooming together off and on for a few months, sharing meals, driving from town to town in one car and exchanging views on every imaginable topic of the day. Our friendship grew and saved me from the isolation of the other reps, not to mention their rabid hostility toward my anti-war views.

As far as the college trustees, I would not have minded being set free by them. On the other hand, I also felt a binding sense of commitment to the others in our admissions department. And there were still a few more Kurt Vonnegut books I wanted to read before ditching what was, in some respects, a fairly decent gig for an extrovert completely full of cow manure.

They didn't want to lose me. High school counselors liked me as I came to them as the bearer of good tidings, a representative of a college that offered unique and pragmatic academic programs in a pristine scholastic environment, a learned community proud of its rich heritage and religious tradition.

More significantly, no one else wanted my job. Plus, I was getting good results from my recruitment efforts.

We were all stuck with each other, for what turned out to be another six months. I kept traveling across Upstate New

York from one small town to another, hitting my high schools, hitting those fat-boy Nam-weed bombers in motel rooms by night, strumming the two guitars I carried and reading as many of Kurt's books as I could get my hands on.

By all appearances I had derived a formula for maintaining my sanity during what was surely an unhinged period of time.

Like many others though, I was being eaten up by a persistently nagging state of alienation. The longer what I considered to be an unacceptable war continued, the more I felt I was truly living in An Alien Nation.

Weird dudes like me tried to channel our pervasive angst through anti-war activities and by talking with people we knew about the subject.

That helped a little. But hating the war while having to endure it became extremely difficult.

As Richard Nixon's White House continued to commit human and physical resources to the death and destruction of factions within Vietnam, tolerating the perceived madness became emotionally impossible.

For one thing I saw the enemy factions as no more than an arbitrary term imposed upon the enemy for the convenience of our aggression.

In that context, it was becoming difficult to see any Vietnamese as being logical enemies regardless of what "side" they appeared to affiliate with.

It was the craziest time of my life.

I couldn't handle it but had to handle it. Making it through another day was beyond my means yet I did my best, surviving many decades into the future.

Still I am quite sure it made me crazy, textbook crazy, at least during that time period. Countless times I said to myself, "This is making me nuts."

It must have been true.

We all know what happens when you don't get oxygen to the brain for more than a few seconds: tissue atrophies, cellular structure erodes, hemoglobin gives up the ghost. As life emerged, experience taught us old peaceniks that people go half-crazy around us all of the time, mostly unnoticed, undocumented, not treated, healed or otherwise redeemed. Just nuts, like most of us others are. We are all raised by brain-damaged parents and continue evoking psychic horror on our offspring as surely as we teach them to use chopsticks.

I'd say my experience with The Vietnam War in late-1969 and into 1970 was way beyond excruciating for every organ in my brain and body.

I couldn't stand it. I became crazier than a partially embalmed laboratory rat.

I shook with anger for so long my shaker quit on me, left me for another Den Mother. I couldn't take it any more. Still, I had no choice.

It was die, change your mind or figure out a way to endure the torture.

I opted for the latter, painful and psychologically destructive as it was.

Years later, much attention was paid to the veterans of this war. They are heroes in my book. They continue to deserve all the support and respect they can gain from a population now sufficiently detached from the struggle to relate to them with open hearts and minds.

I admire them. They were the real heroes of the hour, the pride of our country the very best among us. I can't help repeating this.

They answered the call.

They did what they were asked to do.

They put their lives on the line.

They faced adversity.

Not a one of us who sat out this war back here on stateside will ever have anything resembling a clue of what it took to survive what they went through.

We can only speculate, speculation being less than chump change compared to what our veterans experienced.

I dedicate this book to our Vietnam veterans. Hail to every single one of them.

They answered their nation's call, served admirably saw their buddies die around them.

They fought for their country by fighting for another people's country.

I get it.

Shit Hits Fan

In May 1970, the shit hit the fan in America.

The shootings that occurred at Kent State University in Ohio let the feces fly into the propeller blades of our world. (See Chapter Two.)

Others have their own memories of this gross chapter in history.

If their memories are anything like mine, they recall a deeply depressing interlude between ecstasy and bitter disillusionment, a time when many young people of conscience became semi-unconscious older people as a matter of sheer survival.

My recollections of what happened then and in the years that immediately proceeded and followed that fateful interlude are filtered now through a memory robbed of its original integrity by a lifetime of euphoric self indulgence and other manifestations of normal wear and tear, only to form the alleged content of this book.

Rather than seek to craft an empirically sound account, I've attempted to formulate an open-ended, randomly selected "reader" comprised of varying interpretations. As a result its findings are accurate yet personal, empirical yet moored to personal reflection capped off by a sprig of imagination.

They are ultimately only as consistent with the recall process of the person who formed it as that person can be, in the context of literary freedom.

Literary freedom, in the flawed framework of this work, means every man for himself and more power to the offspring of Elvis.

Accuracy in this context is an illusive concept, a bad joke, really. Bottom line, this extended essay deals in acute subjectivity.

It is gleaned from imperfect recall, captured within the blur of modern-day abstractions, (three fire engines just drove by.)

It is sketched out of the memory of one slightly-skewed observer—an entirely abnormal, narcissistic person not lacking the passion to assemble this less-than-fully-enlightened reminiscence but a flawed person nevertheless, a fingernail-biting extempore still unresolved within the context of traditional maturity.

To balance the stark inadequacy of my views, opinions, biases, this "reader" features a generous mix of other voices, historic interpretations, broader frames of vision, equating I hope to an overage of erudition, enriching this edition.

A Flawed Memory

No one ever said any fool is anywhere near capable of recalling with a modicum of precision events that occurred more than four decades into the rear-view mirror.

This is especially true when said-slacker now has white hairs on his chin and insists on doing this typing against the backdrop of insipid classical music.

All this imposter or any phony intellectual can do is what others do—fake it. Try his best and fake it.

Clearly, many citizens, with an unusual concentration of establishement-types, neo-fascists and dock workers with lousy hygeine endorsed the government's hardened approach to stifling dissent.

Anti-Vietnam War elements were depicted as unpatriotic cowards.

The polarization was extremely worse than disheartening; it was mind numbing.

Over a several year period of time, I became opposed to the war.

As I perceived it by 1969, our actions in Vietnam seemed to have less to do with protecting our country than they did with destroying another one. Practically zero attention was paid to the young men my age who were dying in Southeast Asia. Their names were anonymous, the nature of their death unquestioned or examined.

Bottom-line, I could not accept the challenge of letting our military train me to become a killer, as I did not perceive the anointed enemy as deserving to be killed by me. To have answered the call and willingly gone to the war to participate in the slaughter would have been to tacitly accept the government line -- we deserved to live they deserved to die.

In my increasingly smarty-pants mind, it didn't add up. I came to believe anti-war protestors had it right in concluding the Vietnam War was a lie.

Eventually I endorsed the premise it was the moral responsibility of all detractors to make our voices and opinions heard.

Of course, that is my take on the subject. I feel comfortable asserting it today, many decades later, as it seems to me now at least the tentative prevailing wisdom among historians and other possibly objective sources on this subject is that the Vietnam War was ill-advised, at best, and amoral, at its core.

We've picked that apart for a long time.

Now it is important that we persist in the process of doing our best to learn from history. This seems imperative in order to draw instructive perspectives from our wins and losses, our accomplishments and our disasters, so that in the future our children's children and we have a better chance of avoiding similarly predictable disasters.

Sure, there were some bad actors in the movement, just like there were some textbook creeps persecuting the war on the other side of the rice paddy. How about that? Anyone who ever read a matchbook cover had the intellectual ability to sort through that contradiction.

For the most part, anti-Vietnam War dissidents were everyday people of a certain age group. They (we) were normally complacent individuals who had been stirred from conservative lethargy by a war that by then had been thrust upon John Q. Public for four or five years.

They (we) were typical American young people who shared in common an early instinct that our government was up to no good in Southeast Asia.

America got involved in Vietnam in the early-'60s, the protest movement revved-up in late-1968.

During most of the decade most of the populace was significantly detached from it all. By 1970s, all bets were off, Katie couldn't bar the door because the door wasn't there any more.

Many of us who came of age during that time—especially me—were flipped so far off our rockers we could only roll, with the punches, the putridity, and the pulchritude. Because it was huge, we're still there.

There was plenty of courage to go around in the late-'60s. Soldiers who answered the call of duty and put themselves in harm's way in Vietnam had tons of it.

I honored them then and feel even more strongly about it ten minutes from now. They did what they were told to do. Most of them did it well. Even those who faltered were to be forgiven, as theirs was a difficult task, as in illogical.

On the home side, young Americans who put their own ass on the line to protest the war displayed similar balls although most veterans would argue that point. It is their right to do so. And it was our right as sincere opponents of the war to stand up against our government and plead our own case. In our minds, we were acting within the established boundaries of exalted and previously fought-for American political tradition.

No matter how you sort that out, four students did not need to die that day in northern Ohio. Their demise occurred because our system broke down, allowing poor thinking to overwhelm good intentions.

This Chapter does not attempt to dissect that specific event or somehow address the greater wrongs of that awful day. Rather, it seeks to let the writer engage in what he dares believe is meaningful computer activity this afternoon. In doing so, this creepy empire-builder hopes to leave you with an imagined sense of what it was like to be there with an illegal spiritual hew and a pen that worked.

Others who survived this treacherous passage in time will suggest a great number of us who also claim to have traveled that journey did so amid persistent fumes of burning hemp flower. Accordingly our ascent into adulthood and beyond was flavored in false reverie, transient euphoria, magic carpet riding and Alice in Wonderland fantasy.

I think we might still have a few extra tickets if anyone's interested.

Of course we stopped getting drunk all of the time. Of course we found superior ways to listen to the music of Paul Simon and Artie Garfunkle.

There is a huge difference between marijuana and heroin, as you may learn from reading this.

As a living person with average preceptor skills, I can tell you from experience that probably one in 100 pot smoking regurgitates will gravitate to heroin use, even though the propaganda on the subject asserts otherwise.

(Unfortunately, a decade or so after the previous sentence was crafted North America was under new, previously unimaginable degrees of assault, invaded by waves of heroin, cocaine, and other debilitating agents. Exported by craven Mexican cartels lacking a shred of concern for interests other than their own, this menacing phenomenon gained a foothold across our land in the early-twenty-first century emerging as the scourge of an era. It's worth adding those who gravitated to the abuse of truly dangerous drugs rarely came from a background of marijuana use. Rather their journey to perilous addiction was routed through gross misuse of prescribed pain medications.)

Marijuana circa-1970 was lethal.

A lot of it came from Vietnam, in fact.

Tons of earthy greenish brown flower-top stuff called *cannabis indicus* flowed into our heads through our mailboxes mailed to previously totally straight frat boys like me by dear buddies conscripted into military service, sent by soldiers (former frat boys themselves) to their friends in Kent and throughout the country.

Ridiculously potent ganja flooded sectors of our country, flowing ferociously through UPS warehouses, Fed Ex facilities, U.S. Post Offices, military discharge centers and other obvious portals.

In addition to addicting our forces in Southeast Asia to scarily complacence-inducing narcotic reverie, this herbal onslaught also laid waste to mellow multiples of the friends and family members of those serving their country, back here IN their country.

A good time was allegedly had by all yet in retrospect istalso occurs to this old duffer that something equally dramatic took place – minds were as permanently altered stateside as they were in the jungles and villages of Vietnam.

G.I.s in the Mekong Delta could buy a large fistful of pre-rolled, brain cell destroying dobbins for less than a dollar. Hundreds of thousands of them did, mailing the shit back to real kooks like me in the heartland.

It was devastatingly powerful pot they bought for a nickel a joint, rockin' reefer stronger than a palate of crazy glue and more mind-altering, too.

In many respects, you could safely surmise the stuff was TOO good, TOO strong, although from a real hippie perspective that seems like a misnomer. For objectivity's sake, it was flat-out disabling, disorienting as well as *"Dis is some good shit."*

Too good it turned out, dangerously lethal pot at best and ridiculously overstated in essence.

Although the product filtered into our society compliments of our friends serving in Vietnam who mailed it to us, none of us really needed it, actually, although many surely benefited in ways that seemed compelling in context and even a few of which survived the test of time.

Pot from Nam was one-toke-and-done. It came to us in pre-rolled joints that were twice as large as average cigarettes. A single pull would get you through and two would render you quickly disabled, incapable of doing anything other than dopily contemplating riffs of Led Zeppelin.

Just for the heck of it one early Saturday afternoon after returning from my scheduled morning shift at the office, I decided to experiment, Apparently free of responsibility for the rest of the day, I wanted to find out what would happen if I consumed an entire "Buddha joint" in a single setting.

One-tenth of the way into the experiment I began to sense my curiosity had the potential to lead to any number of variants of calamity. Driven by a deep commitment to medical science, cursed with the heart of an inveterate researcher with an odd penchant for crushing maggots I kept that baby burning long beyond the point of rationality. I sort of remember at the half-way point looking out the window and thinking I was seeing an intense thunderstorm even though the region was deep in the throws of a persistent drought. Nearing the end, I knew for a fact my entire being had walked down the road as far as the eye could see, turned right and headed off into points unknown, still within our Galaxy but indeterminate, Gushy Acres, just so much darned nebuli.

Not knowing it at the time, I had surely wandered into Jerry Garcia'land. I was so far off the planet even Pluto looked funny.

Next thing I knew, there was Frannie again at my door, telling me the college had called and needed me to come back in to take a visiting family on a tour of the campus. I rested my soul, believing she was kidding. She was not. Next thing I knew after that, I was driving the Bug back across the hollows, headed for an encounter with The Twilight Zone, without the light.

Let's see, a mother, a father and their daughter. Drove down from the Pittsburgh area. What a dismal proposition. The father had the disposition of a maligned football coach who could not keep a job. He projected a sullen persona which is to say he wanted to murder me. Why? I don't know, you'd have to ask him.

I sensed they were defensive, knowing they had showed up "unannounced," although I doubt they copped to that. They may have said they had scheduled their visit and that the admissions office had screwed it up. Boy, what a bunch of dumb bells. There I was, in any event, obliged to lead them on a tour of the small but despairing campus. This was going to be about as scintlating as spending a decade in Siberia without long underwear.

Within the first few seconds my cover was blown. I projected such an extreme absence of self confidence even a visiting Martian would have picked up on my comatose state. The degree to which I did not want to be there was so overblown, moribound larvae in our proximity began to emit noxious bad vibes, setting off sensitive monitoring devices as far away as Roanake.

Things deteroirated from there, leading to the complete deterioration of an amalgam of contigous zip codes. After saying they would hate me forever and do everything within Satan's power to ensure my remaining days would be replete in misery, we ended our tour with no real tangible results accruing to the insititution. I imagine the daughter opted instead for the military, perhaps a position in a government laboratory dedicated to the science of lizard dominance among ancient Mayan cultures.

Smoking a whole one proved to be a bad strategy for making sense, eye contact or lifelong friends. Inhaling all that heroin without really knowing what I was doing made the term "disoriented" seem like today's equivalent of "grounded." In woofing down that whole bad dog in about a 20-minute period of now-immortalized time I surely did enter into the zone made famous by the late Rod Sterling, who one night asked his wife, "Have you seen the roach clip?"

This happened 46-years ago, also know as a few minutes less than now.

For the record, the college had never called me in to walk three straight people around after my shift had ended before. And they haven't done it since then. You make sense of that.

I'd figured I'd chosen the perfect time to see what would happen if I huffed down an entire montrous Nam bomber. I found out all right. I learned that there is surely such a concept as "too much" of a good thing.

I played Russian Roulette with my job took a bullet in the skull.

I screwed around with Ma Nature and almost lost my mind, so painful was that walk around the grounds and gulleys, the statues and shrubs and *daggone son* so many buildings that comprised an aspiring academic community in the hills of dungaree.

Everything in moderation, my Mother thought she taught me.

I took a somber walk into the dark reaches of Why In The Hell Did This Happen? Our stroll through the ravines was an experience in hightened excrutiation. What started off bad immediately deteriorated into psychic naseau. I wanted "out of there" so badly every chromosone in my makeup cried out silently but with actual impact on everyone's mood. We engaged in group meltdown. How I ended up not committed to the looney farm eludes me still; surely other-worldly entities did intercede, saving me from a life embedded in hellish institutional inferno.

Part of the price for reaching sufficiently within the memory bank to produce the proceeding vignette is the reinforcement I gain of the sanctity of the fact I never want to get that high again; I greatly prefer having at least one moccasin on the ground. Complete disorientation may appeal to some members of the tribe I chose; I just happen to prefer space flight conducted within the constraint of good judgement.

(Complete findings from that research project can be found on the inside of the cover of the back of this book, printed upside down in both Arabic and Laotian.)

From a current perspective, I can tell you that marijuana from Vietnam was suspiciously potent and devastatingly lethal, to the point of possible conspiracy.

I can only imagine the raw fear experienced by a young American G.I. zoned on 'Nam pot in the middle of a mortar attack in the middle of a strange country where in the fierce illumination of a overly-amped hyper hemp buzz the inherent illogic of the larger military mission surely came home loud and clear.

Our soldiers bought their pot from sources that they assumed were committed to their best interests.

In *wrecked-'o-spect*, it is now obvious the Mama San's who peddled creeper 'Nam weed to cash-rich Government Enlisted American soldiers were likely intent upon debilitating as many white-skinned interlopers as possible. Which leads to a discussion of whether pot, in fact, is good or bad, which leads to closer analysis, which leads to the men's room.

Whether we needed it or not is not the subject of this book. That we smoked trunk lockers' full of it probably gets closer to the theme—we freaked out, some more than others.

Some didn't freak out at all.

Some freaked out so badly, so far, that they could not and therefore did not come back to reality in any recognizable way.

I smoked several pounds of the crap between 1969 and 1972 and became a different person in the process, transposing from abnormal to fringe.

I gave up taking my shirts to the dry cleaners and learned how to play "Heart Of Gold."

I stopped thinking everybody was looking at me and began instead looking at everybody, I mean, really *looking*.

I left My Ego in San Francisco, met my advanced curiosity index in San Jose.

Life as I knew it was no longer about me but about everything else *but* me.

I forgot everything I knew before and rented my brain out to a hurdy-gurdy man. It was a disgusting development in a perfectly cosmic sense that beget much eventual hilarity. Worse yet I lip-kissed stuff I would now regard as taboo during a brief but transforming four-month ascent into permanent addiction.

This occurred in early-1970 when I received in the mail from friends serving in the war several packages of pre-rolled *cannabis indicus* dobbins, many of which were tainted with highly addictive opium and death inducing heroin.

The only good thing you can say about Vietnamese marijuana 50 years after the fact is you can't get it anymore, assuming you got it in the first place. We only had access to that particular product for a relatively short particular period of time. This surely enabled at least a few minds to retain some vestige of mental functionality, some miniscule but biologically redemptive layers of mental particulate sufficient to foster the beleaguered formulation of some kind of lousy example of a logical conclusion to this lengthy and rather pointless sentence if you can really call it that.

The reliance I developed on top-of-the-line, maximum potency Marie Juanita during the time it was showing up in copious amounts in my landlady's mailbox became a permanent phenomenon as I navigated the rest of my life. Some observers noted I liked the stuff "a little too much." Uh yes. Probably still do. Maybe not. Writing about it causes me to question its eternal permanence in my portolio of vices, irrational habits and self-destructive practices, primarily the contruction of persistently protracted sentences.

I place this out in the open as a gesture of honesty revealing artistic commitment, like an attorney in a courtroom adding an exhibit or two in support of a closing argument.

Anyone seeking to understand what happened in Vietnam to America – and the generation of Americans asked to go fight in the war – may benefit from seeing as far within its impact as my story allows that insight to possibly extend.

I share it honestly knowing my infatuation with self-medicating is but one more legacy of the galvanizing event of our youth.

Looking back on it now, I'm certain my story mirrors millions of others, maybe just hundreds-of-thousands. Who's counting?

Based on the experiences of returning veterans I knew at the time, insane amounts of amazing smoke came home packed in large plastic containers within stereo speakers, duffel bags and whatever else they brought home with them, ear of enemy, laundry receipt in foreign tongue.

Killer reefer filtered from the war zone back into every American city and suburb, every hollow and enclave, every town and village, ghetto and country club, no zip codes excluded.

Vietnamese marijuana not only caught on big-time among Americans, it altered the existence of members of a certain age group in the homeland, extending its profound reach into all corners of society.

War.

Pot.

Protest.

Alienation.

Revulsion.

How these dissecting historical points on the compass of the rear-view mirror of the mind alternatively messed with the lives of people who inhabited that world at that unbelievably poignant time is the object of this study of male chimpanzee hygiene.

A person could literally be on the reservation from 1968 through 1972 and still have no idea of who killed Kennedy, or why McNamara ran 3.5 million Americans through the Saigon Airport, or how so much oily hemp plant found its way into our dresser drawers, let alone what really happened during a four or five year run through recorded hegemony.

Take this writer for example. (Take him outside and grill him a cheeseburger.)

Ask him what he remembers.

Like an escaped loon from the old folk's home he'll fill your head with so much psychobabble, you'll think you've died and gone to Art Linkletter University.

As a crazy old guy from the war-era, he'll start mumbling about General Hershey and Dick Nixon's daughters and crack a few jokes about Alexander Haig's inflated expense accounts, possibly let slip a personal anecdote or two about the time he spent spying on the Canadian Embassy.

He thinks he knows a lot but chances are, what he does know would probably fit in a Japanese phone booth, with room to spare for the rickshaw. He's full of blarney, drained of wisdom and absent of anything resembling a moral rudder, relying instead on choral stutter.

But look, he speaks like a real scholar, calls him self an author wears elbow pads on his college fraternity blazer. He stands up tall to make his points organizes his words in published format as if to say *ka-zoon-tyke* to the real literary world.

The events surrounding the time period embellished in this excusable excursion into the historical murk will ring particularly true to people who shared those moments, other turned-on geezers like me and the former governor. Instinctively, like shamans lacking adequate portfolio, they will know in their hearts the author is not making anything up other than the actual facts and the thousands of responses various assignees of different astrological signs had to those non-happenings.

Whether or not any of this bears any resemblance to things as they were will no doubt be sorted out by future librarians and will remain less important than any reader's willingness to embrace the work with an open mind and a pocket full of discounted elk jerky.

Those identifying an overlay of mild sarcasm in the previous summarization have sustained the kind of acuity required to fully assimilate the unquestionably fascinating accounts that follow, specifically a section on best strategies for selecting infant hosiery.

Others See It Differently

You won't have to look far to find others who would disagree with my assessed opinions and all the other left-wing dogma I'm peddling today.

If they have a better handle on all of this than I do, I'd like to exclaim, more cranial capacity to them.

I was then and remain just another pinhead with a point of view, however narrowly endowed the teller of this story is.

After sitting silently on the sidelines watching The American Vietnam War unfold I gradually transformed into a fully venting detractor.

This tale of yore took years to unfold.

A person like me experienced large anxiety in summoning the gall required to speak out against the mainstream and authority structure.

Screaming at The Man was new territory for all of us.
I hitchhiked from Tucson to San Francisco in 1971 to attend an anti-war moratorium.

When I got as close to my destination as Sacramento, the freeway entrance ramps were a swarm of other travelers, seeking to find a ride to The City. Helping to form that floating mass of fellow travelers ranks forever in my memory bank of pristine, exhilarating moments.

Stumbling upon the scene I became one of dozens of similarly oriented young people, all road vagabonds, some from Texas, others from throughout California, all engulfed in a spontaneous swirl of wild headbands, fashionable suitcases, signs, backpacks, excitement, color, conversation casual chaos.

All had stories of their respective journeys to this auspicious juncture. Some had spent days getting there. Relief was palpable as all of us shared the joy of knowing we had made it within 100 miles of our destination, with several hours to spare.

As dissenters we were truly emerging from the woodwork of America when the dominant moratoriums went down. An unmistakable sense of mission united us – individuals merging as a controlled but boiling-at-the-surface aggregate of war objectors.

On the following day, as part of a large demonstration including well in excess of 100,000 culturally similar war-protesting dilettantes, I joined my cohorts on a sunny downtown roadway in San Francisco. We united in beseeching employees watching us from windows in a large federal government facility to stop the war.

As the fervor reached a crescendo and 100,000 voices united as one, we cried out this slogan repeatedly: "Fuck Richard Nixon. Fuck Richard Nixon. Fuck Richard Nixon."

Later, many of us signed a massive petition to be delivered to The White House. I added my name to it, in bold print with a magic marker, aware that doing so may lead to complications in life but not really giving a flying fuck, knowing I had hitchhiked a thousand miles from Tucson to be there, wanting to leave my mark. I was at the zenith of contempt for authority, proud of myself for taking such a public stand against a war that had seized my entire being, consuming me, crushing my heart, causing me to truly detest my own country.

Looking back on that moment from the distant perspective of nearly 50-years later, I'm glad I did my vagabound deal back when I still thought sleeping out all night on the gnarly edge of a craggy freeway entrance ramp was exemplary behavior.

A fair question at this point might be, did that particular demonstration make any discernable difference when it came to lessening the duration of an detestable war? Like all important answers, that one remains blowing in the wind.

Aligning with the war opposition front was dangerous behavior, on one level, but soothing to the conscience on another, knowing somebody had to do something about the runaway train of war that kicked my age group in the gonads.

Taking to the streets was satisfying, to a large degree, and risky behavior in ways we didn't exactly understand. We just knew members of the so-called Silent Majority would have preferred to eviscerate us, send us back to Chairman Mao.

Everyday Americans hated our ass. We were scum. We became "them" in an "us versus them" societal paradigm, a categorical "out group" in a world dominated by clucky, culturally regressive intellectually vacuous citizens of the "in group" variety.

New lines were inter-laid upon the existing national demographic design, adding conflict points to an already-cluttered young vs. old, man vs. woman, rich vs. poor, Catholic vs. Protestant, Black vs. White, west vs. east way of seeing things.

With pro-war vs. anti-war added as yet another identity establishing point of demarcation, America in the late-1960s found itself becoming a more multi-stratified world in which "I am right and you are wrong" thinking gained increasingly prominence.

People became less who they simply were and more a symbol of what they may have believed in, felt about certain issues. More and more, people were reduced to being labeled something – a "this" or a "that."

Dichotomous thinking on every identity found a foothold in 1969 when millions of young Americans chose to rally and speak out against what had been an accepted war. It continued to gain increasing traction in our shared sense of oneness as a country.

If, among other things, you happened to harbor skepticism regarding the validity of our foreign policy in Southeast Asia, you became a ... (fill in the blanks.) That skepticism, at once only a portion of your overall being, became your identity. Period.

Simply remembering this brief interlude in our long national history is enough to transport me back in time to an era I'd hoped to permanently repress. I can't be there again without reattaching my emotions to a period of enormous tumult and concern.

I didn't like being there then and have not changed enough since then to like being there again now. People who would not have even noticed somebody else before began glaring at those same people as the protest movement continued to gain steam.

They cast scowls of hatred at pure strangers whose only shortcoming may have been manifest in chosen hairstyle, a type of garment a definitive wisp of patchouli essence about them. Children became permanently alienated from their parents, siblings from siblings.

Old friends adapted conflicting views and behaviors only to never talk to each other again. Others of us stayed fast friends no matter what our number was in the draft lottery. In fact, it wasn't at all unusual for a war protestor like me to have a friend in the war who because of family background felt obliged to go to 'Nam and "be a hero" for God and country.

Friends could finesse these divergences in opinion and personal action.

Our shared affections forced us to understand one another and expand our willingness and capacity to tolerate differing perspectives and agendas.

We were all directly impacted one way or the other.

My friend who hated the war as much as I did had been a member of the Reserved Officers Training Corp (ROTC) during his college years. He accepted his commission as a lieutenant when he graduated from a university and went off to lead a platoon of Marines in combat for an entire year.

Another close friend was drafted out of law school. He was bright enough to excel academically and also sufficiently learned to be fully aware of the abject absence of logic behind our nation's foreign policy strategies.

Each of their fathers served in WW II.

Each could see through the bullshit that sought to justify our involvement; yet each did what was expected of them in the spirit of something much larger than my dinky ego. Better people simply do not exist, not then, not now. My admiration for each of these gentlemen, then and now, is as big as the horizon as viewed by functioning astronauts. I rub this lather of blather on you to convey a complex reality, that of the protestor and the combatant, lambs and lions in the same field, of the same philosophy and mindset, diverging on a primary issue but remaining forever loyal to the larger vision of enduring friendship, for better or for worse.

In making these kinds of tricky adjustments in our young lives I believe we gained greater intellectual dexterity and became more philosophically adept better prepared to cope with the intricate diversities encountered in later life.

Being a protestor was dangerous in many respects. Adapting that posture positioned me on the wrong side of the law but the right side of morality, at least as I saw it. Half-a-lifetime later, I've become a bit more sanguine about the matter, still not understanding what the word "sanguine" means but really loving the sound of it, the phony sophistication its use imparts, if only to the user.

Less sure if I was right or wrong way back then I find solace in sentiment shared with me by my oldest son. He looks into my tired old eyes with youthful clarity and says he is proud of the positions I took DURING the war, when taking those positions had real meaning.

This dualistic dichotomy approach to existence lingered at the heart of my personality and lifestyle long after the last American G.I. flew out of Saigon International Airport only to return to the undeserved indifference and scorn of the citizenry they had been putting their ass on the line trying "to protect."

Bottom-line, life as a Vietnam War soldier was an exercise in lack of appreciation.

Life as a protester of that horrible ordeal was also a bad day at the beach, when there was a beach.

There were quite a few of us who eventually climbed aboard the "Hell no, we won't go" express, which seemed significant when we were all standing in a pack together. For the most part, though, being a protester was a lonely pursuit within the context of society at large, where most people treated us like creeps.

As noted, the "cool" thing to do at the time was to keep your mouth shut, blend in and make a lot of money.

Most people my age adhered to this hierarchy of goals.

I see them in full regal arrogance at class reunions, cocky in their wealth and freedom and possibly removed from the long-term residual economic and psychic effects of the advocacy hippie dudes like me adapted during the cultural wars of our youth.

For it was then many of us "fell off the bus," abandoned the pursuit of the almighty dollar and took on instead the larger cause (as we saw it) of doing all we could to stop the runaway train of war.

Going to Vietnam required obedience to government, right or wrong, not to mention a shit load of courage, balls and a good upbringing.

Protesting Vietnam required less courage, smaller balls and any background that applied.

It also took a fairly aggressive intellect to digest the evidence, wash it around in the saliva pit of history and eventually make sense of what could never be sensible.

Not every one of war age was capable of independent thinking.

If you were lucky enough to gain a decent education along the way, it became increasingly difficult to do anything but that.

Existing innocently within these two camps became the most common approach.

Protesters were treated like crap throughout their late-'60's quest for sanity. And when the war was finally over in 1975, their place in American society was somewhere between ignored and discredited.

Even though historians began to assess our Vietnam strategy as incorrect and wrong-headed, those of us who exposed those positions when the argument was at-hand were relegated to So What City?

I agree with Vietnam veterans.

Of course they deserved a parade.

These men and women deserve our complete, unconditional, open-ended irrevocable respect.

In fact, in accepting the assignment to go off to war, they demonstrated the kind of character and courage people like me will never know, will never be able to take any kind of pride in.

It was said many went to war because they were afraid not to go. Such a notion strikes me today as suppositional, cynical and probably accurate to a large degree.

My instinct remains to honor those who answered the call, did what they were asked to do. I can't question that, having thought about for most of my life.

They did what they were told to do. There is great dignity in that. I give them all the credit in the world .

If they didn't get the reception they felt they deserved when they came back from Vietnam, I'd say they got screwed, again.

If you protested the war like I did, you got Jack Shit, or, worse. You got a ton of condemnation from just about everybody alive. You got called a coward or worse, a draft dodger or a commie.

There were plenty of words for those who stood up and opposed the war.

On the upside, we did what we thought was right, usually in the face of enormous social consequences.

We may not have been classic bad-asses in the tradition of those magnificent young boys-become-warriors who went off to fight. But we were pretty awesome at times ourselves definitely true to our values and possibly even vindicated by the passage of time and the prevailing read of history.

So you know, we were called "commies" and "fags" and all of that happy horseshit.

But we stood up to the man never knowing when we might get swatted- down by the man or worse yet, shot at like the students at Kent.

On November 15, 1969, when half-a-million of us found our way to Washington D.C. to take part in a moratorium against the war, I later learned the federal government had amassed an army of similar size to engage protestors, an ad hoc group comprised of mostly reserve military personnel from around the country.

I came to understand this situation from a source that told me he was a national guardsman from Wisconsin who became a part of this government contingency force. Based on his story, he and his fellow soldiers were assigned to lay low in waiting in underground facilities close to the Capitol.

If the protests escalated into violence, he said they were fully armed and poised to intervene.

We never saw them that day. Given the tensions of the times, it was a miracle this tinderbox didn't explode on the National Mall that afternoon.

If it had, we might have witnessed another Gettysburg. Half-a-million moderately angry protestors gathered to pass joints and hear speakers decry the war in the shadows of our greatest monuments. I remember thinking at the time I had never seen so many pairs of Levi's in one setting.

Only by the very end of the day did a small radical contingent identifying as the "Red Guard" or some similar title break off from the mass of bodies and begin to create a disturbance on the outer fringe of the event.

In sheer numbers, they may have represented less than one-percent of the overall group, probably half of that as I recall. Volleys of teargas from the Capitol Police stifled their movement, dispersed the extremists in a real jiffy.

I felt at the time and still do that this faction represented the most offensive aspect of the protest movement.

Their instinct was not to reason in a civil manner. Rather, they sought all-out chaos. I understood their radical rationale. For them, the process of cautious protest was not working. Taking a relatively passive approach had failed, in their minds. They were intent upon evoking chaos as a means to eventually end the insanity on distant battlefields.

On Being One of Them

Regardless of our pedigree within the movement, those of us who chose to oppose the war were very visible highly contemptible. Our cause was the opposite of popular and people back home wanted to kill us.

At Kent State, they did just that.

America applauded that atrocity. That's why I hitchhiked out to Vancouver Island a few weeks after it happened. I could no longer handle life in America. This place quickly became entirely inhospitable for anyone with a mustache or hair touching his or her collar.

Many years later, not much has changed. America's Vietnam War veterans were given the memorial they deserve in the nation's capitol. The names of those who died – including a sergeant named "Meadows" --appear on a waving wall of granite and courage.

A person with an actual heart can't help but be moved by the memorial, no matter how you felt about the war when it was waged or how you feel now. You just see valor and heroism in their names and tragedy in the aura surrounding the place, knowing how controversial the war was and how the losses of those military personnel seem so jaded now by the understanding many have gained of the truly controversial nature of the Vietnam engagement.

That's my interpretation. If others remember this differently than I do it is because they lived through the period in different skin than mine.

Great responsibility exists within the realization that all of us came at this thing from diverging angles, different circumstances and places in time. It teaches us we have to accept whatever any of us did when our nation called asking us to off and fight in Vietnam as merely an extension of where we as individuals were coming from. Translating reality with this focus on understanding and acceptance reflects hippie thinking at its best. It is, I believe, a wonderful gift from the bohemian branch of my generation to the larger culture, something redemptive for all open-minded, freethinking unreformed rebels to acknowledge and celebrate.

Here is my most-inner take on the subject.

Others have told me the same thing so I think that I speak for many people my age in stating this yet another way.

We need to forgive one another for whatever we did back then, as we were simply being who were were/are/remain. For each of us had to deal with the matter in ways intrinsic to ourselves, not necessarily others. What was hard to imagine then is quite apparent today.

Others have their own views, all coherent and correct, from the perspective of the varying individuals whose lives were permanently altered by those events.

In the modern era -- Circa 2000 -- the issue of America's involvement in what became known as The Vietnam War remains nearly as controversial as it was during the very persecution of the controversial military strategy.

The war records of the two major political parties' candidates for president were subject to endless review, second-guessing and painful analysis.

Missing from the argument, however, was the issue of whether answering your country's call to duty in the first place was or was not appropriate, given the circumstances. Nearly 30 years after the "end of the war" its implicit logic -- or, illogic -- still raged in the minds of many of our citizens.

What John Kerry did and what George W. Bush did now stand as vivid reminders of the various paths followed by men my age at a time when a less than popular war dominated our lives.

Kerry signed up as an officer in The Navy and went to Vietnam even though many reports from that era indicate he did not support the cause. Kerry was not the only young American who agreed to become part of the killing apparatus with conflict and ambiguity haunting his conscience.

As a candidate for President, he absorbed hellacious amounts of hatred and vitriol from others who questioned his war record, in spite of the fact he actually answered the call and served in a leadership position with valor.

In his own words he has acknowledged as much.

His actions in the war are now seen as either mildly heroic or tacitly objectionable, depending on where you are still coming from and upon whom you listen to on the subject. When he got back, Kerry became an outspoken critic of the war and went as far as to characterize the actions of his comrade's actions in a negative manner.

For his part, Bush did what a lot of us did -- he fudged on his responsibility. There was nothing ignoble – or heroic -- about joining the Air National Guard in Texas. Clearly, he made a commitment while not actually being involved in combat. But still the fact he found a viable loophole like most of the rest of us did haunts him politically.

The presidential election of 2004 was seriously marred by this unfortunate dialogue and suffered to the extent outsiders sought to find clarity in a cauldron of historic murkiness.

In the end, whatever Kerry and Bush did then had less bearing on their potential for being elected then did more important impressions on the pressing matters of the day -- a new war in Iraq, domestic issues and numerous other items on the political agenda.

I believe those of us who survived the Vietnam War and did our best to learn from the lessons it taught are capable now of accepting the mandate of the electorate and supporting our national leader, no matter which imperfect person prevails.

It's called "maturity," folks.

What we know now, and possibly didn't know before, is the importance of getting over it, no matter what the "it" is. The idea is to accept reality on its own terms, to mellow out, move on, accept the past and basically get a life, have a life and stand tall, as that is our shared destiny.

Vanity Or Valor?

To the logical mind, *fessing-up* turns *messing-up* on its head.

When cornered and captured, confession comes easily. Why not spill-all when all else fails?

On the dark side of humiliation awaits abdication.

With liars, however, the inclination to tell the truth is as illogical as breathing under water.

Within a moral psyche, telling the truth is staying in-bounds, and is, therefore, fairly reactive. To have cast morality aside is to operate, full-time, out-of-bounds.

Bill Clinton should not necessarily be criticized for avoiding the Vietnam War. The moral basis of his leadership is another matter. To me, he is suspect merely for being unclear about the "how" and "why" part of it. Throughout his ascendance to the presidency, Clinton and the media who were supposedly covering his sorry ass left the epochal issue of Vietnam to hang, unresolved, unexplored, not-at-all understood.

I may not have adapted the correct posture relative to my lack of involvement in the execution of the Vietnam War. But at least I'm willing to talk about it. And honor my friends who took separate paths.

Speaking of marijuana, truth serum of choice among many college educated, gentle-by-nature men in bib overalls, I'd say Clinton represents "the beast" of my generation. I mean, having spent ten years being between the ages of 20 and 30, taking deep notes in some of America's most stridently bohemian enclaves I have to say, I don't remember EVER meeting ANYONE who smoked pot and didn't inhale. There might have been people who did that and I just didn't ride in a bug with 'em.

At least I liked Spam back then, before the personal computer changed everyone's carpel tunnel syndrome. There is a lot of gray in these lives we lead, as there is black and white. One-time, full-time smugglers I've known speak to me of honor in their ranks, of individuals who on the surface might appear below the law but who, in life, exhibit character ... way beyond the norm.

Belieing their menacing appearance many gnarley Harley owners embody the essence of peace, just as other apparently virtuous clean-shaven businessmen spend their days walking on the wrong side of the street.

You'd think a good-looking American President would embody most if not all of the values we systematically attach to the highest leadership in the land. One-time meth cookers need not apply to this position.

Hey, Bubba. Let's go swimming in the contradictions, with the Contras, in the Meena Airport fountain.

I think about my friends who put their pretty ass on the line in forlorn Vietnam. Two of them in particular come to mind. There are no finer people alive.

Both served in ''Nam because their fathers served in World War II. And that was that. Their willingness to engage in what they and I knew at the time (late-60's) was a dubious-at-best military adventure of "character reveal" in its finest sense.

Clearly, their decision to put their lives on the line in the war was an absolute act of respect for their respective fathers. Their "stand up" approach to navigating their military obligations amazed me then and continues to light up my life now ... and ten seconds from now ... and so on. Because I appear to have little control over what runs around in my hyper active brain, the stories of their lives intercede with mine, every day, past, present future. Our shared wartime encounters took place five decades ago; my brain perceives it as still happening.

I got stuck here. This was the mountaintop moment of my life. Nothing I'd experienced up until then and ever since then ever came close to rivaling the drama of this era.

We were 22 or 23 too old to be young too young to be old. Who cared?

There was a war to be fought, a need for millions of American soldiers to fight it. This was happening in real time. Real people had to make real decisions. Right now. You were dealt your cards and you only had a split second to look at them before you played your hand. Right now. My friends and I at the time were smart enough to be just getting out of college but green peas nonetheless, each of us without a lick of real-world experience, exposure or global awareness. Who cared?

What they did during the war will always engulf all regions of my brain as long as it operates effectively. Past, present, future, their choices will forever exemplify valor, nothing short of it.

Valor walks with each of them, to this day. And the paths they walk lead right through my consciousness.

People fill their lives with nothingness, at least some of them. Others proceed diligently, an otherworldly magical aura about them, revealed in their eyes, their posture, the full flowering of the choices they make, actions they take, the personal vapor trail they leave behind as they go about their existence.

I watched as friends who hated the war as much as I did went off to help prosecute it, nevertheless, compelled by a sense of destiny that meant more to them than their brains may have otherwise dictated.

My own experience during this troubled time was to do everything necessary to remain home and, eventually, to stand up against the war. The more distance I get from the experience, the greater my appreciation of the total despair I experienced.

Not against those who served but, rather, against the very nature of action unexplored. Had our national leaders at the time truly explored the pros and cons of committing men and resources to a distant conflict, we surely would have stayed at home.

Be that as it may, many went, many didn't. Men my age defined ourselves then.

Clinton defined himself by evading the entire process and then, shutting up about it afterwards. His was the ultimate childlike gesture in that he pretended the issue did not exist. Issues, and the evasion thereof, are the issue in this issue.

If Clinton were going to fess-up he would have started at Age 5.

Instead, we have a President who makes Johnson and Nixon look valiant in comparison.

After The Fact

He was my boss. Knowing that might help you understand why it was I couldn't physically assault him when he made a statement that offended me more than any other comment I heard that day, that year, that life.

"The Vietnam War didn't hurt our country," the man said to me in the summer of 1973.

Yes it did, I argued.

The discussion ended after a few minutes of point-counter point. I went back to my telephone. He went back to Denial.

He was considerably older than I had yet to become.

He died in 2004, a few months before I wrote the next sentence.

For all that any of us know, he's still alive in our minds and hearts.

I didn't work for the man for long—three months, to be exact. That was enough for me.

Vietnam wasn't the reason I resigned from that position. There were more important issues, like doing what I really wanted to do, not what someone else wanted me to do.

I moved on, he moved out.

Many years after the official conclusion of America's war against the North Vietnamese people—Communists, allegedly—what I remember is, he was wrong as hell.

Vietnam and the dirty war we waged against its citizenry creamed this country.

(It is said LBJ went off the gold standard in order to pay for the war, forever impacting the sanctity of world economic structuring. This singular consideration extends well outside whatever measure of expertise I bring to the discussion. More serious students of the subject may find infinite intrigue in this sub-topic.)

Vietnam damaged our country by all measurable means of assessment. And his remark hurt me more than anyone could imagine.

Still, in spite of my sense of political correctness—then and now—I've also gained the wisdom and insight required to dare to imagine it was I who was wrong, he who was right. In other words, I'm not so sure now.

In other words, if others saw it differently then, or, see it differently now, that's fine with me. I'm considerably more open-minded as a virtual old man. I no longer pretend to know whether The Vietnam War was bad or neutral or good or otherwise.

I'm simply forever intrigued by what happened to our country at that time, what happened to their country, what happened to my life and to the lives of others my age. I do know the whole son of a bitch flipped me off my rocker, beyond the tarmac.

The heartache I experienced then was so overwhelming I could not possibly be the same person I was before that nightmare came down on our generation. It tore me deeply for a long time. To think I can now just shuck it off and get back to wherever I'd been before is nuttier than a clown reunion in a tequila bar.

For several years, I spent everyday believing the act of enduring an unendurable war was driving me up a large wall. What I felt was unmanageable became somehow doable, only out of necessity.

Surely I wasn't the only one to effectively give up the ghost and slip off into Flip City in the face of such persistent trauma.

Oh well. That is a very small deal in the larger scheme of things. Bottom line, I am most comfortable deferring now to the recollections of others. They were there too.

I wasn't the only one paying attention, even when I was temporarily checked out of Planet Earth. We all experienced this differently.

My friends who went to Vietnam took more traditional courses of action.

Our souls converged in an earlier time. Our lives intersected and our experiences wove in and out of and around each other's respective journeys.

How sweet it sort of was.

What we saw and heard and felt and celebrated and anguished about was a time in our lives when duty and maturity required us to step forth from youth and enter into adulthood (since we had no choice) while the world around us was changing faster than we could imagine, let alone deal with.

All players aspired to dignity and at least one of us may have fulfilled that particular mandate. Speaking on my own behalf, I'd say my specific story lacks honor, grace or nobility.

As you discovered, I was just another will-of-the-wisp rich suburban dilettante/guitarist who could play every Kingston Trio song by heart.

I lacked focus and foresight to such an extent it's hard to explain now how I even got off the Greyhound, let alone on it.

In the final analysis, I think my story provides one person's view of historical dynamics that were, in actuality, extremely more complex than what I can express since I only experienced those dynamics as one single and zealously troubled persona.

Fortunately for society most people my age adapted a more responsible approach to the process known as coming of age than I did.

My take on all this is not the story of Everyman; it is the sordid tale of any man. Any one of us from the era could posit a similarly subjective account of what we went through as Western Civilization indulged in large-scale culture change. All versions are of equal validity to the extent they are true and searching and illuminative.

We were, generally speaking, a confused lot, challenged by ephemeral circumstances to make transcendent choices. The times called for instantaneous decision-making. Where we stood on the key issues was summoned out of us by reality. Only now, some 50 frosty years down the road, do any of us old hippies and hostesses have the relative luxury of truly contemplating the vagaries of what we experienced and mulling over all the large events in a calm, non-emotional manner.

I like this a lot better. It's easier on the arches.

What any of us did in our earlier years did truly take place in the context of genuine upheaval. What any of us do from this time on will be influenced by not only our respective memories but also by our shared commitment to proceed carefully, recognizing the perils of basing national foreign policy on naïve analysis.

We're drawing now on whatever lessons we finally regard as instructive, life instructions handed down from our former selves to our emerging sense of who we are and who we should continue to become, considering all we went through to get here.

Did the Vietnam War hurt our country? Surely, "it" did. The real ambiguity exists in the finite definitions within the premise. History moves much too fast for any consensus-based evaluation to color the conversation. The best any of us can do in deep retrospect is engage the uncertaintly, assess whatever commonly agreed upon facts emerge from the morass of controversy and find guidance from experience, honoring all who gave their lives in the cause of *freedom*.

Decades later, the freedom for which they fought now manifests in our shared responsibility to parlay wisdom into enlightened pursuit.

After Vietnam

The Vietnam War raged in Southeast Asia throughout the decade of the 1960's. People now look back on that decade as being a period of major dissent and anarchy in America. That was hardly the case.

During the first four or five years of the conflict, few in America questioned its persecution. There was no major precedent for refuting the government line. Major news sources reported "the facts" and the citizenry generally ate them up.

Prior to 1969, protesters existed on the outer edge of societal esoterica. After 1969, the tide had turned, the President-elect had gained office on a pledge to end the war and returning veterans began to encounter a country increasingly either hostile to them and their designated cause or indifferent, at best.

A few citizens fully embraced the "logic" of the war -- for more than half-a-decade. For many of them, the rationale for its execution was plausible.

Just about everyone agreed Communism was a pretty bad idea. If we had to face it down in Southeast Asia, so be it. If we had to take casualties in that effort, *C'est La Vie.* Americans granted its government the benefit of the doubt for quite a while, I'd say. Nearly everyone with a pulse bought the government rational.

Even dehumanizing, fully implausible explanations were accepted as binding fact, full justification for invading a foreign land, killing their people and ours as well.

The "enemy" as loosely defined was different than we Americans, human for sure but of another breed altogether, to the extent death itself was supposedly less of an issue for "them" than it is for noble us. To make slaughtering them more palatable, they were labeled "gooks," a dehumanizing term that evoked the gross liquid buildup that occurs around the edge of the human eye.

If readers today find this hard to believe it is because America Circa-1965 was considerably more naïve then than it is today. We came a long way after the horrible Vietnam War ended in terms of gaining better appreciation for the fact that all people ARE the same, that we are all one, together, that it could never again be appropriate to diminish the humanity of any people anywhere for the benefit of the ammunitions industry.

In effect, ever-arriving waves of hundreds and hundreds of thousands of American soldiers were primed for what would follow by a palate of propaganda designed to deceive them into thinking they would encounter sub-human entities.

They were trained to believe they would be going into battle against the equivalent of outer space invaders – odd alien entities in pajamas who deserved to be killed by us for reasons under-explored, rotten rational incapable of standing up to the scrutiny of reason, ultimately evil in intent.

A travesty of galactic proportion played out for more than a decade with the full consent of the same country whose soldiers had only a generation before helped liberate Western Europe.

It may well have been, we were so blinded by the perceived glory of what we had allegedly accomplished in Europe, many years earlier, that we failed to recognize the rot within the structuring of our descent into Southeast Asia.

It was more incomprehensible in real-time than it has ever been in retrospect.

This remains true even as the great weight of cumulative historical assessment continues to conclude with ever-greater consensus that the entire war experience was ill advised, counter-productive and entirely wrong by every possible measure.

During the war, after its conclusion, reticence to posture with such conviction prevented this writer from going so far as to frame these matters within the context of historic surety.

Only now, nearly 50 years after the last American helicopters lifted off from the abandoned embassy roof, does the balance of opinion tilt so affirmative as to cover my back in positing my viewpoint.

I know as well as anyone that others have their own take on this matter.

Our Tragedy

A generation fully invested in the optimism of post World War II America had its illusions shattered in the cauldron that was our war in Vietnam.

The entire notion ours was a chosen age group destined to carry the proud torch of Yankee manifest destiny to its next exultant level came crashing down in a million rice paddies.

The bold lies that sought to justify our military adventure were gradually unmasked. Instead of fighting for a worthy cause, we eventually woke up to the fact the entire premise we were expected to die for was in fact a morally bankrupt, deeply flawed and tragically incorrect lie.

Years after our retreat the thick dust of history began to lift, revealing monstrously deceptive manipulation, inept strategies and wholesale failure of leadership.

We had no choice but to pick up the pieces and start building a new model of what the land of our birth truly represented.

Having seen it for its best and then its worst we took on the challenge of integrating the good and the bad.

We surrendered youthful ardor, worked through the disgust and committed to resolving the extremes ... and to replacing them with sober clarity and mature acceptance.

To those who remember, and anyone else listening in, any effort to chronicle the nature of *this extended interlude* is obliged to engage "in fact."

However, in this context, anecdote and assiduous reporting facilitate an elastic approach to defining fact, differentiating it from opinion or larger hyperbole and assisting the curious-minded among you in gaining better appreciation of the nuances of a long, pointless war.

As revealed, I never made it to this particular theater of conflict, many thousands of miles from our heartland, across the Pacific Ocean and far into the unknown realm of unfamiliarity, in a land mostly misunderstood, under-valued and culturally denigrated.

Vietnam to me was entirely indistinct, off my radar—a giant void of incomprehension.

All of that changed in the mid-to-late-1960s.

Everybody was in on that learning curve, especially men of my age group, especially men challenged by the rigors of staying enrolled in college.

Like probably eight or ten million others of my suspicious ilk, I did in fact matriculate, gesticulate, exacerbate, regurgitate and remain enrolled somewhere in an accredited institution of higher learning long enough to eventually skate around the system and more or less avoid the call of duty.

Merely recalling my own sad truth hits like a large piece of weather-treated lumber, a two-by-four to the side of the head. Speaking for myself, we did not see ourselves as virtuous in any way. We were game-players, pure and simple.

There was no honor, no self-satisfaction in the devious steps we took to keep our ass out of a war we also gradually came to despise. I take no comfort asserting any inside knowledge pertaining to this unfortunate story.

I was age-appropriate and consumed in it like we all were, those of us born after Hiroshima and raised on patriotic love of country and allegiance to its foreign policy.

I never stopped trying to learn, listening to others, reading as much as I could find on the subject of the American War in Vietnam.

Over the years I have barely scratched the surface, even as I've sought to dive in without forgetting to make dinner tonight.

This much is certain: I am artistically sustained by my reliance on the thoughts of others who remember all of this through their own experiences and insights.

Revisiting Vietnam

In response to another State of the Union speech from another American President, National Public Radio (NPR) in early-2006 corralled a group of Dayton, Ohio-area voters into a broadcast focus group.

Their objective was to capture and broadcast reactions to the speech from half-a-dozen or so voting citizens.

Turned out, this apparently "randomly selected" group was made up mostly of adult men who were identified as "war babies" and "Vietnam War veterans."

Grandpa lit up his pipe and listened in.

To a man, the thrust of their remarks focused on perceived parallels between *their* war and our current crusade against "the enemy" in Iraq. There was no variance in opinion.
Each speaker alluded to why America "lost" in Vietnam – because our political leadership capitulated.
They as soldiers didn't lose the war; defeat came from inside The Beltway.
And, by-God, they said, we'd better not make the same mistake again in Iraq.
Grandpa put away the tobacco and started tapping *these-here* plastic keys.
Key-resistors, he thought to himself.
Listening to each speaker repeat the same mantra – "we could and should have won that war" – he was immersed in both compassion and disagreement.
Compassion because his primary instinct was to respect veterans of this controversial war, disagreement because he felt their historical interpretations were flawed.
Amid all of that he was reminded human nature dictates we grasp for justification in our actions, strive to believe we are "right" about all matters even as common sense suggests otherwise.
Forty years later people from my generation continue to be stratified as ever regarding The Vietnam War.
Legions of detractors say we lost it. Some say we won it.
We did kill two or three million of their citizenry, two million more Cambodians and Laotians, spent billions of American dollars bombing the daylights out of the place.
We must have accomplished something.
They're still resolving lawsuits regarding the deathly effects of Agent Orange, a nasty defoliant our military drenched on the country we assaulted back in the glorious '60s. Of course this war remains in the news.

It was huge. The sharp edge engendered by its controversial nature lingers forever auspicious. Clearly, the old man realized, those of us from the late-'60s remain pretty well locked-in to the positions we took back then, all these many decades later.

If you were there, you invested large portions of yourself into the decisions you made. All of us from the Vietnam War era had big-time skin in the game. Those who answered the call and did their time in the combat arena surely paid the greatest price in terms of leaving much of themselves in those troubled rice paddies.

As for those of us who stayed home and eventually joined the protest movement, we too made sacrifices, although clearly of a different nature.

To compare what we went through with the toll of real battle is a harsh insult to the gravity of war and to the courage of those who in doing their duty effected such action.

Way more than a decade ago my job required persistent travel. As creative director for a national training program, I journeyed to nearly all States, staying in the air, in rental cars, hotel rooms and predictable restaurants for the better part of 12-years. The best experiences emanated from chance contacts made, usually in the back of commercial airliners.

One night in the dark skies 30,000-ft. above the American heartland, I found myself engaged in an illuminating conversation with a person seated next to me who turned out to be a U.S. Navy officer who served in Vietnam.

We talked for hours and connected for eternity, as far as I was concerned.

We shared a peculiar sense of humor. He laughed at nearly everything I said, especially when I noted there was what appeared to be a small applesauce stain on his Passport. Considering we were not drinking we were goofy, like lifelong buddies with much in common and nothing better to do than celebrate. We discovered we were fairly similar in some respects although his resume made mine look like a chewing gum wrapper.

He was an Annapolis graduate. Upon learning this, I sensed an opportunity to permanently secure our new friendship by confessing to him that I dated a girl named Ann Appolis in high school. At that point, he was forced to decide whether I was kidding or simply trying to impress our stewardess.

Because he brought at least half-a-dozen more I.Q. points to this showdown in the sky, the man seated next to me acknowledged his awareness that I was breaking out all the stops to make this conversation among the most memorable of a lengthy era of working essentially way above the clouds.

He was sincere, friendly, intelligent willing to wile away this flight in conversation. We exchanged personal histories. I told him Ann's father had been a Greek mobster with an odd obsession for pastel-shaded upholstery; he said his own Dad was a diabolical despot despised by everyone he ever knew, but winked while talking indicating he was committed to extracting at least as much levity from our conversation as I was obviously racking up.

Inserting elements of mirth into our conversation had the effect of providing some relief to an inherently somber topic.

For the most part, we exchanged serious thoughts on the war. In doing so, we both acknowledged harboring profound doubts about the positions we adapted then. Our thoughts circled around each other. He questioned the validity of the war; I questioned my own opposition.
The more we backslid the closer we came to consensus. Hindsight proved extremely helpful.
As the plane began its approach to an airport in who-knows-where, we endeavored to summarize our points and bring finality to our discussion.
I told him I admired him as a person and a veteran who did what he was asked to do. He told me he completely agreed with my views on the war, appreciated my honesty and courage required to take my protest to the streets, more than once, and my willingness to stand-back from my position of opposition to the degree exhibited in our dialogue.
We shared a moment of mutual affection, two previous strangers connected now by our willingness to "get real." He concluded saying if he had it to do over he would again don the uniform. For as dubious as he had come to perceive our strategies in Viet Nam really were, he said in the final analysis, when they ask you to go, you go. He was raised to think that way.
He still bought-into the patriotic model -- the principle of duty and honor however questionable the circumstance.
I couldn't top that. Instead, I shook his hand again for the sixth or seventh time and told him what he already knew; he and his fellow veterans were and are always heroes to me.
Saying good-bye to this former stranger I knew I'd been in the presence of a true Spartan, a man-and-a-half, a walking/talking smiling manifestation of exemplary

I was driving from Syracuse, New York to Boston, Massachusetts when I heard the news that four students had been killed by National Guard troops in Ohio.

As the radio announcer droned on I looked out the windows of my Volkswagen, beheld the Berkshires and realized everything was different.

My whole world changed. In less than a minute, I concluded America as I thought I had known it was less like home sweet home and more like alien territory. So I decided to freak out.

I knew all about Kent—a friend lived there. I'd been through the place as a political lackey; later on, a close confidante matriculated at the university enabling me to buy her dinner a few more times even after her real Mr. Right had intervened artfully, stealing one of the finest hearts on the old prairie.

Yes, indeed. Kent, Ohio. *Hmmmm.*

Located near Cleveland, it is/was a hotbed of political rancor, a swelling cesspool of left-wing radicalism and a legendary citadel of exceptionally brilliant beer stores.

Months before the Kent shootings, I had driven from Scranton, Pennsylvania to Kent, Ohio one snowy winter's day in my old German sled with erratic windshield wipers in order to supposedly procure a bag 'o hemp, only to later discover no such product was available.

Pardon me?

Only genuine stoners will appreciate the blanket of despair that accompanies such moments. I was more disappointed than a groom on the first night of his honeymoon who discovers the *woman* he thought he just married is actually the boxer, Sugar Ray Leonard.

My friend who encouraged me to drive six hours in order to pick up a bag of something that was no longer available humanity. I'd felt honored to share the flight with such an open and distinguished personality and to have experienced his acceptance, given our disparate patriotic pedigree.

Walking down a familiar airport corridor I felt taller, fuller less encumbered in all respects. Something clicked in my head. I felt suddenly reborn in the present tense, delivered from the past tense. A random conversation had vanquished whatever lingering Vietnam War-related angst had still been festering in my soul.

Being in this great person's proximity for this brief interlude and earning his blessing of my wartime conduct lifted me measurably from whatever funk I might have been in, elevated my peace of mind.

I experienced myself as a slightly better person for having imbued his revelations and perspectives.

I luxuriated in his respect for my views. Everything felt better. He was OK with me. I was OK with him.

The lingering weight of The American Vietnam War lessened a few degrees in my psyche on that flight, at that moment. I still carry much of it and always will as long as my carrier still works. I try to shed it whenever any opportunity presents itself, in an airliner or in the quiet of morning, when I find myself awake and alive.

It is then I remember that sheer existence on our glorious planet is a gift, extended to you and me by "The Almighty" as well as the valor and sacrifice of others we should never forget.

Final Thoughts

Into this document I've dropped a mass of Vietnam War mental montages, capsules of fact and opinion that for the past five decades have swirled around in my memory, defining perpetuity. By sharing them I've been able to clear out my noggin' open up some new space for the endless parade of current exigency that seizes up an older person's agenda.

In order to accomplish this important piece of mental housekeeping I shifted my brain into Reverse, committed to spending another year absorbed in Vietnam, immersed in the depression that characterized the era during which our country found itself bogged down in the mire of illogical war.

I found being there again wasn't nearly as difficult as being there the first time. Surely hints of familiar despair sought to enter my consciousness as I put the present aside and journeyed back in time. Fortunately, I found myself more adept at sidestepping the angst, processing it now with greater insight and maturity. I suppose.

Then again, none of this strikes me as absolute certainty. Living through the war – then and now – has been a dominant element of my life. The entire episode permeates my existence, past, present and future. My thoughts about our war in Southeast Asia seem to permanently bang around in my brain, for better or worse, like neurons in an atom, or atoms in a neuron.

I've done my best to present them in logical linear order. I've also become so overly familiar with these narratives many now strike me as trite, pedestrian, hyperbolic, grandiose – all the things I don't like about New Yorkers. When concocted, these contributions struck me as relevant, fresh, drawn from the cauldron of personal experience and worthy of inclusion in this or any neo-scholarly screed. Factoring in both views, I come up with "let her rip."

When asked to express my thoughts about our Vietnam War, I share this stock answer: Anyone from my age group is A-OK with me– people born in the first few years after

World War II -- veteran, protestor, anomaly, hippie, yuppie, narcotics agent, Moonie, theater usher or usherette, cartel hit man, angel. I'm permanently enamored of each and every one of them, of us.

You see it's "a generation thing." This 70-year-old happens to like other 70-year-olds.

Veterans of our war in Vietnam have special appeal to me, whether they opt for invisibility or choose to be recognized by the hats they wear or the bumper stickers they slap on the backs of their pickup trucks. I really dig this crowd, perhaps more than this crowd digs me.

I know many Vietnam War veterans would just as soon dig me a hole in the ground and park my ass in there before I take this exercise any farther.

Their contempt for me, the "me" who is now identified as an old war protestor, is entirely comprehensible. It also reflects a larger communications breakdown.

Veterans tend to believe that war protestors on the home front encouraged the enemy, made their lives worse. Protestors believed our actions would help end a senseless war, save our soldiers, bring them home out of the killing zone. The two sides simply did not understand each other. I remember thinking then that a lot of our soldiers didn't really comprehend the full range of motivations that led people like me to resist the war, attend demonstrations, scream at federal building employees, all while appearing to tacitly encourage "the enemy," as defined at the time. Many veterans perceived protestors as *the enemy at home*, people whose objection to the war was implicitly making their lives more difficult. There was no arguing that position.

For a protestor, it became a sad fact of life – trying to stop a war may have actually perpetuated it, even worsened it. That was not what we had in mind.

Our objective was to stop what we considered to be an indefensible war. We wanted to do it as soon as possible, to save soldiers' lives, not exacerbate the problem. Alas, the two sides weren't listening to each other.

The fleeting random nature of everyday encounters did little to enhance careful explanation. What you saw was what you got. It was crazy to think a returning soldier had any obligation, let alone desire to sort out the nuances of protest.

I certainly never expected a veteran to expend any mental money trying to grasp what made me tick let alone seek to cultivate a mind capable of grasping the complexities of speaking out against your own government.

That was our job. They had enough on their plate. Those were and remain separate realities.

At this point, it's all "on me" to fully grasp and embrace the model of obedience that led others in various directions. I'll never know what it was like to board the plane fully aware there was a good likelihood you would not come back, in one piece or not at all.

This life will not afford me the opportunity to experience what it is like to put on the uniform of my country, fly off to the other side of the world, step down onto the tarmac into the intense heat, ever-present danger and sheer ambiguity of Vietnamese society.

To understand the raw experience of war I can only rely on imagination.

Similarly, a person who never experienced the intense nervousness and deep personal conflict war protestors felt every second they expressed dissent can themselves only speculate what it was like to say "no" to the man.

What all of us *should* know is the war is over we don't have to resent one another any more, if we ever did. Our only obligation now is to demonstrate our shared desire to dump the angst and get on with the larger cause of understanding ourselves and the positions we took during the war.

Bottom line: All vets by now are all good with me.

Chapter Two
Epochal Events

A number of distinct events occurred as The American War in Vietnam wore on some exerting considerable influence on the political and military landscape of war. Following are my "takes" on seven of those "epochal events."

Kent State

Forgetting the shootings at Kent State University will always be impossible in the minds of those us who were paying attention that day, May 4, 1970, when a small squadron of nervous and unqualified Ohio National Guardsmen shot and killed four college students and wounded nine others.

Politically minded zealots captured that event in our permanent mental reservoirs. There it exists forever along with other indelible dates like November 22, 1963. Most of us can go back and place our souls on the Kent State shootings as easily as we can recall what we had for lunch five minutes ago.

Anti-war protests in Kent had erupted following President Nixon's TV speech on April 30 announcing that U.S. forces had invaded Cambodia, thus enlarging a war he had once pledged to end.

The next day Nixon derided students everywhere as bums, encouraging most of us to plead guilty as charged.

The disturbances in Kent grew particularly nasty.

When the college ROTC buildings were set ablaze— supposedly by students although that has never been verified—The Guard went on edge.

On May 3, sitting governor James Rhodes called antiwar students worse than brown shirts and the Communist element and also the night riders and vigilantes.

They are the worst type people we harbor in America, he screeched.

Rhodes was wrong.

In retrospect, neo-reactionaries like him come across as more sinister. Others surely disagree.

They may write their own books.

I was there and can attest more than two-thirds of the people who protested the Vietnam War were cream-of-the-crop people, bright, sensitive and as patriotic as the next guy.

More than anything, they were onto something important even if they were still slightly ahead of their time.

While others may see this differently, it is my opinion that whole Vietnam mess was a bad war, as opposed to a good war.

I may be wrong. I could very easily be wrong.

None of that discourages this effort.

When he cast his profane analysis Rhodes was spewing hate and a false, self-serving summary of an infinitely more complex manifestation of protest.

Gov. Rhodes' dim-witted interpretation derived from a hillbilly brain in the body of a chauvinistic bully.

He was a shallow yet politically successful man with a crazed look in his eye and a frightful incapacity to interpret reality with a precise measure of accuracy.

He flourished in a system based upon work ethic, political instinct, a general willingness to play by the (lack of) rules and an abiding capacity to consume copious amounts of alcoholic beverages without throwing up on the shoes of your alderman.

Rhodes was a hayseed made good. I was a man/child, gone south.

This writer began working for the Republican Party in Ohio in 1968, one week after I got out of college and two years before the Kent State shootings took place.

I met Rhodes more than once, finding him to be singularly unique, an animated, vibrant character who embodied the rich texture of his native Ohio.

I joined him and hundreds of other extremely inebriated party insiders in attending that year's sodden and guaranteed insane Republican Party Convention in hotter-than-fuck Miami, Florida.

Encouraged by media predictions, Rhodes actually thought Richard "Dollhouse" Nixon might choose him as his running mate in '68.

Perhaps they had a secret deal.

Perhaps no one cares.

Ohio *was* a must-win state for The Trickster.

Even if he hadn't been officially promised a place on the ticket, Rhodes as an over-the-top opportunist/should-have-been carnival barker could have mistakenly construed his destiny, multiplied by three-dozen tall glasses of cheap vodka.

I sure as hell don't give a flying fig one-way or the other. I am only here to tell you he was but one or two steps removed from common lout.

At the very moment when Rhodes learned Spiro Agnew got the call instead of His Ignorance, he threw an enormous pout in an elevator in a hotel in Miami, where thousands of Republican shooters like Rhodes had gathered for a week of incredible alcohol consumption conducted in the guise of a convention.

In all, there were four people in the elevator.

It was going up. It was early in the morning.

It occurred to one of the elevator occupants—me, incidentally—that at least a few of the people in the elevator had been up all night drinking.

Whether or not that was the case, it was clear Rhodes was a poor loser with a discouraging contempt for hotel property.

When someone told him Agnew was Nixon's choice, Rhodes started kicking the elevator wall and cursing loudly, his anger unreserved, his stature forever reduced. He snarled and fizzled and came just about completely unglued although I don't recall any actual weeping or sobbing, at least on the part of the other three of us.

We quietly observed his odd behavior like sociologists assessing the decomposition of an incorrigible juvenile delinquent.

I remember thinking at the time the country was probably better off with this particular nut off rather than on the ticket. Although the other cross-dressing transsexual we got proved to be more than a horse's ass, himself, until Nixon eventually threw *him* under the bus, after Agnew had hurled Nixon himself beneath the semi.

Oh my. These were people of intrigue.

Destiny offered me an opportunity to watch them in action. They had about as much stature as a disposable birdbath.

In May 1970 it was then-Governor Rhodes who ordered his state's National Guardsmen to help quell demonstrations on the Kent State campus.

Students at Kent State were allegedly armed with weapons. But none were found.

Still, the men of Troop B opened fire.

And the shit hit the fan.

picked up on my faltering spirit, came up with another plan he thought would placate my desire for some mid-range variant of self medication.

Offered heroin as an alternative, I quickly declined, drove off decisively to a liquor store bought a 6-pack of Miller High Life and beat it back across the Appalachian Mountains, copping along the way a good old-fashioned American beer buzz in lieu of boo.

Hit Shit Fan

When the shit hit the fan at Kent State the shift change became more like a global waltz with couples swapping partners and partners changing couples, with enzymes entering the vernacular and hibernation giving way to short naps.

America changed 437-degrees after Kent State, only to revert to normal again before flinging off into caffeine addicted pure free-fall by the time of Nixon's reelection, just before Watergate fall-out rocked his—and my—world.

So many things took place in the same relatively short time frame, most people gave up trying to keep track of the various sequences and simply opened disco clubs or at least hired nannies.

That was a long time ago, more than 46 years by golly.

The shit hit the fan and the novice took notice.

As for the young people who were murdered at Kent State, let the record show there was nothing fundamentally wrong with them.

They knew the history of our country.

They appreciated the terms of being a citizen of this noble experiment in representative government.

Like all of us, they assumed certain precepts:

- Dissent is an honored tradition and is tolerable, even laudable in the land of the free and the home of the caveman.
- If you think something is wrong, you have the right to act on your feelings as long as in doing so you don't disenfranchise others.

Spring 1970 peaked with the Kent State shootings, in early May.

Insanely pissed off protestors were throwing rocks at National Guard soldiers and burning down buildings.

Straight America would have no part of it.

When the protests turned violent, the response did, too.

At Kent State, the response became more violent than the provocations.

As noted, four students were shot to death.

They died and the entire anti-war movement suffered a major defeat. Straight America farted and snorted and strutted proudly after the shootings.

Average people in the country defended the government's actions in Ohio.

Anti-war types like me didn't stand a chance.

If you presented an easy-going manner, revealed denim in your wardrobe or wore a discreet mustache, mainstream citizens marked you as *one of them*.

Apparently my freak flag was more apparent to The Silent Majority than it was to me, still wearing a coat and tie for my job and submitting to occasional barbershop visits.

After Kent State, I began getting disturbingly bad vibes from types of people who previously did not focus on me at all.

I went from being culturally invisible to Mr. Walking Bad News.

Keep in mind, my only sin was to adapt to changing times, drive a VW bug, carry a bunch of guitars around and have enough intellectual curiosity to begin to question policy and authority.

I was guilty of exercising the skills I had learned in school to question, probe and analyze evidence, sort through inconsistency and formulate thought based on honest assessment.

The more any of us learned "to think" the more open-mindedly we thought. As we saw things, it wasn't our fault our brains had actually begun to work efficiently.

My alienation reached the point of suffocation.

The Kent State protestors took their chances when they chose to provoke the skittish Ohio National Guardsmen. But the abnormal ones that day were the conscripts who obeyed the evil command to shoot unarmed students.

Like Nazi prison guards gassing people of the Jewish faith only a few years earlier, they probably felt they didn't have any choice other than to obey their commanding officer ... and defile their Lord.

What I learned between 1968 and 1972 was that there are certain times in the life of a purposeful being when it's imperative to stand up to amoral garbage and exercise your endowed-in-America right to speak truth to power.

My generation was instructed to go kill Asians.

A few of us thought about it, rejected the premise and lived the consequences of our actions.

Earlier we were told Civil Rights demonstrators were provocateurs.

We spit-out that garbage, too,

We actually joined the ranks with the brave pioneers who rectified that particular realm of gigantic injustice.

Later we were told marijuana was evil.

That was laughable.

Soon we shoved aside archaic environmentally destructive practices, let Gays out of the closet, stood aside so women could gain positions of leadership and embraced multiple dimensions of diversity in any number of additional ways. When all the issues were sorted out, however, nothing really compared with Nam.

Most Americans bought the Vietnam War rationale for many years, before events in that theatre began to change perceptions.

By May 1970, the tide of public opinion was changing quickly.

The Kent students may have been in the vanguard. But they weren't too far off from a historical perspective.

And they didn't deserve to die.

Straight, obedient America accepted the rationale that the Kent State students asked for the bullets that killed them, that the Guardsmen were correct in shooting at them.

A line was drawn in American society.

To set the record straight, most everyday Americans supported the authorities in this unfortunate but galvanizing episode now known simply as Kent State. Protestors even as late as 1970 were still a decided minority.

The movement as it were was still gaining momentum when Rhodes' conscripts sullied history.

Their sinful shots resonated and ultimately gave additional credence and support to the emerging opposition to the prosecution of the Vietnam War, ultimately galvanizing the inevitable logic of the cause.

Whatever disaster beset the young troublemakers (read heroes) on the Ohio campus, they had asked for it in the minds of the Silent Majority a phrase cooked-up by

Republican myth makers to describe the American status quo, a realm within which rocking the boat was greatly discouraged.

Perhaps with a few of *them-there* hippie-dippy protestors dead they'd shut up about the war and go back to their Budweiser stupor.

Historians and those of us who posture as such draw back from broad-brushing the complexities of the subjects at hand.

Many elements comprised the silent majority.

And disparate sources filled the ranks of protestors, from earnest individuals to self-serving sycophants, from Communist plotters to government spies and informants.

You never knew who was passing you a joint. And you never knew what was in the joint.

You could pretend to draw from the joint without actually doing so or you could pocket the joint and share it with your old lady afterwards, even if she was just 19.

And keep in mind—I was only one more peon back then.

I can't speak for everyone.

I did have my antenna up.

But my radio didn't always work.

Not everyone protested in those days.

Most people did what they were told to do and towed the company line.

Of the approximately 125 other males in my high school graduating class of 1963, I'm sure only a dozen or so of us became anti-war activists during the Vietnam War.

Most men my age did what was expected of them joined a branch of service.

We weren't necessarily smarter or dumber than they were.

Back then; people simply did what they felt they had to do.

In fact, that is among the primary lessons learned from that military excursion.

Only a fringe minority successfully put two and two together, realized the war was wrong and went nuts trying to figure out creative ways to somehow try to help stop it.

The decisive events of May 1970 changed the paradigm. Kent State made it painfully clear America was tough on dissidents.

But America was changing.

America was on the verge of becoming permanently different than it had been before.

A new dimension of introspection was infecting the body politic, the body cultural the body beautiful.

A new capacity to see ourselves objectively, good and bad, was gradually cleansing our thought processes while elevating the national character, escalating the rate with we were about to become capable of assimilating the full picture and able to adjust our agendas consistent with a larger view.

Four dead in Ohio equated to a large loss of innocence and an even greater emancipation from the constraints of our charmed and childlike naiveté.

OK, we inferred.

You shoot back, with real bullets intended to kill, like real bullets do.

Your indelicate response silences the stone-throwers, mutes the voices of some elements of your most passionate youth ostensibly sets the record straight just as to who is running this rodeo.

Yes, sir.

As you might know, the authorities got away with killing students at Kent State; just like many years later the

Chinese bosses would succeed in killing more than a thousand protestors in Beijing.

In a world where thugs rule, thugs have a tendency to rule and to prevail with certainty.

Of course, none of those thugs can stop me from writing this sentence nor can they prevent masochists like you from reading it.

You've basically had enough of this anti-war business, haven't you?

And you would prefer if those of us who have hitherto felt inclined to speak out against the nasty son of a bitch would instead stifle our instincts in favor of some alternative form of mutation.

OK, we understand that.

Of course, we did not shut up.

We did take one step backwards reassessed the means by which legitimate dissent could be effectively channeled in the name of rational discourse.

Four dead in Ohio inspired four million others to join the anti-war movement.

The National Guardsmen killed a few kids.

But all that did was finally give us the rallying cry we needed to turn our minority into an eventual majority and, in fact, stop what we saw as the insanity in Vietnam.

After Kent State, we approached the anti-war equation with a more informed mind-set.

We read a few more books, consulted with members of the clergy, slept in a wigwam, smoked a few placebo joints and thought about the role of creativity in altering the course of human events.

Soon we realized there was more than one door to the barn.

And it began to occur to us you didn't necessarily have to enter the building in physical form to free the ghosts from the shackles of misery.

There was also the matter of the soul and the subconscious mind and the ethereal self and the timeless waif and the eternal concept, the almighty OM. Some of us may have gone temporarily insane at that point, around that joint.

The shootings that took place on the campus of Kent State University in May 1970 represented both the high and low points of the anti-war movement. The loss of lives shocked everyone, especially the millions of protestors who also took to the streets that day in cities across the country.

In a small way, we may have cowered in fear, knowing any of us could meet a similar fate simply by speaking out against what we felt was an insane, pointless war.

Yet at the same time we gained greater solidarity in the aftermath of sorrow, experienced a greater sense of oneness within our growing ranks.

Grow they did.

Kent State was a turning point, a dramatic moment in American history.

Four students were shot to death on campus. But their loss signaled to America the protest movement was anything but dead, more like increasingly energized.

Within five years Nixon, Kissinger, Gerald Ford the whole mess of them would pull the final plug on The American War in Vietnam.

Thank God.

The Vietnam Wall

Its formal name is The Vietnam Veterans Memorial.

It's also called "The Wall That Heals."

Its value in the context of national healing is inestimable.

As a symbol of the need for a divided nation after the war to reunite as one in the spirit of honoring veterans from the Vietnam War, the Wall was established by a non-profit charitable entity -- the Vietnam Veteran's Fund (VMF).

In setting this process in motion, the VMF cited two objectives. It wanted Americans to have a tangible symbol of recognition for war veterans. It also hoped "to begin a process of national reconciliation by separating the issue of service of the individual men and women from the issue of U.S. policy in Vietnam."

Legislation was introduced in the U.S. Congress in 1979 to authorize a site for the memorial. Subsequent funding amounting to more than $8 million was raised from various sources, primarily from the donations of 275,000 individual American citizens.

Design concepts were accepted in 1981. Ground was broken and the monument was completed in the following year.

The VMF established four criteria for Wall design. It mandated the Wall be reflective, contemplative in character and that it harmonize with its surroundings. In addition, the design had to contain the names of all dead and missing American service members, and make no political statement about the war.

The names of the dead Americans are inscribed in order of the dates of casualty, showing the war as a series of individual sacrifices and giving each name a special place in history.

Built with polished black granite, the two-section Memorial features a mirror-like surface that reflects images of trees, lawn and other monuments in its immediate proximity.

The Wall is located on a two-acre site northeast of The Lincoln Memorial in Washington, D.C. It hosts three million visitors each year and is maintained by the National Park Service.

In 1984, the first "traveling" Wall was built in Tyler, Texas. It was a half-size replica of the actual Wall. Three traveling Walls have been built since then; one was retired due to wear.

Also known as "Moving Walls," the replicas travel to towns and cities around the country, usually staying five or six days. Local arrangements to bring this stirring portable memorial are made by veteran's groups and civic associations. Millions have visited these Walls, millions more marveled from afar inspired by the amazing tribute they represent.

The first person killed whose same appears on the Wall was Richard B. Fitzgibbons, Jar, killed in Vietnam on June 8, 1956.

His son Richard B. Fitzgibbons III who was killed in action on September 7, 1965 is also honored, his name forever engraved in granite.

The youngest solider killed, Dan Bullock, was 15-years old.

You can find his name solemnly set in stone along with 58,194 other names.

The oldest soldier killed was Dwaine McGriff, age 63. His name is there too, along with the essence of valor he exemplified in his life.

The most common name on the Wall is Smith – (667 veterans.)

The Wall includes the names of 14 soldiers named "Meadows" – Artis, Calvin, Charles Thomas, Carroll Fayne, Chad David, Jerry Roger, David Lewis, Eugene

Thomas, John William, Lee David, Lester Leejo, Merle Russell, Millard Franklin and Roy Lester.

Jerry Roger Meadows of Regina, Kentucky is listed as a sergeant.

Presuming Jerry Roger Meadows to be the "Sergeant Meadows" who served under the command of Col. David Hackworth I began calling people with his name who still live in his native Pike County, Kentucky.

A notably friendly soul by the name of "Keith Meadows" with whom I spoke identified himself as being either a 4th or 5th cousin of Jerry Meadows. He directed me to another family member, "Christine" whose maiden name was Meadows. She said Jerry Meadows was her Dad's brother's boy.

Keith Meadows told me family legend recalls Jerry Rogers Meadows as a country boy from a coal mining community. His grandfather's name was Francis "Bud" Meadows.

"I've talked to people who knew Jerry," Keith said. "He was known as a hard-worker who was raised by good people. Like everyone else from down here, Jerry was very diligent in everything he did. When there was a job to do, he would just bear down and do it. He followed orders to a tee, didn't question authority. He just stood up, put his head down and got the job done."

Keith went to the Veteran's Memorial outside the Pike County courthouse and checked on Jerry's name, engraved for all to see along with the names of other area war veterans who died in defense of their country. According to what he found, Jerry Roger Meadows died on May 2, 1969.

I went back to Col. David Hackworth's book, **About Face: the Odyssey of an American Warrior**, hoping to revisit the passage about the loss of Sergeant Meadows.

American soldiers from Team 50 providing support in the delta to the 7th ARVN Division were fighting to help protect little mud forts of the Regional Forces from being overrun by the Viet Cong.

Their final "victory" was bitter as two of Hackworth's men were severely wounded while serving as members of Major Allen Gezelman's Mobile Training Team. Hack wrote the two had taken charge and saved the day when the Viets went to ground.

"One of them died," Hackworth wrote. "A fine sergeant named Meadows. Regardless of the number of men I'd had die under my command – and Meadows was the last – it still got to me."

There are five Pomeroy's listed on the Wall – Alexander, Carlyle, David, Dean and Jack.

David Keith Pomeroy was from Lutesville, Missouri.

There are two Trout's on the Wall – Bradford and Michael. Each of the 58,195 names is reverently etched into the magnificent marble edifice that resides in natural harmony within the landscape it renders sacred.

Veterans, protestors, widows, orphans, grandparents bearing shattered hearts and dreams alike find enormous solace in the presence of this beautiful monument.

Each name signifies an American soldier that answered his or her country's call, went to war, engaged in battle stepped into harm's way. In doing so each believed what they were doing had value in the greater scheme of things. Beholding their eternal presence in the profound aura of the Wall, that is *a given.*

The name of Army Col. Harry G. Summers Jr. is often associated with the Wall. He was twice wounded in action in Vietnam and twice decorated for valor as a combat infantryman.

Summers drew attention when he lamented the disappearance of what had been a "noble cause" characterization of the Vietnam War that prevailed in the Reagan years.

As George H.W. Bush (Bush 41) sought to curry favor with Congress Summers wrote his "first victim" proved to be a group often sacrificed to political expediency – the men and women who fought the war in Vietnam.

Summers quoted Bush as saying to Congress: "Our great parties have too often been far apart and untrusting of each other. It's been this way since Vietnam. That war cleaves us still. But, friends, that war began in earnest a quarter of a century ago; and surely the statute of limitations has been reached. This is a fact: The final lesson of Vietnam is that no great nation can long afford to be sundered by a memory."

Summers found Bush's goal laudable – a return to an era when "our disputes ended at the water's edge." But he found nothing laudable in damning many millions of Americans in the process.

He pointed out "a statute of limitations" applies only to a crime, and, wittingly or unwittingly, by using that phrase "characterized all the nine million Americans who served bravely and honorably on active duty in the Armed Forces during the Vietnam era as criminals."

Summers also pointed out two of Bush's draft-age sons sat out the war, one – a la Dan Quayle – in the Texas National Guard the other in college.

Summers wrote Bush put himself in the company of those who "still take it as an article of faith that the Vietnam War was uniquely illegal, immoral and unjust."

Some of those take it further, believing the only ones entitled to take pride in the war are those who stood in opposition. "Thus," the retired general and author of **On Strategy** and **The Vietnam War Almanac** "the resurgence of pride engendered by the dedication of the Memorial is seen as a direct affront to their sensibilities." Some who opposed the war began attempts to discredit the Memorial. One writer spoke of "a monument to a loss of life that is seen as shameful and dishonorable."

From the heart of this writer, a war protestor in that era, I could not disagree more.

People with heart, soul and brains unite in celebration of this Memorial, for every conceivable reason. It is stunning in presence, way beyond appropriate, silently stirring for every visitor.

It honors the deceased brave Americans whose only sin was doing what they were asked to do by their government. It is not like the TV news shows of the day that chronicled America's alleged achievements on the battlefield with anonymous weekly death tolls. Instead the Vietnam War Memorial brings the human dimension of loss home as it contains the names of all of lost military heroes.

Each name illumines on the wall as the person it embodied did in life.

In a way you could say the Wall did not make it in time to save the lives of those whose names now appear upon it.

Such a cheeky appraisal dances with sarcasm.

Had the network news shows in the mid-'60s added names to the statistics they promulgated for a long nasty number of years things might have turned out differently.

They didn't, though.

Few attached lives to numbers.

The real truth of the matter was, there was nothing but sheer valor in their actions during the time period in which most of them gave their lives to help the South Vietnamese resist Communism.

Each name now is a person, finally, permanently.

It's damn near perfect, close enough for now.

Their sacrifices occurred in an atmosphere of overall societal acceptance of the risk and reward nature of war, of support for our foreign policy in Southeast Asia and a time when a pervasive belief in the sanctity of our mission dominated thought.

Beholding the incredible examples of more than 58,000 soldiers as projected through the profound wonderment of this Memorial the question of whether we should or should not have gone off to war in Vietnam gives way instead to a massive surge of multi-emotional respect and love.

Never once did I hear a single person make anything resembling a negative remark when the memorial was dedicated, nor in the intervening years. I find it nearly impossible to imagine a person so deprived as to harbor animus toward such a perfectly wrought memorial.

Honest to God.

The Pentagon Papers

Daniel Ellsberg had an inside view, leading to a permanent place in history. He was your standard scholar a federal government functioning bureaucrat working the intelligence beat during the lead-up to the war and the years that followed.

With the war still being waged although in a wind-down context Ellsberg, then 40, discovered and released what became known as The Pentagon Papers -- a history of the United States' political-military involvement in Vietnam from 1945 to 1967.

The papers first were brought to the attention of the public on the front page of *The New York Times* in 1971. Public response was quite overwhelming. Other newspapers around the country picked up the series of reports, including *The Arizona Daily Star*, which was at the time the primary daily paper in Tucson where I attended graduate school, drove a truck for a construction company, performed music in bars and helped support the illegal importation of brain-pleasing flowers of weeds.

Ellsberg gained access to the study after leaving government service and going to work for the Rand Corp., which had copies of the 47-volume Pentagon report.

In mid-June, 1971, *The Times* voluntarily turned over to the government the list of secret documents upon which the newspaper based its series on the origins of the war. *The Times* had begun publishing the series, dealing at the onset with escalation of the Vietnam War by former President Lyndon Johnson. Within days the government filed suit, asking an injunction to bar further publication of the series.

At the time it was reported the majority of the approximately 36 authors who wrote the narrative-analysis sections of the papers were career military and civilian officials who were promised anonymity when they were recruited for the project.

The promise of anonymity was given to enable the authors to make candid judgments in the documentary histories they were writing and not to have these judgments later affect their careers by displeasing higher authorities.

The project took one year to complete and came at a time of great personal disenchantment with what was often called then, "the Indochina war." Many of those who compiled the report had helped to develop the policies that they were asked to evaluate and some of who were simultaneously active in the debates that changed the course of those policies.

The report amounted to the equivalent of 40 books, nearly 7,000 pages and 1.5 million words of historical narratives plus a million words of documents – enough to fill a small crate. It contained many inconsistencies and lacked a single, all-embracing summary, according to *The Times* news service. Limited in ways, the report did shine light on the unfolding commitment of America to South Vietnam and the way the U.S. engaged in that conflict. It was also rich in insights into how government works and the thought processes of the men who run government. Strange as it may seem decades after this episode, the historic backdrop to our involvement was fundamentally unknown particularly among the public, most of who were too consumed with common banality to care about the actual context of our engagement.

Ellsberg's subject matter was highly esoteric, then and now. Yet what he revealed does more to explain our involvement than any other source outside the realm of extant academia.

In Tucson, publication of the papers caused a major stir, as interpreted from its daily newspaper's placement of breaking news stories detailing elements that emerged from the papers. On some occasions, a day's story would appear on the top of the front page, above the masthead. The "news of the day" became, to a large extent, the news of the past as minute details from the papers filled large news holes in every day's editions. Prominent politicians chimed-in either in support of or opposition to publication of the papers; federal courts issued rulings upholding or dismissing lower court rulings

In the final edition of its June 20, 1971 paper, the *Daily Star* ran this bold headline: "Ban on NY Times Vietnam Articles Lifted, Reinstated." An accompanying story from the Times news service led off, "U.S. District Judge Murray I. Gurfein refused Saturday to enjoin *The Times* from publishing further articles based upon a secret Pentagon study of the origins of the Vietnam War. However, Judge Irving R. Kaufman of the United States 2nd Circuit Court of Appeals, to whom the government immediately appealed, blocked *The Times* from resuming publication of the material in today's issue."

Headlines from subsequent editions chronicled what were then major bombshells, jarring readers each day with new revelations.

- "New War Article Details JFK's Role in Conflict"
- "New Article Reveals JFK Knew of Diem Coup Plans"
- "Secret Papers Cases Taken to High Court"
- "Ike Sought Downfall of Hanoi"
- "LBJ Saw 'Victory' in 1963"
- "Woman Xeroxed 'Some Documents' For Ellsberg, She Testifies"
- "McNamara Felt Doubts About Pacification In '65"
- "Ho Asked U.S. Aid After War"
- "Tucsonans Queried On War Report Issue"
- "Ike Decided Geneva Pact "Was A Disaster,' Study Reports"
- "Study Hits JFK Hard, Post Says"
- "War Deception Continues, Ellsberg Colleague Says"
- "Aftermath to Tet Stalled Army's Escalation Push"
- "Rusk's Talk Of Using Nuclear Arms Revealed"

As the articles continued to dominate the local paper, other war-related reports were also prominent in the news.

On June 27, under the headline "Communists Still Control Countryside in Cambodia," readers learned that one year after the departure of the last American forces from Cambodia, the Vietnamese Communists were still in control of three-quarters of the sparsely populated countryside.

Surveys at the time revealed that a majority of American opinion disapproved of the government effort at suppression of the documents. A majority also felt that the government kept too much information secret.

On June 30, The Supreme Court ruled 6 to 3 that *The Times* and *The Washington Post* could resume publishing the articles. The majority held that the government had not proved that the national interest would be damaged if the Pentagon papers were made public.

Ellsberg, who admitted leaking the papers and was under indictment for theft of government property, said of the ruling: "It's obviously a great decision. I'm delighted that the justices have decided that the American people should have the opportunity to read these documents in their entirety. I'm hoping that the justices themselves will take the opportunity to read every page."

An article that appeared on July 1 under the headline "Kennedy Abandoned 'Limited Risk'" quoted the Pentagon study as concluding that President Kennedy transformed the 'limited risk gamble' of the Eisenhower administration into "a broad commitment' to prevent Communist domination of South Vietnam.

The study also indicated that President Kennedy knew and approved of plans for the military coup d'etat that ousted President Ngo Dinh Diem of South Vietnam in 1963. Early troop commitments were kept secret, in an apparent effort to prevent what was in effect a formal breach of the Geneva accords. The U.S. had not signed the 1954 Geneva accords ending the French war with Vietnam, but had agreed not to undermine them.

Kennedy's tactics deepened the American involvement piecemeal, the report read. Each step minimized public recognition that the American role was expanding.

On July 4, a massive article under the headline "Bunker Recommended Laos Invasion In 1967" occupied the entirety of Page 12 of *The Daily Star*.

Two days later the paper cited a quotation from "an informed source" in *The Atlanta Journal-Constitution* as saying the late Robert Kennedy probably had a hand in preparation of the so-called Pentagon papers and "wanted to be certain that President Lyndon Johnson got 'full credit' for botching up the war.

As off-the-graph as this news item seems in retrospect, it fell on mostly deaf ears when it surfaced, perhaps because of the frenzied nature of the day's cluttered news cycle.

For their part, the Pentagon Papers rocked the world, or at least, the domestic political world.

The papers demonstrated substantially that the Kennedy and Johnson Administrations had systematically lied, not only to the public but also to Congress.

According to the interpretative "filters" of the various sources that began to interpret the significance of their release, the papers revealed more specifically that the U.S. had secretly enlarged the scale of the Vietnam War with the bombings of nearby Cambodia and Laos, coastal raids on North Vietnam and Marine Corps attacks, none of which were reported in the mainstream media.

In June 2011, the entirety of the Pentagon Papers was declassified and publicly released.

Although President Johnson insisted that the aim of the Vietnam War was to secure an independent, non Communist South Vietnam, it turned out that version of the truth was less-than-fully-candid.

In fact, a January 1965 memorandum by Secretary of Defense McNamara stated that the real U.S. goal was "not to help a friend, but to contain China."

McNamara accused China of harboring "imperial aspirations, just like Nazi Germany and Imperial Japan," according to *Wikipedia*, which quoted McNamara as saying the Chinese, were conspiring to menacingly organize all of Asia against the United States.

Nevertheless, McNamara was said to have admitted that the containment of China would ultimately sacrifice time, lives and financial resources.

In order to encircle the Chinese, the United States aimed to establish "three fronts" as part of a "long-run effort to contain China":

The Japan-Korean front.

The India-Pakistan front.

The Southeast Asia front.

McNamara, a so-called "whiz kid" former top executive at Ford Motor Company recruited to be a large player in Kennedy's Administration, inherited an active portfolio.

Since 1950, the U.S. had provided large-scale military equipment to what was known as "the French colonial empire" in its fight against the Viet Minh.

By 1954, the U.S. had begun to engage in acts of sabotage and terror warfare against North Vietnam and within another year was encouraging and directly assisting South Vietnamese President Ngo Dinh Diem's rise to power.

Lo and behold, by 1963 the U.S. encouraged and directly assisted in his overthrow.

One year later following the Gulf of Tonkin incident the U.S. "manipulated public opinion in its preparation for open warfare," according to *Wikipedia's* narrative.

Years before the 2 August 1964 Gulf of Tonkin so-called "incident" Gulf of occurred, the account of The Pentagon Papers in *Wikipedia* attests the U.S. government was directly interfering in Vietnam's internal affairs.

The most damaging revelations in the papers revealed that four administrations (Truman, Eisenhower, Kennedy, and Johnson), had misled the public regarding their intentions. Even well into the twenty-first century, many decades after the war's end, virtually no one professing to know about how we ended up in Vietnam expressed any cogent understanding of how far back our manipulation of events in Southeast Asia extended.

This part of the publication of The Pentagon Papers shocked the masses.

The Eisenhower administration actively worked against the Geneva Accords.

The Kennedy Administration knew of plans to overthrow Diem before his death in the November, 1963 coup.

The Johnson Administration had decided to expand the war while promising "we seek no wider war" during LBJ's 1964 campaign, including plans to bomb North Vietnam well before the 1964 election.

Kind of twisted when you factor in LBJ's outspoken assault on his opponent Barry Goldwater, who he claimed was the real Vietnam hawk. In fact, Johnson drubbed Goldwater imposing a humiliating defeat on his opponent. He successfully portrayed him in dramatic TV ads as a president who would lead us to war, actually nuclear war as Johnson's effective ads implicitly suggested.

After the release of The Pentagon Papers, Goldwater said, "During the campaign, President Johnson kept reiterating that he would never send American boys to fight in Vietnam. As I say, he knew at the time that American boys were going to be sent. In fact, I knew about 10 days before the Republican Convention. You see I was being called trigger-happy, warmonger, bomb happy, and all the time Johnson was sayiing he would never send American boys. I knew damn well he would."

Clearly, the most damaging revelations in the papers revealed that four administrations had misled the public regarding their intentions.

According to the papers, the U.S. government played a key role in the 1963 coup, in which President Diem was assassinated. While maintaining "clandestine contact" with Vietnamese generals planning a coup, the U.S. cut off its aid to President Diem and openly supported a successor government in what the authors called an *"essentially leaderless Vietnam"*:

For the military coup against Diem, many sources contend the U.S. must accept its full share of responsibility. Beginning in August 1963 we variously authorized, sanctioned and encouraged the coup efforts of the Vietnamese generals and offered full support for a successor government.

In October we cut off aid to Diem in a direct rebuff, giving a green light to the generals. We maintained clandestine contact with them throughout the planning and execution of the coup and sought to review their operational plans and proposed new government.

Thus, as the nine-year rule of Diem came to a bloody end, our complicity in his overthrow heightened our responsibilities and our commitment "in an essentially leaderless Vietnam."

As early as August 1963, an unnamed U.S. representative had met with Vietnamese generals planning a coup against President Diem. According to newspaper reports this U.S. representative was later identified to be a CIA agent.

In publishing the papers in *The New York Times*, its writer James Reston added these words in a set-up piece: "One of the many extraordinary things about this collection is how seldom anyone in the Kennedy or Johnson administrations ever seems to have questioned the moral basis of the American war effort. ... They seem to have concentrated on the pragmatic questions of whether proposed policies, from bombing to getting rid of Diem, would work rather than whether they were justifiable for a great nation fighting for what it proclaimed were moral purposes." Johnson seemed not to have been able to conceive of the notion that these enemy soldiers, about whose character and culture he knew little, could withstand the threats, let alone the use, of American military power.

Regarding the papers, Reston wrote, "Ironically, McNamara was personally responsible for ordering this vast study of what went wrong, and in the process has furnished compelling evidence against himself and his colleagues in the Johnson and Kennedy administrations." At the time of the book's publication, *Detroit Free Press* columnist Susan Ager asked, "How can anyone defend a man who admits he was 'wrong, terribly wrong' in his involvement in the Vietnam War? His critics say Robert McNamara stayed quiet too long, that his book is 30 years tardy, that once he decided the war was un-winnable, he ought to have stood outside the White House screaming. Instead, he moved to a comfortable job as president of the World Bank. He remained publicly silent on Vietnam until now, when all the men and women who fought there are well into midlife, except for those who never came home to build sandboxes for their children or take their mothers to church on Easter Sunday."

Ager not only read the book, she also digested every editorial condemning him for his bad decisions and his long silence. She found herself wondering if any of those writers "ever admitted in print their much smaller misjudgments."

She thought about all the times "we begin enterprises casually, then find ourselves neck-deep in the Big Muddy, dragging others behind us, not sure whether to push on or turn back."

All of us, she ventured in thought, find ourselves trapped in circumstance, "the same way everyone once knew that if South Vietnam fell to the communists all the nations of Southeast Asia would tumble like dominoes."

She said we live, as did McNamara and his cohorts, by "bedrock assumptions we fail to challenge out of inertia or fear that they will shatter."

McNamara's choices she concluded were small and careless. And early chances to reverse things passed "because the men were tired or distracted or afraid, as we all are, stumbling through our lives."

She called Vietnam "a tragedy by increments. Our own challenges are smaller and less bloody." But, she wrote, we can learn from McNamara and Vietnam that we must be wary over every small first step, "that getting out is harder than getting in. And that when there seems no exit, there always is, but it will not be easy, and it will not feel like victory."

Writer's Notes

I clipped articles containing excerpts of The Pentagon Papers from *The Arizona Daily Star*, the daily newspaper inTucson, Arizona, several arroyos from the Beltway. America was still fairly dim on the background of the Vietnam War. Everyone within my range of human contact was hungry for explanation as the war continued to chew through American lives, resources and essential optimism. On the other hand, I don't remember most people being singularly obsessed with the content of this modern-day history of a war still barely waging on, more like fading into the mauve.

Nothing had been resolved. But the dynamics were changing.

Outside of dusty Old Pueblo, Arizona a larger degree of interest may have permeated society. Out there most of the populace was more interested in "getting along little doggie." The spectacle of historic detail was essentially off the radar.

The publication of papers was enormous in context although it didn't exactly alter the unfolding of human history.

Our war in Vietnam had been winding down since the election of Richard Nixon in the 1968 elections. Domestic political pressure insisted upon gradual withdrawel of troops, a tacit abandonment of mission. America had lost its stomach for war, as America would do other times in its future.

But the light of optimism continued to shine in its heart and soul.

Looking back decades later, the detail revealed within *The Papers* is riveting, clarifying, instructive and quite sad a lot of the time.

Reviewing this information lo these many years later one is reminded American policy makers were bent on manipulating events in any venue where their presence led them to engage.

Eventual "outcomes" were as much a result of the natural unfolding of events as they were of constucts of our intentions.

I'm too removed from the center of power to know for sure whether our intenstions were noble or otherwise.

I only know what the novelist knew – something happened.

The Best and the Brightest

David Halberstam began working on the book that would become **The Best and the Brightest** in January 1969, according to the associate editor of the Book-of-the-Month Club newsletter, Joyce Illig.

As a reporter for *The New York Times* in Vietnam in 1962 and 1963, his dispatches earned him the Pulitzer Prize and several other awards.

Halberstam was educated at Harvard, worked at small dailies and the Nashville *Tennessean,* before joining *The Times*.

For six years, he served as a correspondent in Leopoldville and Warsaw, before going to Saigon.

His first major book, **The Making of a Quagmire** was published in 1965. It was regarded as a pessimistic and prophetic report on Vietnam. He also wrote **Ho** and **The Unfinished Odyssey of Robert Ke**nnedy and a novel, **One Very Hot Day,** considered by some to be required reading for anyone seeking insight into this war.

Best and Brightest emerged when Halberstam began to wonder how and why this conflict could possibly be initiated by "intelligent, rational men who would have known the obvious, how unlikely bombing was to work, and how dangerous it was to send combat troops, and that if we sent American units we would be following the French."

Setting out to study the men and their decisions, he ended up writing a book not about Vietnam but about America, in particular about power and success in our country.

His goal was to create a 600-page document. But three years, 500 interviews and no vacations later, the work had doubled in length to 1,200 pages (672-pages in small type in the published version from Random House.)

Halberstam said at the time, "Vietnam was the worst tragedy to befall this country since the Civil War, yet the architects of the national shame and national horror were seemingly the best and the brightest of a generation. We had a right to know what happened and why."

The author said in an interview with Illig published in *The Detroit Free Press* in late-1972 that as a reporter at the time he had a feeling in early-1961 when the Kennedy Administration came to power that there was a certain degree of hubris about his team.

"I remember having a feeling that there was too much arrogance. I thought they were awfully cocky."

Hubris was the right word to use to describe the Kennedy Crew.

"They really thought, oh boy, they were so good. We're the best and we climb mountains and win prizes, read poetry and our wives are good-looking – all that sort of thing."

Halberstam visited Vietnam and began to suspect Kennedy and team were on their way to "a first-class foreign policy disaster." Along with fellow reporter Neil Sheehan, Halberstam felt the two of them were "terribly clued-in" to this pending train-wreck.

In covering the Kennedy's and their war, Halberstam said he did not set out to make friends or "to be welcome at the ambassador's house." The only questions in his mind were: Was he reasonably fair? Did he treat their decisions in an honorable sense of the context as it existed then?

He knew certain people in power would not like his book. "That really doesn't concern me very much" he told Illig. In 1964-'65, Lyndon Johnson had called him "a traitor to his country."

In 1972, he had become the celebrated author of what was regarded as a brilliant and probing book that was to become the most quoted study of the decade on the Kennedy/Johnson years.

Kennedy brought to Washington what reporter Robert Boyd described as "proud, ebullient, self-assured young men who swarmed into Washington with him – and screwed it up."

These gifted young men, Boyd wrote, gave us the nation's worst mistake in a century.

Halberstam's book brought to life *The Pentagon Papers*, which had been published one year earlier.

"He populates with flesh-and-blood human beings that all-but-unreadable wasteland of memos, cables, faceless committee reports and abstruse option papers brought to life by Daniel Ellsberg."

Boyd wrote that Halberstam "piled real-life quotes, anecdotes and incidents on top of each other, recreating the mood and motivations of the early sixties, it vanities and illusions."

In his review of the book, Boyd found it to be "repetitious, loosely organized and badly in need of tight editing, flawed but fascinating."

Halberstam begins by painting word portraits of the main players of the day – McNamara, Rusk, Bundy, Rostow, Westmoreland, Taylor, as well as JFK and LBJ. The rest of the text is a reconstruction of "the slow, dreary, disillusioning process by which we slipped into Vietnam – never really wanting to, never realizing the consequences, but seemingly as unable to help ourselves as characters in a nightmare."

Halberstam found Vietnam to be a tiny issue overclouded by the great issues. It rose to pre-imminence partly because of neglect and omission, "a policy that had evolved not because a group of westerners had sat down years before and determined what the future should be, but precisely because they had not."

The author traced the beginning to the Potsdam Conference in 1945 when the new President, Harry Truman, made his first major trip abroad.

The decision to permit the British to accept the Japanese surrender in Vietnam seemed inconsequential at the time, Boyd wrote. But it led one small step at a time to the French returning to struggle against the Vietnamese communists, and later to "creeping escalation" under Eisenhower and Kennedy and all-out war under Johnson. Sparing in his assessment of Truman and Eisenhower, Halberstam comes down heavily on JFK who he charges, "Knew better but lacked the political courage to stop the slide into the Asian quagmire." He faulted Kennedy's team's "passionate desire to at least appear to be tough, realistic and hard-nosed especially against communism." Only recently, some of them had been dubbed "soft" during the McCarthy years explaining perhaps in large part why they rallied to the Cold War banner while the Democratic Party became more committed to military spending than The Republicans.

Totalitarianism had been stopped by force so force became recognized as the primary means to wage philosophic war. "They justified each decision to use power by their own conviction that the communists were worse, which justified our dirty tricks, our toughness."

Kennedy eventually fell victim to:

- Serious misreading of the aspirations of a non-white nation
- Bringing Western, Caucasian anti-communism to a place where it was less applicable
- Institutions pushing forward with their own momentum
- Too much secrecy with too many experts who knew remarkably little either about the country involved or their own country
- Too many decisions by the private men of the administration as opposed to the public ones
- Too little moral reference and later too little common sense.

In *Best and Brightest*, Halberstam portrays Kennedy as more of a right-winger than is commonly perceived, a leader who believed in sending off troops to Vietnam we would "sober the enemy and discourage escalation." Kennedy's bravado in Vietnam was inspired in no small part by the contemptuous way he felt his Russian counterpart Nikita Khrushchev was treating him, believing the Soviet found him inexperienced and without guts. "Until we remove those ideas we won't get anywhere with him, so we have to act," he told reporter James Reston. And so it was Kennedy began to increase U.S. advisory forces in Vietnam, turning an internal conflict into an international war.

The author found this somewhat astounding. He felt Kennedy was sensitive to changes in the political world and as a political figure cautious and even timid. He weighed his moves carefully, with a constant eye on the future.

Halberstam made this assessment:

"It was the irony of the Kennedy administration that John Kennedy, rationalist, pledged above all else to rationality, should continue the most irrational of all major American foreign policies, that policy toward China and the rest of Asia."

Halberstam dropped the hammer on Kennedy like a pissed-off carpenter banging the first nail of the morning.

"He failed to deal with Vietnam as a political problem. He worked to conceal the truth about Vietnam from the public and had markedly increased the American commitment. He deepened the commitment there and he had, in a way, always known better. He preached in his book and in his speeches about the importance of political courage, but his administration had been reasonably free from acts of courage, such as turning around the irrationality of the China policy. In this most critical area, the record was largely one of timidity."

As a reporter in Vietnam, Halberstam found Kennedy guilty of employing secrecy and deception to covering up his escalation of the war, well in advance of the LBJ years to follow.

American commanders began to corrupt intelligence reports while reports from fact-finding tours in 1961 were blatantly misread, altered, obscured from even close officials or even disregarded. Soon came the advent of "war by public relations," featuring overly optimistic yet entirely untrustworthy statements as commonly accepted propaganda fare within policy papers and other briefs. Halberstam traces the pattern of deception in nauseating detail, horrifying the reader with elements of actuality capable of inducing repulsion. So much lying began to take place even mirrors lied to other mirrors. Truth was in complete retreat, replaced by empty endless subterfuge.

By 1965, LBJ was sending U.S troops in batches to the battlefield, including up to 125,000 at that point – a number that was officially understated by two-thirds. The war's mounting costs were also cast in unbelievable terms, adding to the pointlessness of citing numbers in an era of suspended acuity.

LBJ hoped the worst would not come true, Halberstam wrote. He hoped it would remain a short war and feared he would lose his cherished Great Society programs at home if its real costs became known. Therefore his economic planning became "a living lie" and his administration took us into "economic chaos."

The American public had been manipulated from the start, as well as the Congress, the press. All had been told half-truths about why we were going in, how deeply we were going in, how much we were spending and how long we were in it for.

Predictions turned out to be hopelessly inaccurate, Halberstam reported.

When the public realized they'd been hoodwinked, annoyed at being manipulated, they soured on the war. This caused its architects to feel aggrieved so they turned on those very symbols of the democratic society they had once manipulated, criticizing them "for their lack of fiber, stamina and belief."

LBJ was convinced he could accomplish things by reasoning with leaders and that all men had a price. His instinct to personalize with the Vietnamese helped bring him trouble. He would find "the price" of Ho Chi Minh, his weakness, perhaps. Maybe it would be threats of more bombing, or expanding troop presence. Then he might offer Ho a lollipop – massive economic aid regional development.

Alas, LBJ found him self confronting a contradiction to the Western mind, a George Washington-caliber nationalist leader of unusual stature who Halberstam called "a true revolutionary, incorruptible, a man who had no price, or at least no price that Lyndon Johnson with his Western bombs and Western dollars could meet."

Best and Brightest dominated bookstore shelves for many years. Many decades later following publication of his epochal account of the antecedents of America's involvement in Vietnam, Halberstam died in an automobile accident.

He left behind a rich study of an important event, a book that was generally regarded as a "must read" assessment of the war.

Best and Brightest seems aptly titled in retrospect as its scholarship reflects the ultimate in thorough, insightful, colorful on the spot reporting, real history on a page.

His commitment to sharing what he reported on remains a beacon of light to this writer as well as everyone interested in a subject each of us continue to find of lasting importance.

On Agent Orange

In the 1960s the United States blanketed the Mekong River delta and the areas around the Vietnam/Cambodian border with Agent Orange, a chemical defoliant more devastating than napalm. Nearly 50 years after the end of the Vietnam War, the poisoned legacy lives on in the children whose deformities it is said to have caused.

In Vietnam, between 1961 and 1971, the high command of the United States decided that, since tree cover was apparently protecting a guerrilla struggle, a useful first step might be to "defoliate" those same trees.

Corporations such as Dow and Monsanto were given the task of attacking and withering the natural order of a country. The resulting chemical weaponry was euphemistically named by color: Agent Purple, Agent Blue, Agent White and – spoken often in whispers – Agent Orange.

The name "Orange" derived from the color of tape that wrapped the large canisters of the chemicals that arrived on ships and were subsequently distributed to air force bases around the peninsula.

Its key constituent is dioxin: a horrible chemical that makes total war not just on vegetation but also on the roots and essences of life itself.

About 12 million gallons of lethal toxin, in Orange form alone, were sprayed on Vietnam, on the Vietnamese, and on the American forces who were fighting in the same jungles.

Agent Orange – or, Herbicide Orange – was one of the herbicides used by the U.S. military as part of its herbicide warfare program. It existed under the code name, Operation Ranch Hand.

Precedent for using herbicides in warfare was established by the British who years before had used similar chemical agents to confront rebel movements in its Malaysian colony.

In 1961, President Ngo Dinh Diem asked the U.S. to conduct spraying and the country's Air Force initiated operations with American help, authorized by President John Kennedy. The Monsanto Corporation and the Dow Chemical Company manufactured most of the extremely toxic agents of war. It is estimated that four million Vietnamese citizens were exposed and at least three million of them were left suffering from resulting illnesses. In the 1970s, high levels of dioxin were found in the breast milk of South Vietnamese women and in the blood of American military personnel who served in Vietnam. The highest levels of residual chemicals were found around Air Force bases and in 28 other former military bases where it was stored and loaded onto airplanes.

Contaminated soil and residue continues to affect the citizens of Vietnam poisoning their water, food chain and causing illnesses.

It is estimated that 17.8 percent of the country of Vietnam was sprayed during the American war, or about 12,000 square miles.

The persistent nature of dioxins and other factors has rendered reforestation difficult-to-impossible a condition made even more severe by the incursion of invasive pioneer species bamboo and cogon grass.

Dioxins have settled into soil and sediment allowing them to enter the food chain through animals and fish that feed in the contaminated areas.

Spraying permanently life-destroying chemicals on those we considered to be "the enemy" during this long war had additional goals beyond eliminating possible cover for the Viet Cong.

In advancing Operation Ranch Hand military planners were responding to the fact the Viet Cong got most of their food from the neutral population. This dictated the destruction of civilian crops that resulted in the destruction of an estimated 50-percent of the rural economy. At the same time, tens of thousands of American military personnel were inadvertently exposed to a veritable stew of highly toxic herbicides, causing adverse medical conditions for many of them, even affecting many of their own eventual offspring.

Studies have shown American veterans of the Vietnam War have increased rates of a multiple of diseases and other acute disorders; vets exposed to Agent Orange suffer more than twice the rate of highly aggressive prostate cancers. Such exposure also doubles the risk of invasive skin cancers.

While in Vietnam veterans were told not to worry about the effects of their exposure to Agent Orange and other dioxin-based chemicals. But when they got home many began to experience illness, saw their wives suffer miscarriages or have children born with birth defects. Believing there might be a relationship between this emerging disease pattern and their wartime exposure some veterans began filing claims for benefits with the Veterans Administration; most claims were denied.

As of 1993, 39,419 veterans had filed disability claims yet only 486 were compensated. Since the 1970s, several class action lawsuits were also filed against the chemical companies that manufactured Agent Orange. Corporate defendants sought to escape culpability by blaming the U.S. government. They also denied that there was any link between Agent Orange and veterans' medical problems. Before going to court in 1984, seven companies agreed to pay $180 million as compensation if veterans dropped all claims against them. This decision angered veterans many of whom felt betrayed by lawyers involved in the decision. By 1989 it was determined a totally disabled vet would receive a maximum of $12,000 spread out over 10 years. The Veterans Administration now provides medical care and disability compensation for the recognized list of Agent Orange illnesses.

In a separate legal action, Vietnamese victims groups filed a lawsuit against several chemical companies in U.S. District Court. A judge dismissed their suit, ruling it had no legal basis.

The judge concluded that:

- Agent Orange was not considered to be a poison under international law at the time of its use by the U.S.
- The U.S. was not prohibited from using it as an herbicide
- Companies that produced the substance were not liable for the method of use by the U.S. government.

To assist those who have been affected by Agent Orange/dioxin, the Vietnamese have established "peace villages", which each host between 50 and 100 victims, giving them medical and psychological help. According to the online encyclopedia *Wikipedia,* as of 2006, there were 11 such villages, thus granting some social protection to fewer than a thousand victims. U.S. veterans of the war in Vietnam and individuals who are aware and sympathetic to the impacts of Agent Orange have supported these programs in Vietnam. An international group of veterans from the U.S. and its allies during the Vietnam War working with their former enemy — veterans from the Vietnam Veterans Association — established the Vietnam Friendship Village near Hanoi.

George Romney Vietnam War Remark

In the mid-1960s George Romney was the immensely popular moderate governor of Michigan. His appeal extended into all age groups, demographics, gender and other sectors of political identification.
Non-ideological, rock-solid handsome, incredibly energized the squeaky clean Mormon embodied the essence of non-partisan neutrality, defined "the middle" in both style and political instinct.
After the rout of the distinctly Conservative-flavored Barry Goldwater in the 1964 presidential election, the national Republican Party was looking for a centrist candidate like Romney to run in 1968, someone with demonstrable ability to appeal to voters of each party.
The square-jawed governor of the Great Lakes State appeared to fill the bill.
Time magazine featured Romney on its cover. Polling results projected his prospects as exceptional. There was also an absence of other competitors, other than the ever-stirring ghost of Richard Nixon and New York Governor Nelson Rockefeller, long associated with the East Coast "liberal" establishment.
While he originally supported Romney's candidacy, Rockefeller did eventually jump into the race after Romney later suspended his efforts.

In spite of its initial surge of interest among voters, Romney's quest for the presidency never caught fire. As I recall, Romney did not exactly convey genuine "fire in the belly" for the office of the presidency. An unbridled pursuit of raw power wasn't in his nature. Not lacking in ambition, he was understated in disposition, smart as hell but mystifyingly inarticulate mostly inclined to serve his second term as governor as effectively as he could, and let other considerations evolve as they might. It may well have been, his reticence contributed to his early appeal yet also ensured his final departure from the national political stage.

Being on the cover of then-prominent news magazines had given Romney a real inside advantage. However before his campaign had officially begun, Governor Romney made a statement that effectively scuttled his chances of getting the nomination.

Romney had been reluctant to discuss Vietnam, while he was also beginning to earn a reputation as being slightly gaffe-prone -- something of a plodder. Skills that had served him well as a successful business executive and State governor began to appear as liabilities in the national political arena.

In August 1967 in a taped interview with the host of a relatively obscure weekend TV current events show in Detroit, Romney discussed among other subjects his take-away from an earlier fact-finding trip to Vietnam.

"When I came back from Viet Nam [in November 1965], I'd just had the greatest brainwashing that anybody can get," he told host Lou Gordon, who was a brainy muckraker dealing in political scuttlebutt and other common forms of news and entertainment way back in the pre-Cable era.

The remark seemed fairly innocent at the time. It did not elicit any tangible follow-up questioning from the host. Nor did the local media appear interested in acknowledging what the governor said, let alone tracking it in the week that followed.

Soon, however, it became crystal clear his comment had legs – major legs.

In its account of his biography, *Wikepedia* suggests Romney then shifted his remarks to Gordon to opposing the war:

"I no longer believe that it was necessary for us to get involved in South Vietnam to stop Communist aggression in Southeast Asia," he declared. Decrying the "tragic" conflict, he urged "a sound peace in South Vietnam at an early time."

Thus Romney disavowed the war and reversed himself from his earlier stated belief that the war was "morally right and necessary."

According to the Internet encyclopedia, the "brainwashing" reference had been an offhand, unplanned remark that came at the end of a long, behind-schedule day of campaigning.

By September 7 it had found its way into prominence in certain daily newspapers. Eight other governors who had been on the same 1965 trip as Romney said no such activity had taken place, with one of them saying Romney's remarks were "outrageous, kind of stinking ... Either he's a most naïve man or he lacks judgment."

Brainwashing was a controversial concept at the time. Popular films of the era rendered it fairly plausible as the term "Manchurian candidate" entered the realm of cinematic reality.

To say you had been brainwashed was thoughtless candor before its time. Conveying any semblance of political softness was potentially fatal behavior, especially on TV even if it was broadcast on a relatively obscure channel in a second tier market like Detroit.

Going so far as so reveal ones self as subject to mental manipulation was akin to political suicide.

For Romney, the remark had devastating effect as it reinforced the negative image of Romney's abilities that had already been developed, as noted in the online encyclopedia.

Romney's perceived naiveté became the brunt of newspaper editorials and TV commentary. The consensus emerged that anyone capable of being brainwashed was therefore incapable of being President.

In the meantime, his only real competitor for the GOP nomination, Richard Nixon, began to out-poll Romney, who eventually withdrew from the race in February 1968. Rockefeller put up a good fight but never stood a chance, given the baggage he carried as a divorcee, nearly as bad at the time as being "dumb enough" to buy the lies of the generals in Vietnam.

Romney's sudden fade from prominence coupled with the subsequent ascent of Richard Nixon represented a seminal change in policy direction for the Republican Party.

It was generally agreed that had he been nominated and later elected to the Presidency Romney would have sought to lessen our involvement, leading to a more immediate cessation of our prosecution of the Vietnam War.

That's all 100-percent speculation now. Romney's son, Mitt, eventually ran for the nation's highest office. Like his father, he did not quite resonate sufficiently to crack the final barrier and make it to the White House.

George Romney did serve as Secretary of Housing and Urban Development in the Nixon Administration.

In the case of Nixon, history is clear: while he and his foreign policy advisor Henry Kissinger endeavored to gradually withdraw without tacitly surrendering, the war dragged on throughout Nixon's first term; in fact, deliberation to achieve the Paris Peace Accord was announced on the night before the election was held to decide Nixon's second term.

It is estimated, another 15,000 American soldiers were killed in combat during the four years of his first tem as Nixon's administration attempted to end the war.

For decades, I labored under the assumption that Romney's presidential hopes were completely dashed not by his candor but by sinister forces from within the Nixon camp that did what they could to sustain excessive press attention on Romney's Vietnam remarks.

However it played out, I now realize it was quite a bit more complicated than that.

Of course American military commanders on the ground in Vietnam were not above painting deceptively optimistic portrayals of our prospects for visiting politicians.

In *About Face*, Hackworth frequently draws attention to this persistent syndrome, airing out a thorough rational for advancing what now seems as garden-variety propaganda. The generals may have sold then-Governor Romney a bill of goods. However that went down, he didn't do his presidential aspirations any good by flaunting the receipt on TV.

The Things They Carried

Tim O'Brien's epic work of fiction, **The Things They Carried** was first published in 1990. Critics responded with effusive praise, showering accolades on what was generally considered to be a masterpiece.

In adding it to its "Books of the Century" category, *The New York Times* said it "belongs high on the list of best fiction about any war … crystallizes the Vietnam experience for everyone (and) exposes the nature of all war stories."

The Times added the book "gives the reader a shockingly visceral sense of what it felt like to tramp through a booby-trapped jungle, carrying 20 pounds of supplies, 14 pounds of ammunition, along with radios, machine guns, assault rifles and grenades."

Those were not the only items the members of O'Brien's platoon carried.

Each also bore his own emotions, spirituality, romantic impulses, sentiment, superstition, macabre trophies of war, ancestral urgings as well as fear, anger, sadness, regret, faint hope and optimism.

This book is not for every reader. Those well advised to skip this 233-page incursion into the reality of Vietnam would include anyone unwilling to behold the raw essence of war as perceived by young American soldiers.

Fate has delivered them to hellish circumstance. Thanks to O'Brien's deft story-telling skills, encountering them there can be as difficult as experiencing them in fictitious format.

O'Brien created vivid characters, literary artifacts who the reader identifies as immediately real, singularly believable instantly identifiable.

Diving in, the reader is instantly transformed to the jungles of Vietnam where O'Brien's small platoon of soldiers confront an incomprehensibly harsh environment, danger at every turn invisible enemies in every imaginable guise, not to mention many anxieties.

The author not only identifies their location, individual identities and personalities, he also brings the reader into the vagaries of what they're doing, what it's like to be in their boots, what they're thinking, feeling and fearing.

We enter their daydreams, tour their personal histories engage their ambitions as they exist in a theater of wall-to-wall existential uncertainty.

O'Brien's ability to evoke a credible backdrop of war draws us fully into the drama, challenges the reader to confront the toll our war-making takes on the conscripts who must execute the impossible missions endowed upon them.

Two-dozen pages into this book, its characters become as real as your best friend, exemplifying a complete mix of human characteristics that endear them as real, cherished sources of absolute familiarity.

As this infatuation continues we are led to ask ourselves what are our leaders are thinking when they send our very best young men and women to war, in this case, the most vague and improbable of all conflicts.

O'Brien's literary conscripts have no idea who they're fighting, why they're fighting, where they're fighting or what their overall objectives are, other than to kill every person they encounter along the way as practical means by which to survive them selves.

They don't carry things, they "hump" them, through swamps, mountainous terrain, into tunnels and in the many villages they encounter and often eviscerate. As they proceed from anywhere to somewhere else, their largest and smallest thoughts form the basis of each chapter's content, ever revealing the true essence of war, beyond the platitudes, statistics and assessments.

Amid all the intense onslaught of forceful prose, the reader cannot escape the spectacle of how war's many unintended, residual affects of conflict show up long after the battles are fought, how sending young soldiers into such an unlikely, unholy, non-redemptive milieu will alter their souls, flip a vital switch in their makeup, dehumanize them beyond the point of recognition.

Book reviewers broke out all the superlatives when this modern-day epic tale emerged.

To wit:

Chicago Sun-Times – **The Things They Carried** is as good as any piece of literature can get ... It is the perfect approach to this sort of material, and O'Brien does it with vast skill and grace ... It is controlled and wild, deep and tough, perceptive and shrewd."

Milwaukee Journal – This is writing so powerful that it steals your breath ... it perfectly captures the moral confusion that is the legacy of the Vietnam War ... **The Things They Carried** about more than war, of course. It is about the human heart and emotional baggage and loyalty and love. It is about the difference between 'truth' and 'reality.' It is about death – and life. It is successful on every level.

USA Today – Nobody else can make me feel ... what I imagine to have been the reality of that war.

New York Times Book Review – By moving beyond the horror of the fighting to examine with sensitivity and insight the nature of courage and fear, by questioning the role that imagination plays in helping to form our memories and our own versions of truth, he places **The Things They Carried** high up on the list of best fiction about any war … A stunning performance. The overall effect of these original tales is devastating.

Hartford Courant – O'Brien has unmistakably forged one of the most persuasive works of any kind to arise out of any war.

Detroit Free Press – The search for the great American novel will never end, but it gets a step closer to realization with **The Things They Carried**.

The Veteran – Go out and get this book and read it. Read it slowly, and let O'Brien's masterful storytelling and his eloquent philosophizing about the nature of war wash over you.

Booklist – Just when you thought there was nothing left to say about the Vietnam experience … there's plenty.

Chapter Three
On The Learning Continuum

The American War in Vietnam concluded in the mid-1970s but remained deeply mired in my consciousness existed in a timeless dimension within the core of my being. As the years proceded and the demands of adult life took over my life, the war I opposed receded gradually, giving way to other urgencies, mainly seeking to perfect the writer's craft.

Like many from my generation, I was fully caught up by the impact of the work of the newspaper reporters who followed up on the break-in at an apartment/office complex in Washington D.C. and helped shape American history in the process.

Those of us who opposed the war were seriously seared by the flames of dissent decidedly contemptous of authority. Not surpisingly, then, the Watergate tale that became the basis for the book, **All The President's Men** siezed our attention helping shape many a destiny, mine included.

Prior to that, the exuberent uplift of Kurt Vonnegut's novels had enabled me to survive the war, mentally and in other incalculable ways. His entertaining, morally profound and typically hilarious visions offered an alternative roadmap into existence one that led from irony to complete transcendence.

With each book I took on I knew this writer's imagination and devotion to task was *quite literally* saving me from complete despair. And so it was, Dr. Frued, that I resolved to follow his path, believing I owed it to "K" himself as his family members called him.

Eventually I finessed my way into the newspaper business, took on the mantel of semi-serious scribe, did it long enough to turn the corner on achieving some redemptive measure of competence.

Decades past, new fascinations flourished. But I never lost interest in trying to understand the war that came down like a asteroid on my age group.

Vietnam stuck in my being a permanently imbedded splinter.

As I could I committed to learning more about a topic I once professed to comprehend, only to come to see as too intrinsically complex to categorize.

In the process, I've been influenced by the writings and experiences of dozens of uniquely informed sources, from writers of letters to newspapers to well-known scholars, military leaders and historians as well as dozens of contemporaries who served in the war.

They include a handful of close friends who answered the call (in the affirmative) and shared vivid accounts of their experiences with me.

Also of great influence have been the writings of the novelist Tim O'Brien and the late U.S. Army Col. David H, Hackworth, among others.

Their respective imprints mirror the content of this book to a significant degree, which is not to say they reflect its entire content.

Other's thoughts directly contradict many core assertions of my primary sources.

Taking this "mixed bag" approach enables me to imagine this as being "a Vietnam reader" of sorts; a collection of divergent views intended to offer the reader an open-ended view of a very dicey matter.

I first learned of L.A. native Hackworth in 1989 while reading an article wrtiten by Jim Webb that was published in a popular weekly news magazine that was included within many prominent Sunday newspapers.

The story of Hack's life captivated me. He was orphaned at birth and raised by his grandmother. Early in his teenage years joined the Merchant Marines and later the military at the end of World War II.

He faked his age like so many others did at the time in order to serve in what most felt was a noble pursuit.

He was known as "Hack" and Hack did surely love the Army, as his friend Ward Just recalled, "with the indiscriminate ardor and lavish expectations of any moonstruck Romeo."

Hack learned "to soldier" in Italy during WW II and later as a highly decorated commander in the Korean War.

He gained instruction from war-tested sergeants perfected his chops on the battlefield knew the score by heart.

Instinctively he came to care for his men, maintain discipline, and always set an example, "Keep your head, think in danger's midst, avoid paralysis master your own fear."

The vivid recollections of Col. Hackworth inform much of the content of this study.

I dug this cat big-time when first encountering his writings.

Hack came across as informed, credible, larger-than-life regal to the bone.

A soldier at heart, he gained astute writing skills during his years of service that gave wings to the real-world military mindset that informed his prose.

Hack brought both substance and style to the page. And did surely kick my butt in the process.

I saw in him the ultimate man's man, a true Stud, "you gotta' be kidding" bold, dominant in presence, funny, sardonic, a classic person-magnet, friendly to all adored to the point of mindless hero worship by his men, dazzlingly creative and heroic in leadership on the battlefield.

In Hack I also found a source whose views mirrored m own with remarkable consistency.

What I had come to regard as personal biases about how and why we found ourselves in that war were largely substantiated by reading Hack's take on the subject.

His eyes were rendered wide-open after spending a few years in Vietnam in various leadership capacities enabling him to take accurate measure of how deeply flawed our mission was.

The more acquainted we became, the more my imagination surrendered to the revealing nature of his stunning accounts.

I found his stories stark, uncloaked in fanciful notions, alive in sheer immediacy.

His national best-selling book, **About Face: Odyssey of An American Warrior** (Touchstone/Simon And Schuster-1989) is regarded as an accurate, unflinchingly candid, objective assessment of America's military engagement in Southeast Asia.

I've taken liberty extracting generous portions of his book verbatim, paraphrasing hundreds of other elements basically retelling his story for a contemporary audience. This degree of wholesale literary larceny offends the purist in me. But it also finds justification in the instructive power of Hack's various accounts.

He was there, I wasn't. He can tell this story a heck of a lot better than I can.

So here we go, letting him do that, with apologies to previous publishers, agents, co-conspirators and others.

I go comfortably, knowing I was able to engage Hack in shared email messaging during the later years of his life when his work appeared on *WorldNetDaily.com*. I was between jobs and had nothing better to do with my time then wallow in whatever intrigued me.

Because I feel genuine eternal love for the man – gone now but with us in spirit -- I'm sufficiently delusional to believe he is all right with me repeating his story, in my own words.

The moment seems entirely appropriate.

Many years after the American War in Vietnam ended in 1975, those interested in learning from our experience retain a deep yearning for objective analysis, comprehensive overview, and well-marinated historical retrospect.

In assembling the material contained herein, this writer sought first to air-out his own, subjective account, as it is if nothing else valid in its simple actuality.

Destiny divined my sense of the matter.

For it was my generation, approximately speaking, that was asked, instructed, required to join the military, willingly or otherwise, and go off and fight against fellow human beings anointed "the enemy."

Clearly most people of my age are permanently bound to this singular chapter of history as it came to define us, color our sense of self-identity.

Considerable disagreement continues to cloud any centrist interpretation of why America did not appear to prevail in this controversial war.

Among prevailing myths shared by both Vietnam veterans and the general public is that the combat performance of individual GIs determined and was responsible for the outcome of the war.

Research presented here asserts 82% of Veterans who saw heavy combat strongly believe the war was lost because the nation's political leaders would not permit our troops to win a traditional military victory.

In that spirit, nearly 75% of the general public agrees it was a failure of political "will to fight," not of arms.

For what it's worth, this observer of this war finds neither of those positions tenable against the backdrop of how native Vietnamese people processed these matters.

My impression is they were prepared to fight us to the last woman and child.

America to them was but one more interloper in a long sequence of invading forces.

It was their country.

We called them North Vietnamese and South Vietnamese.

To themselves, they were all brothers and sisters.

Getting Into Hackworth

Distracted by other concerns, I did not respond to an article sent to me by a family member whose intent was to enlarge my thinking on a controversial subject.

It asserted America could have won the war in Vietnam if we had taken a different approach, perhaps, adapted better strategies or followed a better course.

Its author claimed to be telling "the real truth" about the war.

I am familiar with this approximate point of view, I thought to myself in ignoring the article, conveyed to me as an email attachment.

What the heck, man?

My brain kept babbling.

No one needs to remind me others see this differently than I do.

I've also come to terms with how limited my own views are, as so much continues to escape me.

Yet on a larger plain of reality I believe the truth has many faces. Therefore I am skeptical of anyone who claims to possess it. The same applied to the material sent me that I regarded as unworthy of consideration.

In my opinion, its writer did not have special access to the truth.

No one does.

Those who claim to "know the truth" are playing games with the masses.

Their intellectual arrogance is a sin unto itself.

The article was conveyed to me in early 2015 by a family member who believed in sharing it with me he or she was doing me a favor by providing thoughts worthy of my consideration.

I ignored it; yet its arrival in my in-box subsequently prompted me to write this book.

To do so, I immersed myself in a sea of related materials from my decades-old Vietnam file. The more I've read, the broader my outlook has become.

At this point, the idea of another voice claiming to be telling "the real truth about the war" has actually become more palatable.

Just as I know "the real truth" will never be fully agreed upon, I also know that any element of partial truth bears consideration.

I've directed my research within my own personal files, bulging with pieces I saved but didn't pause to read along the way.

I began preparing for this effort nearly 50 years ago about the time *The Pentagon Papers* was published, along about 1971.

Since then I've kept anything and everything I could find on the topic, squirreling away a wide variety of related materials for the time I could lavish over them, gain new perspective become more informed generally.

Along the way I allude to what are considered to be among the most highly regarded books on Vietnam and the war we waged. In citing these titles I feel satisfied I've aided the reader, a person who may be more curious about all of this than I've been. If reading more books on the subject appeals to you reading *this* book will give you plenty of good leads.

For primary guidance I settled on David Hackworth's autobiographic treatise of his military career, 870-pages of riveting accounts from the battlefield, the brothel and the officer's club – settings of scintillating detail describing the in-between maneuvering that defines such a life.

Destiny did not divine me a place in this war.

I would later behold it from afar, attentive yet detached. Hackworth's writing took me there in print, vicariously, safely allowing me to experience conflict in the comfort of my office. The Vietnam I came to partially comprehend existed within my imagination between two softbound covers. I read it twice for good measure.

Hackworth entered the theater of battle with faith in the mission, only to completely change his mind after beholding the specific dynamics at play.

I urge anyone with a sincere interest in discovering one man's version of the truth to read *About Face*, his best-selling book.

Or, you can follow my text from here.

I've identified what I feel are the most salient passages regarding Vietnam recast them in my own voice, systematically following Hack's *About Face*.

My re-telling of his story is detailed and true to his text, as constructed with the assistance of Julie Sherman.

His story begins in the 1940's, when he lies about his age in order to go fight in WW II.

By the time of the Korean conflict Col. Hackworth emerges as a brave effective leader in the field.

"Hack" as the men he led affectionately called him, was a columnist on *World Net Daily* before he died in 2007.

As such, he was able to receive email messages from readers and answer them if inclined. I wrote often as his published articles were always of great interest to me, especially his views on the Vietnam War.

He responded to my emails from his home in exile in Australia where he gained refuge after really pissing off his former employer by telling his version of the truth about our war in Vietnam to an ABC TV news crew in the early-70s.

Feeling we had established a small bond of sorts, I committed to learning more about him, leading to the acquisition of *About Face*.

Hackworth was the youngest full colonel in Vietnam and to this day remains one of America's most decorated soldiers.

From age 15 to 40, he devoted himself to the U.S. Army, fast becoming a living legend.

Hackworth after decades of distinguished service in battle, turned into what James Webb called "an albatross" that carried with him "the ghost of an Army" that, in his view, failed itself and the nation by not winning the war in Vietnam.

To others Hackworth was "a warrior who became an eccentric."

Jim Webb, former Secretary of the Navy, presidential candidate and novelist, is a recipient of the Navy Cross and the Silver Star.

He wrote the article that appeared in *Parade Magazine* on April 2, 1989 featuring Hackworth's journey through the military and elements of his later careers.

Webb was familiar with Hackworth's reputation, the odds he overcame as a boy (he ran away from an orphanage at age 14, largely educated himself and enlisted in the Army at age 15), his courage and dedication to the battlefields of WW II and Korea.

He also knew of the circumstances surrounding Hackworth's decision to later leave the Army amid the controversies of the war in Vietnam.

In Hack Webb encountered a uniquely capable soldier whose personal force was synonymous with discipline whose unique acuity in battle had established a legacy of valor.

He had entered Vietnam like all of his contemporaries with a belief that the enemy could and should be soundly defeated.

He was known as "Hack." He spent four years on the battlefield, adding four Purple Hearts for wounds in action to the four he had received in Korea. He was also awarded two Distinguished Service Crosses, second only to the Medal of Honor; nine Silver Stars, four Legions of Merit and eight Bronze Stars. He was among the most decorated living American soldiers.

Webb wrote Hack's combat exploits in both wars were "the stuff of legend."

A West Pointer who served under Hack as platoon leader, Brig. Gen. John Howard called Hack the finest combat leader he had ever seen.

"He had no peer. He simply had an innate sense of the battlefield."

Another legendary warrior, Lt. Gen. Hank Emerson called Hack "the very best we ever had. There is no solider I respect more. He could do it all. He could write, speak, fight – you name it. He would have had at least three stars. And he came to a terrible end."

Hack was a respected thinker, a bold tactician who became a protégé of noted military historian S.L.A. Marshall and a favorite of former Army Secretary Stanley Resor.

His life, Webb wrote, was filled with "great heroism and grand flaws ….his improbable successes seemed almost a magnification of the opportunities the Army provided; his disentanglement provided a harsh judgment of its foibles and travails."

Hack's military career began with a brief stint in the Merchant Marine before reporting to the 752nd Tank Battalion in Italy as WW II was winding down.

He then served as a squad leader in the elite Trieste United States Troops. He was tough and thoroughly motivated, pushing his squad to perfection.

From there he volunteered for Korea.

He fought from Pusan to the Yalu River and back again during the difficult early days of the war.

He earned a battlefield commission at the age of 20 and finished the war with three Silver Stars, two Bronze Stars, four Purple Hearts and what Webb called "a reputation for charismatic, independent leadership."

Hackworth spent four more years in Vietnam, beginning with the 101st Airborne Division.

During that period, he also logged two years serving at the Pentagon, before returning to the war theater as a battalion commander with the 9th Infantry Division and with a number of Vietnamese units and advisory commands.

Along the way, he became increasingly frustrated with the Army's lack of overall objectives and failure to adapt its tactics to the enemy.

He became a critic of "ticket punching" – a policy that sent officers into the battlefield for short periods of time in order to give them some combat experience in order to "round out their resumes," as Webb phrased it, instead of focusing on leaders "who could fight more effectively, stay longer and win the war."

Hack came to believe a capable combat leader had traits, which are inconsistent with criteria for high-level positions.

As a result men who knew how to win in battle just did not get ahead.

He later wrote that "ticket-punching" was the Army's "death blow," a response to demand from top civilian leaders for "officers who would not only command fighting men but also teach physics, serve as statesmen and advise industry. This produced officers conversant in many matters, and proficient in very few."

In January 1969, Hack took over a downtrodden battalion in the 39th Infantry Brigade and turned them into a proficient unit by emphasizing surprise, deception, mobility and imagination.

Nevertheless, he discovered there was little interest in his adaptive tactics. He wrote extensive reports on how to prevail as the Army continued to repeat its mistakes and push ticket punchers through the rice paddies and Central Highlands "like tourists."

He deemed *"Vietnamization"* a doomed effort, saying the South Vietnamese failure to develop mid-level management had been a disaster, as it was populated by political appointees who "betrayed their nation by being more concerned about stealing than fighting."

About Face was an important undertaking for the former top-shelf combatant.

"As I wrote it, the bitterness went away. I was so affected by Vietnam. The book gave me the catharsis I had needed."

He told Webb after a long 20-year exile in Australia he hoped to return to Colorado and become a military commentator.

A few of his pieces from that era appear later in this work. Webb said we have much to learn from Hackworth, with respect to personal courage, human resilience and what it takes to train and lead combat soldiers.

Webb added Hackworth had much to learn from the America he would return to, about its continuing obligation to lead the free world and how we slowly but honestly have been coming to grips with our national failure in Southeast Asia.

"Perhaps we can relearn together the lesson of tolerance," Webb wrote. "We all burned out in some fashion toward the end of the Vietnam War. But beyond that anger and disappointment, there are hands to shake and wounds that may yet heal."

Hack's Story

Hack's story begins in the 1940's, when he lies about his age in order to go fight in WW II. He hooked up with the Merchant Marines, enlisted in the Army at fifteen, received a battlefield commission in Korea at twenty, was four times wounded before he was twenty-one.

He was among the most decorated officers in the American Army by the time of his retirement as a full colonel in

1971. It is not an exaggeration to note that by the Korean conflict Col. Hackworth has emerged as an incredibly brave and effective leader in the field.

In the introduction to *About Face* Ward Just wrote, "By his own account, Hackworth was not an obedient protégé, and tact was never his long suit; but his heroics in Korea were a powerful credential."

At this point, I let Hack tell his own story within the following exerpts drawn from *About Face..*

"Throughout my Germany years, it had become increasingly clear that among the world's 'little wars' one with no end in sight was that of Vietnam. There had been little peace in that country since the French defeat at Dien Bien Phu.

"The U.S. had sunk $1.9 billion in South Vietnam since its birth in 1954 (which helped President Ngo Dinh Diem rebuild the war-torn country), but the $80 million spent per year specifically to strengthen South Vietnam's military capabilities had done nothing to slow down Viet Cong (VC) guerrilla activity all over the countryside.

"The Cold War dimension of the struggle in Vietnam was stated (in general terms) by Khrushchev in Moscow, four days before Kennedy's inauguration: 'There will be liberation wars as long as imperialism exists, as long as colonialism exists … Communists support such wars fully and without reservation and march in the vanguard of the people fighting for liberation.'

And stated by the President, after the nightmare of the Kennedy-Khrushchev Vienna talks, when he reportedly told James Reston, then Washington bureau chief of *The New York Times*: "Now we have a problem in trying to make our power credible, and Vietnam looks like the place."

"A month later, in July 1961, the Americans pledged to increase their advisory "training mission" from 685 men to almost a thousand, and now, more than a year later, there were more than three thousand American soldiers serving as "trainers" for the Army of the Republic of Vietnam (ARVN), with the "the number" according to a 26 February 1962 *Newsweek* magazine piece, to "shortly double."

Hack wanted to go.

"Whether or not the conflict would grow into a full-bloom war I didn't know or care; for me it was just a great opportunity sharpens my skills."

His first effort to be sent to the war was rejected.

Too much combat experience, the guys at Personnel said. Keep in mind; the Vietnamese had already been fighting for 20 years.

He saw inexperienced colleagues being sent.

"How could sending highly motivated but inexperienced young lieutenants to train indigenous troops result in anything more than what was reportedly already there – an inept, inefficient South Vietnamese army?

"It was early days yet, but it seemed as if the primary purpose of our being there had already been compromised; only now did it occur to me that in 1962 Vietnam was not just 'the only war we've got' for me as a combat infantryman who didn't particularly want to go to a stateside staff assignment, but for the entire U.S. military establishment."

He ended up with the 101st Airborne Division at Fort Campbell, Kentucky. "I'd wanted Vietnam but I couldn't bitch."

As a major he was assigned with one of the best divisions of them all, one of the U.S. Army's top units.

Then came the Cuban missile crisis.

"It shook all of us, both military and civilian, out of our complacency, at least momentarily.

"For the very first time, the war of ideology between East and West was not being fought by proxy in China, Greece, Korea, or Southeast Asia, but by the superpowers themselves. And neither Kennedy nor Khrushchev looked as if he intended to back away."

Writer's Notes

Safe to say, nearly every attentive adult on the planet took a deep breath in tandem at that moment.

Russia and America appeared ready to set the whole planet ablaze.

Shared mutual destruction felt imminent.

Everyone's worst fears appeared on the verge of being realized.

It was undeniably the scariest moment any of us had experienced.

Decades later, it's hard to think of any other crisis that rendered our species as utterly despondent, despairing mankind's final chapter.

My computer keyboard isn't used to casting expressions in such dire vernacular.

My memory doesn't lie, nor does my sense of the relative nature of historic events succumb to hyperbole.

As a 10th Grade student at Groves High School in Birmingham, Michigan at the time of the Cuban missile crisis I experienced a pervasive degree of intense concern projected by the adults in our presence, teachers, counselors, administrators and others.

As we processed *en mass* along endless hallways and corridors in our building, heads were down, normal chatter subdued.

Few of us had much grasp of the full severity of the moment.

We knew what we knew, not much really.

We knew school was hard, days were long life was tough even for upper middle class suburban kids like us.

Our families were well to do but the pressures creating anxiety for us were similar to the experiences of 15-year-olds everywhere.

Back to Hack

Hackworth notes at the eleventh hour Khrushchev accepted Kennedy's firm "suggestion" that he dismantle and remove his missile sites from Cuba *muy pronto*.

Neither U.S. air strikes nor an invasion proved necessary; the Kennedy Administration's naval blockade coupled with our military advantages within our own hemisphere combined to help stabilize the situation.

Hackworth called the confrontation in Cuba "undoubtedly the most dangerous 13 days civilization has ever known." In a way it provided a pause in the Cold War.

"But the only real lesson the two powers came away with in this brinkmanship duel was that each needed bigger, faster, and longer-range weapons. In the end, all the Cuban missile crisis led to was a new round in the nuclear arms race from which there'd be no turning back."

Hackworth was at Fort Benning attending an Infantry Career Course, remaining on alert should the planned Cuban invasion become a reality. Counterinsurgency was becoming a primary focus point, endorsed enthusiastically by Kennedy and his brain trust.

Hackworth was struck that little emphasis was placed on the late-forties to early-fifties French experience in Indochina.

"The guerilla techniques taught to our class were of Napoleonic vintage, and, according to the dozen or so of my classmates who'd just returned from U.S. Special Forces assignments in Southeast Asia, would be of little use in the Highlands and paddies of Vietnam in the 1960s. Moreover, Benning's mentality was first and foremost one of stopping the Soviets on the plains of Europe."

He was introduced to a new weapon, the AR-15 an all-metal rifle that looked "about as lethal as a child's toy." Known as an Air Force survival weapon, it was small, light and it jammed, far more than it fired.

Hack felt it never would be worth a pinch of salt as an infantry weapon. It just wasn't rugged enough. It wasn't GI-proof.

"To me, sending a trooper into combat with it would be sending him on a suicide mission."

Hack was surprised to find, two years later the rifle the 101st Division was issued to carry into battle in Vietnam – now called the M-16 – was "the shit-piece AR-15 down to the last detail" except the new version now had a stock. Hack beheld inter-service rivalry that pitted the Army vs. the Air Force to define the bottom line of training activities.

"There was no small truth in the joke that our Army, Navy, and Air Force hated one another as much as, if not more than they hated the Soviets."

There was continuous turnover in his division as more and more people got orders to man the advisory effort in Vietnam. Hack still wanted to go but remained stateside. That year, Ngo Dinh Diem, who had governed South Vietnam since its creation in 1954, was assassinated. Hack wrote, "Over the years the once respected Diem had grown further and further away from the needs of his people even as he insisted that he knew what was best for them.

"Despite the millions of dollars the U.S. provided in both economic and military aid, Diem, the head of a Catholic regime in a predominantly Buddhist culture, had paid only lip service to the U.S.-suggested reforms that might have eliminated the base cause of the ongoing war of liberation in his country.

"Assassinated with the president was his brother, Ngo Dinh Nhu, a power-hungry mandarin who, with his wife Madame Nhu, had actually run the country in recent years as the weak, ineffective Diem retreated into personal isolation in the face of the escalating crisis in Vietnam."

Twenty-one days later, President John F Kennedy was shot to death in Dallas.

At first, Hack thought it was "some Orson Wells hoax." As was the case with the death of Diem, the facts of the case would never be fully known.

In any event, November 1963 marked the end of an era in both Vietnam and America.

"The violent deaths of their leaders set both countries careening toward each other like runaway trains, before hardly anyone – certainly not the American people, or even Lyndon Johnson, the new President, himself – even knew they'd jumped the tracks."

On two days in early August 1964, North Vietnamese patrol boats attacked two U.S. destroyers in the Gulf of Tonkin, 30 miles off the coast of North Vietnam.

Hack was outraged.

The second episode prompted President Johnson to order U.S. air attacks on mainland North Vietnamese military installations – the first use of overt American force in the conflict.

An instructor whose opinions Hack found believable said the whole thing was an election-year sham.

He compared the Tonkin Gulf incidents to Hitler's chicanery just prior to invading Poland.

He deemed Johnson's proclamation that "we seek no wider war" to be bullshit of the first order, asserting that the exercise had been orchestrated to give the President the popular support of the American people.

Hack continued to feel the North Vietnamese, not the U.S., had been the aggressor at Tonkin and that such acts had to be dealt with.

He bought that rationale but quietly disagreed ..."as I was just a few weeks shy of finals and then graduation. I just bit my tongue and kept silent."

In the meantime, U.S. Senator Wayne Morse raged on: "We are going to be bogged down in Southeast Asia for years to come if we follow this course of action, and we are going to kill thousands of American boys until finally ... the American people are going to say what the French people finally said – 'We have had enough!'"

As the 1964 presidential election closed in, Vietnam also was pressing ever closer on U.S. forces, both in the war-torn country itself and at home.

More than 100 American lives had been lost there so far. The U.S. was spending $1.5 million every day, as the Viet Cong grew bolder.

Following Diem's death U.S. support was fragile. It had occurred in an increasingly unstable, coup-plagued country. Its leaders agreed on nothing and paid scant attention to American wishes anyway, in Hack's mind.

Our ambassador to Vietnam, Maxwell Taylor, observed: "The ability of the Viet Cong to continuously rebuild their units and to make good their losses is one of the mysteries of this guerilla war."

As the South Vietnamese Army grew weaker, it became clear Americans would find themselves even more involved in the struggle.

U.S. estimates counted 40,000 full-time Viet Cong guerrillas in South Vietnam in early 1965.

Another 100,000 part-time civilian/farmers were added to the tally.

The 30,000 U.S. advisory and support people in the country to assist the poorly trained South Vietnamese were losing ground as the South lost a battalion a week.

"Time was not on our side," Hack wrote.

In February during the Vietnamese New Year (TET), the Viet Cong attacked American camps triggering a 49-aircraft raid on a North Vietnamese town, evoking yet-another enemy guerilla attack.

The *tit-for-tat* continued with more air raids and a decision by President Johnson to send 3,500 U.S. Marines to Vietnam with the sole mission of protecting our air base at Da Nang.

Three weeks later, the VC bombed the U.S. Embassy in Saigon and within two days LBJ made the Marines available for 'combat support' for the first time.

"Regardless of what anybody said, we were in the war now, boots and all," Hack wrote.

Within months, Hack's boots would show up there as well. His Screaming Eagles 1st Brigade arrived in Vietnam in July 1965, bringing the total number of American personnel in the country to 79,000.

Insufficient stateside training

Hack noted the Army was "made up of predominantly city boys who not only had not grown up with a rifle in their hands, but also had no idea about coping with the bush either."

This particular incongruity congealed with many other emerging points of troubled recognition, continuing to fuel Hack's disillusionment.

He wrote, "War was ongoing, everywhere, no safe areas, no front lines. The war was a sniper on the safe road, a child with a grenade, the old woman or young girl who sold Coca-Cola who just happened to be scooping out your position who spent her off hours planting booby traps and manure-tipped bamboo punji stakes along patrol paths." Impediments to success were omnipotent.

- All the Vietnamese, friend and foe alike, spoke the same language, a difficult tonal tongue that few Americans understood.
- Our cunning evasive opponent had the overwhelming (80%) support of the people.
- Key roads from the coast into the Central Highlands were the ones where France's foremost forces had been annihilated 11-years before at the end of the Indochina war. "The burned-out hulls of French vehicles, still dotting both sides of the road, provided a sobering image for even the most gung-ho guys in the brigade."
- Americans could not fire unless fired upon.
- Booby-traps were a primary source of casualty. They were attached to the doorways of vacant houses and shrines, on gates, along the tops of paddy walls. Hand-grenade booby traps contained one or multiple trip wires; traps were made of dud Air Force cluster bombs, anything any careless American soldier left behind formed the basis of a

lethal enemy device. "It was hell never knowing if you were going to have a foot after your next step."

- Coastal monsoons turned rice paddies into flooded immersion zones.

Problems began when Hack realized that on the user level his battalion was playing guinea pig for the Research and Development (R&D) people back in the States.

"Every time I turned around, our unit was being given some new piece of equipment to test on the battlefield." When what he considered to be "unreasonable requirements" were sent down, he responded, "We are here to fight a war. Our primary purpose is to kick Charlie's ass, not to write reports."

He believed few of the new toys were practical, GI proof, or "applicable to what we were doing in this war."

As Hack and his team members were scrounging equipment, supplies, the basics, he wrote that Service support units lived in Fat City, even as combat units struggled to survive.

Ho Chi Minh had taunted the French, saying, "You will kill ten of our men and we will kill one of yours, and in the end it will be you who will tire of it."

Hack's respect for the enemy's forbearance was based on battlefield observation.

"The NVA stood its ground in the face of our awesome firepower, allowing diabolical casualties among its ranks." In doing so it was theorized they were able to figure out how to beat the American's incredible firepower and amazing mobility afforded by the capabilities and worth of the helicopter for the movement of troops and artillery. From the fight they learned to 'hug the belt' of their enemy, to come in as close as they could in order to neutralize the killing power of our artillery and air support.

"The enemy was not stupid. He rigged up and hid huge logs in trees; an unlucky infantryman who tripped the concealed trap wire found 210 lbs. of teak catapulting down dense uncompromising bush that rose into double and triple canopy, making day like night."

In one instance, 15,000 troops searching for the enemy failed, providing what Hack characterized as "ample illustration of the limitation of the American's large-scale, incredibly expensive multi-battalion operations." They were simply no match for a cunning foe who lived by Mao's conviction, "Give me a path wide enough to move a mule and I will move an army."

Hack over ruled superiors – "selective insubordination" that he truly believed would benefit the whole battalion. A stateside report asserting American success stopped him cold.

"It was a bolt from the sky. We were all being told – even the President was being told – that our combat power, unleashed on the enemy, would either blast him back to the Stone Age or make him give up. We were being told that our air power would, ultimately, be the magic panacea to cure Vietnam of all its Communist ills.

"But if we on the ground were using it as precisely (and as excessively, some might say) as I'd just done on one tiny position and it wasn't doing the job, then what the hell good was all the saturation bombing in North Vietnam?"

Air power, he wrote, was great if you caught the enemy out in the open. But he was fighting from well-dug-in positions.

"They didn't give up even after their eardrums had burst from the concussion of our bombs and blood was pouring out of their noses and their ears."

The exercise was almost counterproductive. "All it did was make the enemy hate us even more, and become that much more determined."

Hack's perspectives were subject to what he saw, leading to what he felt to be true.

"Whatever the answer to this war was I certainly didn't know, but one thing I could confidently say was that bombing alone would never be it."

He mused introspectively, trying to assemble his thoughts amid the shock of realizing our mission was destined for failure due to its own illogic.

"For now, all I knew was our losses were far too heavy to claim 'victory' (although that was how the news people and higher headquarters would describe the battle, with the price in U.S. lives only moderate.) The fact was we'd been sucked in and eaten alive. We had attacked machines guns as the British and the French had in WW I, and I was heartsick at the result."

Hack said the hardest part of the soldier's life "was having to live like an animal for months on end."

Battle scenes were gruesome on a good day, hellish on most others. They featured medics trying to save lives by flashlight in muddy holes in the middle of the night and a lot of on-the-job-training – OJT.

He described a "deceptively quiet battlefield, where you could feel the enemy's presence within."

Hack thought back on the book, **Street Without Joy**, by the French on-the-ground scholar of the Indochina war, Bernard Fall.

He began looking for the enemy not with unwieldy company-size formations, but with small patrols fanning out in all directions of the battlefield.

"Nighttime patrols allowed us to interdict the enemy's ingress-egress routes – in essence, take the battle away from our foe. The VC strong point was patience -- a characteristic that gave the enemy the inner resources to collect, flatten and tack together empty beer cans, one onto the next and the next, like shingles, until he'd made a metal roof."

After a battle briefing, he was instructed to "Pursue, pursue, pursue," by none other than Gen. William Westmoreland.

"Did he really mean he wanted us to charge into the woods and get our ass torn apart by the enemy's inevitable delaying screen of snipers and booby traps? In WW II there were numerous cases of one sniper stopping a rifle battalion for hours, killing and wounding dozens of soldiers in the process. Did Westy really want us to make that investment in lives here in Vietnam for so little return? Surely not.

"This was not the same kind of war as WW II. This was not a war of terrain objectives (a fact I'd come to appreciate the hard way at My Canh) each one worth the price in lives if in taking it you moved closer to your final objective, your Berlin, your Tokyo or Pyongyang.

"Vietnam was a war where more often than not our elusive enemy just went to ground or ran away while we swept through and 'cleared' a village, only to return, rebuild, and reoccupy it again the minute we'd moved on."

My Phu was a classic example. At My Phu, 21 of Hack's men were dead in a battle for real estate that had no strategic or tactical value, and that would be abandoned by our "pursuing" forces as soon as the dust settled. My Canh had not been a set-piece battle either.

As the battles were fought, Hack realized paratroopers were innately unfit for guerilla warfare.

"The main thing I learned at Tuy Hoa was that there was simply no point in taking an objective you had no intention of holding, no point of using men when firepower could do the job. Tuy Hoa's battlefields may have looked like the hedgerows of Normandy, but if (as was the case,) the taking of such objectives one by one wasn't going to lead you anyplace, and if (as was also the case) you were going to abandon each objective after you'd taken it, only to take it again and abandon it again, *again and again and again*, as the French did before us and as we were doing now – well, it wasn't worth the life of even a single soldier."

Eight months in Vietnam, Hack's troops had dealt death and seen death in numbers none could have imagined. They'd endured leeches and jungle rot, constant, heavy rains and clammy clothes that chilled them in their sleep, and the "wait-a-minute" bushes that could hold a trooper as tenaciously as a strand of barbed wire.

Many fought malaria and hepatitis; all fought fear, not just of the enemy but of the snakes, the tigers of the Central Highlands that reportedly pounced on troopers, the monkeys that dropped out of trees at night like stealthy Viet Cong (at least one of these was hacked to death by a trooper with a machete in the dark), and of course the night itself.

"I began to suspect that … whatever we thought, we were really playing the game by their rules."

His men launched operations at Nhon Co, inland along the Cambodian border amid triple-canopied jungle obscured by the maze of solid bamboo below.

For the troops, it was one nasty slog.

The soldiers were plagued by the presence of pernicious leeches, bites from which led to infection on top of infection. There was little to no sunlight for days on end, only endless monsoons.

Well known at the highest levels in Vietnam and proved beyond a doubt at the bayonet level at Bu Gia Mop, the North Vietnamese were operating out of Cambodia.

This information would be big news in the U.S.A., news that by day's end would be vehemently denied by the Secretaries of State and Defense.

This incident well characterized one of the biggest problems in the war, which only got worse as the conflict went on.

Hack wrote, "Out there, every day, American men were playing for the ultimate stakes. Yet back home, it seemed as if the politicians and bureaucrats who sent them there were playing by a different set of rules, if not a completely different game."

There were NVA in Cambodia – so far, four to six regiments' worth – who were already killing American soldiers in South Vietnam. If they remained unstopped, they would kill many, many more.

"To the guys like myself on the ground, it was just as simple as that. So none of us could figure out why things were not that simple."

Soldiers in Vietnam served on a one-year rotation policy – when people "got short," Hack observed, "they just wanted to go back to the base camp and hide under a rock. They were deadweight in an outfit; they didn't do their share and their lousy attitude was infectious."

Men thought it was stupid. Infantry couldn't fight through this terrain. Their weapons could not even penetrate the bush.

Writer Remembers 1966

At the same time, this writer was midway through my college years, jumping from one unlikely institution of higher learning (and higher beer consumption) to another. I was busy doing everything I could to remain matriculated at an accredited college – the primary requisite for maintaining a buffer between my freedom and the omnipotent draft system.

My first memory of hearing anything of real substance about the American War in Vietnam occurred in June 1966 – the same approximate time in this chronology of Major Hackworth's experience in the theater.

Prior to then, it only crossed my mind in a distant, general sense.

Everyone in my sphere of contact knew it was waging on. We also knew college students needed to remain enrolled at an accredited college or university in order to maintain a student deferment and therefore avoid being drafted.

In this time frame I think it is safe to say at least 20-30 percent of male students were majoring in avoidance.

There was no shame in doing so. Playing this card was standard, non-controversial, widely accepted behavior for all personality types.

Informing me, and any others who chose to bask in his presence, was a college student named Michael Harrison. The two of us had recently matriculated at a small liberal arts institution in the hills of West Virginia; we became the only two new students at the school at the beginning of its third-of-four terms.

This became my fourth college; I'd flunked out of one and got thrown out of another.

Now I was ready to get serious about staying enrolled somewhere, anywhere where I could gain refuge from what was heating up as a big deal event for people of my age.

Michael was in his mid-20, older than any of us in the dormitory. We soon learned he was a returning veteran from a war none of us understood whatsoever.

Even the very notion of a place called Vietnam exceeded our frame of reference. He had to show us a map.

Even then, it seemed remote, difficult to imagine let alone understand. Within a few years, everyone had undergone a steep learning curve.

Michael Harrison was an unforgettable personage, instantly.

He wore military fatigues.

He told stories we couldn't believe.

He described the confusing battlefield, the decadence of life among the populace, the utter incredulity of the entire exercise.

Lacking any frame of reference, the scenarios he vividly depicted were on the outer edge of conception for those of us who spent endless nights in his dormitory room listening to his gripping tales of war.

He was a prince among peons. He had his own way different than anyone we'd known. Administrators acknowledged his exceptional aura, gave him his own dorm room.

It became a late-night Mecca for curious-minded undergraduates seeking stimulation and eccentricity after they locked the front doors of the girl's dorms and turned out the lights at The Moose Club on State Rt. 119.

Mature Michael was larger than life, magnetic in all respects.

His was a suave demeanor that earned him a way with petite ladies not to mention several of us larger sweatier gonads who flocked most nights to his bohemian setting, exotic, worldly somehow featuring something most of us hadn't even seen at the time—a coffee-making machine. None of us could figure out how it worked. It was not only cutting edge radical in its time it also produced brain-riveting java that wired our emerging psyches, enlarged our sense of the impossible.

He would make a fresh pot every two hours, or less, deep into the night. Buzzed on his brew we imbued fantastic stories from a distant place in time, descriptions of bizarre occurrences that transcended anyone's capacity to envision the specific references that enlivened his endless chronicles.

Vietnam was coming home in the wildly implausible tales of an early-returning veteran and in the consciousness of those of us who worshiped at The Alter of a uniquely world-wise fellow student.

Michael had gazed far into the wacky vortex of what Hack was discovering – a genuinely insane military adventure that lacked purpose, comprehensibility and rational redemption – a war that was about to engage the full attention of 3.5 million will-be combatants.

Back to Hack

Hack continues: "Like most of the men in the battalion, I went from the sixth to the twelfth of June with no sleep. I was a walking zombie by the time we pulled back for the B-52 strike."

Seriously fatigued, he contemplated the role of the medical personnel in his midst.

"I didn't know what it was about medics. I used to think they joined the Medical Corps because they had a double load of courage, but maybe it was just the title itself that transformed them into the most valiant band of men I ever knew. Medics didn't wait for a miracle to pull the wounded to a safe shelter –they *were* the miracle that pulled, slid, dragged, and packed shattered bodies out of danger. And they performed miracles: stopping bleeding, stopping shock, relieving pain with morphine, and getting IVs going to pump life into broken fighters."

The valor of the medical teams made a big impact on Hack.

"Many packed M-16s along with their forty-pound medical kits, but their job was to save lives, not take them, and they risked their own, again and again, answering calls that took them right into the line of fire – machine gun, mortar, sniper, mines – without hesitation.

"Their most powerful medicine was their encouragement ('You got it made … just a scratch … you'll see that girl again.'), a never-ending patter to keep minds occupied while deft hands administered aid or tried to sort out a stomach or a chest ripped open by shot."

"Seriously the brave pilots who performed Medivac missions further assisted wounded soldiers, but it was the medics who made the difference on the ground, until the choppers could get in. Selfless and serving beyond good sense, countless medics died in the line of duty to save not just their buddies but the life of every man who fell on the battlefield.

"From two wars, it is these men, the medics – the 'docs' – who hold the most special place of respect and trust in this infantryman's heart, and I'm sure there are a couple of million other men in the United States alone who feel the exact same way."

I've read that passage many times.

Way deep inside its essence Hackworth conveys a sincere depth of respect and understanding. It continues to help explain why I feel such genuine affection for the cerebral warrior whose reminiscences of his Vietnam experiences so profoundly inform my sense of what happened there. And why it occurred, how it was our country of origin went so wildly astray in this ill-conceived eventuality. His assignments changed, from the theater of war to stateside again where Hack fulfilled many assignments between deployments.

At one point, Hack found himself in the immediate company of the Chief of Staff, General Harold K. Johnson. He aligned with Brigadier /General S.L.A. (SLAM) Marshall, the ultimate historian considered to be the American expert on soldiers in combat, author of **Battles In The Monsoon**. Hack became his aide.Gen Johnson set it up. Hack became chief of military history. His perspectives proved prophetic.

"We've had U.S. Army units in Vietnam for 18-months. Almost one-third of the Army is committed to that war. But at Fort Benning there is only a handful of field-grade officers with Vietnam experience, and half of these were advisors. They weren't with U.S. units. We're just not putting our best and most recently experienced combat officers into the school system, which is where I believe they belong. We're sending them everywhere else to get their tickets punched, as if their careers took priority over the war. Vietnam is the toughest war we've ever fought, and we're going at it as though we're fighting World War II all over again."

He went on to tell Johnson, "The only people who really know how to fight this thing are the Australians and the Viet Cong."

They shared time with the former Chief of Staff of the Israeli Army, Gen. Moshe Dayan. He'd been to Vietnam, examined the landscape and had come away incredulous over the American style of war – too eager to rush to battle at any price, crazy use of firepower, absence of initiative on the battlefield.

The Israeli's thoughts mirrored Hack's instincts although Gen Marshall countered them with, "Well, we'll wear them out. No one can take the kind of punishment we're dishing out and win. Look at the Germans and the Japs." Twice in one day Hack had heard the Army's top boss and one of America's top military analysts compare Vietnam to World War II.

Before going into the field he and Gen. Marshall received a briefing that Hack found "suspiciously rosy" in its assessment of how the war was going; in any event it matched the General's views as they embarked upon what Marshall referred to as his "journey into disillusion."

Their first stop was the 1st Air Cav Division's base camp at An Khe, where a village of 2,500 mostly mountain people had sprung up into a ticky-tacky cardboard instant city with more than 18,000 Viet camp followers.

The jungle was gone, becoming a large barricade eighteen kilometers in circumference – inside containing the base camp, a fine airfield and an actual mountain.

Base camps were opulent, "obscenely disconnected" with the mud and horror of field soldier life.

Hilton-like VIP quarters featured lavish gourmet meals presented on fine china embossed with the Cav insignia and served by black waiters in starched white jackets – probably line infantrymen who'd found a home in the rear. After-dinner cigars, liqueurs, coffee and other accouterments were standard-fare for the officer class, while frontline soldiers existed on hard scrapple prepackaged particulate.

The base camps had even less place in this war than they had in Korea, where many of the current generals had been majors and lieutenant colonels on the outside looking enviously into this insidious scenario that created a need for up to one-third of combat forces at an base being assigned security detail – for the base itself.

Hack noted these massive installations were really as much the enemy as the enemy himself.

On tour of facilities with the General Hack beheld illogic imposed upon *Alice in Wonderland* imagination.

He witnessed Major General DePuy turn entire regions into parking lots, utilizing huge bulldozers to plow, rip and shear through the jungle and using ditch digging machines to slash into the Viet Cong's ingenious network of underground tunnels and bunkers.

Undetected throughout the U.S. involvement, they were like a poor man's subway system, running through various war zones.

DePuy left destruction in his wake in pursuit of the point beyond which he believed "the enemy could not sustain the punishment we were inflicting, also known as the threshold of pain."

As they gathered information, Hack was depressed to find the same problems occurring, the same lethal mistakes being made again and again. And they were the exact same mistakes we'd made earlier.

The Viet Cong, those dumb country hicks or so we perceived them, were still fleecing us city slickers every day.

Our casualties were fewer than theirs but we still "danced to the enemy's tune," a tune written years before during the Indochina war.

The VC initiated or controlled almost every action. U.S. units were being devastated without meeting the enemy at all, often by booby traps generally constructed of American "debris."

The enemy could sustain their losses and so were not losing the war, whatever "defeats" their foe ascribed to them.

And there was no reason to believe they would not be able to continue to sustain their losses, even in the face of Westy and DePuy's search-and-destroy tactics and the rich man's war the Americans were waging.

No one wanted to know.

Complacency did not see the need for self-examination leading to what appeared to be a total absence of curiosity about what was happening around them.

William Eugene DePuy was considered by insiders to be the prime architect of America's war in Vietnam.

Hack and Slam Marshall met DePuy in Di An in 1966. During a cease-fire, a VC unit ambushed a 1st Division platoon whose patrol also violated the truce.

DePuy dashed into the general's mess and told Slam they were going off to battle.

Hack regarded this as "an incredible example of over supervision: a division commander rushing to the scene of one of his platoon's open-and-shut screw-ups."

Absent were company and battalion commanders, who most likely were overhead in choppers issuing orders amid absolute chaos in an already confused situation.

"Such was not the way to win a war, but the longer the war went on, the worse this situation got as many senior officers saw their unit's fights and patrols only in terms of the glory it could bring them, or in terms of the medals and ribbons they could win (awards so common that they only became conspicuous by their absence in a guy's fruit salad.)"

At Bien Hoa, attached to the 173d -- at that point the oldest serving U.S. Army maneuver unit fighting in Vietnam -- Hack beheld a group that was battle-scarred but not battle-wise.

"Commanders seemed preoccupied with the big picture. They didn't notice that the small things, the things that made a unit effective and prevented unnecessary casualties, were slipping and slipping badly. Guys were using soap, toothpaste and shaving cream before operations. They were smoking and wearing mosquito repellent on patrol."

Slam Marshall was the well-known author of **War Night Drop**, **The River**, **The Gauntlet** and **Pork Chop Hill**.

He and Hack proposed to visit each of the ten divisions and separate brigades in Vietnam.

They went up to Pleiku, met with the 4th Division and told the G-3 they wanted to review what he considered one of the more significant actions his unit had been involved in. The general chose Paul Revere IV, an operation that had been conducted along the Cambodian border the previous November.

At a briefing, officers appeared before them with a set of full-color charts and graphs.

The operation was presented to them as a classic encounter.

Army intelligence had ostensibly heard intelligence and deployed troops around a large enemy element.

As the story went, they had proceeded to push the foe into a trap in which the enemy was savagely punished and all but destroyed.

Hack began interviewing witnesses including 4th Div participants and POWs taken during the battle.

"This examination of the POWs, coupled with the horror stories of 4th Div troops, whose squads or platoons were chewed up and spat out by their NVA opponents, revealed there was almost no correlation between the official Army report on Paul Revere IV and was actually happened on the ground. I was astonished."

Yes, American forces prevailed. More than one thousand enemy were killed-in-action, victims of awesome American firepower. But if Paul Revere IV was examined from the perspective of the war of insurgency that it was, then we did not win and we were not brilliant, Hack wrote. "In fact, we were stupid, lethally so, and Charles won the day."

The enemy had initiated the action using NVA decoys to entice U.S. forces into an airmobile action. The enemy had sucked the American units into well-dug-in killing zones along the Cambodian border, killing more than 140 and wounding more than 560 men on terrain that favored them completely. "Once they'd accomplished their mission, they could scoot right across the border to regroup"

Worse than that, Hack realized for the first time "that probably no one at the very top had any idea that the official reports were wrong."

Pencils were being applied at every level "to put our debacles in the best light." From the company level embellishments were added all the way up the chain of command.

"Whatever underpinnings of truth remained by the time these reports got to division and corps were probably incidental – full of relatively honest but totally false optimism, making it all the way to Washington, eventually becoming the basis of critical decisions made on the war." Slam later chided Hack for his "almost childlike faith" in the honesty of the after-action reporting system.

"Slam saw what was going on. He didn't raise a finger or utter a word to try to change it, although he was centrally involved in the effort to keep the American pubic informed of how the war was going." He wrote books, had a syndicated column and appeared on TV and radio shows. Hack was disheartened. He felt Slam had the responsibility to tell Westmoreland and the rest of the establishment about the truth about what was happening to the war effort. "Instead he continued to ruffle no feathers, even while calling Westmoreland 'a dumb shit.'"

Hack sensed we were not only losing the war … he'd sensed that for some time. He also could not have guessed how much faster we were losing. As we dispatched new units, the NVA matched them, upped the ante, confident we could be tapped out.

At the end of 1966, an end to the war was nowhere in sight. Hack believed the emphasis on body count was taking its toll on the war effort. It made everyone a bounty hunter and a liar, he wrote. It had outlived its usefulness as a reliable measure of anything, he felt.

"The more bodies we counted it was believed the better we were doing." Hack concluded the pressure for a high and instant body count interrupted the flow of battle, tied up communications and created unnecessary casualties among soldiers tasked with doing the counting during a fight. "Leaders did not challenge suspicious figures that too often were actively inflated as they rose up the ladder of authority. Sometimes body counts were completely made up to mask screwed-up missions. Whatever, it assuaged sectors of the public and a government that might otherwise had begun to discern the stench."

Companies in the field were operating at about 50 percent of their authorized strength. Half the men were on R&R, or sick, or lost in logistical mazes. Hack compared it to driving a car with only two tires.

"Nor did anyone seem to notice the pungent smell of marijuana that now permeated many a base camp. It was sold everywhere for a nickel a joint or in a pack of 20 disguised as a sealed box of Marlboros.

"Three-quarters of the soldiers in Vietnam were draftees; regular Army booze was taking a backseat to weed. Our commanders denied there was a problem even after 1967 when heroin found its way into those Buddha grass "Marlboro" joints, eventually turning some 20-30 percent of the U.S. military in Vietnam into junkies before you could say "Far out, man."

Writer's Notes

Like "wow," Colonel.

Three years after the heroin found its way into those Buddha grass joints, those Buddha grass joints also began to find their way into my landlady's mailbox.

They came to my attention in small boxes, mailed to me from Vietnam. Most boxes that size contained audio cassettes recorded by servicemen and sent to their family members as expedient alternatives to traditional letters.

"The tapes" in the boxes I received were actually about 20 pre-rolled doobies bigger than beefy jerky strips and stronger than a pallate of alluminum. This was without any doubt the strongest marijuana ever cultivated on the planet, excessively debilitating, whacked out beyond comprehension. Only in the larger disorientation of the times did consuming anything this powerful make any sense. Given the stark palor of a war without end, gestures of supernatural mind numbing occurred in perfect context. Distortion trumped reality, no matter the zip code.

"Frannie," my landlady's mentally handicapped daughter brought the packages over to my small house located on the edge of their property in an abandoned coal mine town with fewer residents than hawks and other sky birds.

She waited for me to show up: most of the time I was gone performing my job, meeting high school students and counselors, telling them about the programs at a small liberal arts college located atop a hill in a mountainous area.

The shame that accompanies my recollection of all of this is quite a bit bigger than the characters on the screen in front of me. I'd rather show you a box of bounced checks or alimony payments I ignored, which is a fictitious concept evoked strictly in the name of trying to make this point as honestly as possible.

Greeting her at my door, accepting the packages from her, was far short of glorious behavior. Write it off to war animus. I was more upset about a war I couldn't stop than I was wise enough to recognize the sheer depravity of my overall posture.

This was Vietnam, ladies and gentlemen.

There were few actual heroes, certainly not me in this situation.

Here is how I saw it at the time: I felt fortunate to have friends mailing me this stuff. I felt blessed to be able to light up a monster Buddha bud super J. I'd flip on "Led Zeppelin" or "The Beatles" and drift off into a slightly different dimension, often associated with staring at patterns in the wallpaper.

The pre-roll lads and ladies were of a distinct variety. One or two puffs were enough to transform a sullen sad lad into more of a sullen sad lad … lacking any vestige of stability. At this point, they were shaped more like "Pall Mall's" than Marlboro's, considerably larger, longer and a few trillion percent more lethal.

The pre-rolled reefers I received were larger than the extended middle finger of a pro basketball player. They were at least twice the size of an average joint, fatter than a "before shot" in a weight loss ad stronger than several thousand palates of crazy glue.

As I began to smoke this Vietnamese weed my relationship with the "drug" or whatever you want to call it changed profoundly.

In a short matter of time, I went from being a generally take-it-or-leave-it disinterested user to a fulltime burn artist.

Because I traveled for my job at the time, I was used to being gone for a week at a time, even longer.

On most Sundays when I packed up and hit the road, I'd leave my "stash" at home, figuring I'd be OK without it, knowing it would be there when I returned.

After the packages began arriving every few weeks or so, I found myself taking the stash with me.

I really need to stop typing here for a second. I'm not used to being this honest, with myself or otherwise.

Standing outside my self, looking way back at the person I once was, it's hard not to posture objective, knowing the purpose of writing this book is to share with others my Vietnam experience, as honestly as I'm able to lay it out for you.

Hack says Vietnamese heroin-laced marijuana began to really mess with the troops, beginning in 1967. This writer says the same thing began to happen at about the same time back here, stateside, *Reverend Strainmeuhler.*

Cynics, detractors, alleged purists, old girlfriends, deposing attorneys and other saints might question how I can even remember this moment when I first chose to take my buzz bag on the road.

Are you kidding me?

Existentially, it was less than .08 seconds ago. Keep in mind I was paying attention. The significance of the moment was never lost on me.

Eight million pounds of marijuana later I can still remember just about everything that happened to me in my entire life, and specifically I recall this day, this era with crystalline clarity.

First of all, it wasn't THAT long ago, darlings. Second of all, refer back to "first of all."

Life, in the end, is but a mere gallop. We mount the stead ride off into the mountains.

Our time here is a mere snapshot. Sure, it seems to last forever. Of course that is but a mere illusion. Generally, existence rushes past in a fleeting blur.

Anyhow thank you very much, Buddha grass.

For surely you did kick <u>my</u> ass, as well as the ass of so many millions of other then-young Americans like myself (eventual hippies.)

You done "f'-'ed wit me big time, homey bone."

Whup up da side 'o da' head, Mama San, Papa San, all dem-dare San people over in the war zone, growing that bud, dipping that bud in THE WORST addictive additives, pushing that bud on our boys, growing it, pushing it, all the way back to any sufficiently demented associate.

Yes, I answered the door. I accepted the packages. I willfully dove into them.

Put yourself in my shoes.

Better yet, stay in your shoes.

Thanks to you, good buddy, rockin' ganja stick dude, we found ourselves in the bulls-eye of a lifestyle-changing avalanche of tsunami force, imposed in an atmosphere of blinding cultural upheaval.

We got whacked out, Billy Bob.

Instant addicts surfaced everywhere, from the PX in the delta to the post office in Butte Falls.

Once-straight farmhands and drug store cowboys alike encountered the herb, tried the herb liked the herb most living happily ever after.

In the spirit of literary candor, I've never been absolutely sure whether that happy ever after shoe fit me.

I like to think I've been a mostly cheery person during my sprint from diapers to Diaspora although such assessment strikes me right now as slightly saccharine.

I do know some pot is stronger than some other pot.

In that spirit, some pot is also too strong for most people.

We were taken to school on this subject.

Important lessons were learned

Access to heroin-laced Vietnamese marijuana discontinued just in time to save the last vestiges of clear-thinking capacity, in my case at least.

I certainly can't speak for everybody on this issue.

Looking back now, it seems I had open-ended amounts of the lethal Asian stuff available to me for perhaps four or five months.

It was long enough to permanently transform my usage profile, short enough to sustain contentment with relatively pedestrian herb of a less seriously narcotic nature.

Wait. Hold on a minute.

Truth be told, in the early-1970s while living in the San Francisco Bay area friends and I had little difficulty finding similarly disabling "Thai sticks" for sale -- $35 for a seven-gram stick of mind-bendingly distorting and oily flowerage.

For those of us from the war generation this temporary availability of yet more lunacy from distant countries bordering the South China Sea equated to déjà vu, nothing new, thanks again, President Thieu.

Thai stick pot ruled.

The good news was, it was good. The bad news was, $35 was a lot of money in those days.

So most of us only indulged on special occasions – also known as Tuesday mornings, Thursday afternoons, all day Saturday and Sunday.

So as far as looking back goes, I trace what became known as my present-day identity back to that special Sunday afternoon in north central West Virginia when I opted to take my little sack of herb with me on the road, rather than leave it behind.

To myself I tacitly said, "I do believe I will use this all of the time."

Of course, I did from then on.

Fifty years have past. I've only stopped when I had to, usually because I could not find any.

Other times I stopped temporarily for other reasons, always assuming I'd resume using it eventually.

I've never sought "help" to understand what happened to me.

I've just blamed it on, or credited, the radically disabling marijuana I smoked from Vietnam.

More than anything, it led to my turning point.

Only when reading *About Face* the first time through did I finally discover the truth of what was in "that pot" that shot me through the vortex connecting casual use to dependent addictive obsessive/compulsive behavior, doctor.

A few years later, when I read the book a second time, Hack's reference to the heroin factor gave me pause, made my entire torso shiver.

For better or worse, the person I became in the hours after I drove off in my VW bug that afternoon is the person creating the following words on a computer keyboard early in the eighth decade of my life.

I've yet to undergo similar change in my makeup.

Some would say I never grew up, stayed the same, took on life in a false shroud of euphoria, skipped weathering the emotional challenges of getting older, hid in THC-induced neo-reverie, perhaps or perhaps not.

Everyone my age got whacked over the head by our war. American soldiers in Vietnam who inexplicably or otherwise became addicted to heroin-laced marijuana experienced equal variants of hyper bliss and hyper stress. They got knocked around like dodge-'em cars.

American dilettantes back home exposed to Whack City Nam pot were similarly redirected, in an entirely different context but no better for the wear.

Before departing this subject I'd like to add this point of possible clarification: None of us at the time knew the pot we smoked from Vietnam contained elements of heroin. It just turned out that way.

Years later I am reasonably certain had we known that we would have left it alone.

I turned down heroin more than once. I gave away a quarter-ounce of opium a friend from Vietnam mailed me, asking me to save it for him until he came back. I couldn't get that shit out of my hands fast enough.

Only when I read Hack's book did I grasp what happened to us when we took a toke on one of those rocket reefer submarine sized muscular monsters.

Had we known we were smoking heroin I believe 99 out of 100 people carrying guitar picks would have rubbed that giant joint out on the spot, thrown away the bag and beat it to the nearest beer store instead.

Turns out, we were dumber than heck. Most of us have progressed somewhat although in my own case it occurs to me the person I was then is the same person I am now, only today's version is perhaps a bit more enlightened when it comes to understanding the war of our youth.

Back to Hack

Slam knew nothing of the history of the Vietnam conflict. He had not even read Jules Roy's recently translated **The Battle of Dien Bien Phu**.

Slam was right. Our forces were pounding the enemy who was getting physically weaker but was also growing stronger.

Hack continued to interview prisoners to gain perspective, posing as a disinterested historian. He came away convinced that our opponent wasn't invincible, his ability to endure was. He had the will he had the numbers. He knew he had time on his side.

It had taken him a thousand years to kick out the Chinese, and less than one hundred to get rid of the French. What did it matter how long for the Americans, who actually made things easier by repeating the mistakes of the French?

When he asked them how long they were prepared to fight, prisoners told Hack from 15-20 years. They were going to win, they said, and they were prepared to stay in South Vietnam as long as necessary to do so.

"Are you?" one asked.

Hack felt Slam was similarly aware that we were sinking deeper and deeper into a quagmire. But he refused to add up the facts, or at least wouldn't let the facts get in the way of his prejudgment of the situation.

"Meanwhile, body bags were filling with American youths at a rate of 200-400 a week, and somehow in all this madness someone, somewhere, had to know what he was doing."

Hack found himself in Saigon during the 1967 Tet celebrations. "A year later it would come as little surprise to me how easily the Viet Cong's Tet Offensive got under way."

He experienced huge crowds, people screaming to be heard against the din of wall-to-wall exploding firecrackers. There was much noise and confusion an ideal backdrop for a surprise assault as would prove to be the case one year later.

Hack found that Slam hated the press. It galled him that the slants of many of the young journalists work appeared "antiwar." He branded David Halberstam "a Commie" actually believing it.

Slam continued to project a "we got 'em on the ropes" assessment, a view that was accepted as unquestionable for reasons Hack could only guess; he concluded that "most of these guys didn't have a clue as to what the war was all about in the first place."

Over bourbon, Hack told Slam for the millionth time that the summing-up he invariably gave to the top brass bore no relation to facts the two had gleaned over recent months and he knew it.

Hack began working on early drafts of **The Vietnam Primer,** drawing on a list of his observations of our Army's repeated tactical failings as well the details of his discussions with over one hundred POWs. The book went on to become the Army's official source of combat knowledge and was circulated among all the rank and file after its publication about halfway through the war.

Hack was soon back to work at the Pentagon and then Slam was home in what also happens to be my hometown -- Birmingham, Michigan. Slam was writing **lZ Bird**, **Ambush, West to Cambodia** and **The Fields of Bamboo**, the four books that ultimately came out of their visits to military engagement theaters.

Hack's new duty at the Pentagon duty was with The Directorate of Individual Training (DIT). There were more than 400,000 American forces in Vietnam at that time. Casualties were constantly removing personnel from the theater. This rendered the group in a constant state of expansion.

Hack became Chief of the Individual Training Branch and later Chief of the Schools Branch where he was responsible on the policy level for the operation and functioning of all U.S. Army service schools in the U.S. He found infantry schools were still teaching tactics that were more appropriate to World War II. They were ill suited for Vietnam.

Meanwhile, our guerilla, non-conventional enemy was "making hay while the sun shone" on our conventional approach to the conflict. Hack felt even as everyone around him agreed something had to be done, "the general feeling was that Vietnam was a hiccup; we could not scuttle our basic mission, i.e., preparation for war in Europe or Korea, for an aberration soon to pass."

As it was, our forces in Korea and Europe were reduced to skeleton staffing, a situation that should have proved to those in charge that the Russians had no intention of making war on Europe at that time, "if they didn't attack when we were so vulnerable."

At the Pentagon, Hack felt his most significant contribution was a study of U.S. friendly fire casualties in the war.

"If my tour with Slam told me anything, it was that the U.S. Army was its own worst enemy in Vietnam." During the study he was surprised to discover that a new system had been developed to count KIA's. Officers were using a clever, cynical ploy that clouded distinctions between killed in action and died of wounds – (DOW) that reduced KIA numbers rendering them more palatable to the public. Hack's studies indicated a staggering 15-20 percent of all U.S. casualties in Vietnam were caused by friendly fire. On the basis of their calculations, of the 58,000 Americans who died in Vietnam between 8,700 and 11,600 of them shouldn't have.

AWOLs were a large and growing problem. Hack believed if they had been trained properly in the first place the problem would not have exploded as it did.

Slam's book **Battles In the Monsoon** had been published. Slam wrote glowingly about Hack's role with the 1st Battalion, 327 during the Dak to fight making him an instant celebrity in Washington circles.

Hack was chosen to be part of a Distinguished Speakers team and later selected by the Department of Defense as a representative to a presidential briefing team whose job it was to sell the war through a lecture tour.

"Our presentation was a slick dog and pony show designed to convince our listeners that America's purpose in

Vietnam was pure, that our effort there would bring peace and democracy to a war-savaged land."

All in all, the tour was tremendously successful. "The only problem for me was the more I did the rounds with it, the more I knew what we were saying was bullshit."

Soon he realized he couldn't stand deceiving the American people.

Hack's view of the war was taking on a schizophrenic quality.

One voice in his head said, maybe we shouldn't be there at all.

Another voice said, but we are there and we're not leaving, so let's get with it.

He was drawn to the second voice, as he was able to do something about it.

The Pentagon library contained stacks of after-action reports covering the French experience in Indochina, 1946-1954. They had documented every operation and the reports had been translated into English, expressing the full range of frustration, failure and lessons learned, which were exactly the same as those that U.S. troops were experiencing in '67-'68.

"Yet a lot of people really must have believed the American four-star general who suggested that since the French hadn't won a war since Napoleon, nothing could be learned from them."

Hack discovered none of these books had ever been checked out. Neither had **Modern Warfare**, the insurgency treatise of one of Hack's renegade mentors, French Colonel Roger Trinquier.

"The fight against the guerrilla must be organized methodically and conducted with unremitting patience and resolution," wrote Trinquier. "Except for the rare exception it will never achieve spectacular results so dear to laurel-seeking military leaders."

As the unread Trinquier work gathered dust in the Pentagon library, the American military was "getting wrapped around the axle with big-unit missions just like the French before us, arrogantly looking for the decisive battle and the attendant glory," Hack wrote.

Hack reconnected with journalist Ward Just, who had been injured while covering the Tigers at Dak To. Just had recently completed his book, **To What End**, a collection of pieces borne of his Vietnam experience.

Just asked Hack to review it, and the manuscript brought home to Hack that not only was the war effort madness, we were also probably fighting on the wrong side.

Hack began to look at the political side of the war; a war that he began to see was much more of America's own making than he'd ever thought before.

It became clear to him that an American victory would not address the fundamental problems that had fueled the conflict all along and sent so much of the population down the Communist road.

Instead, what the goal had to be was the rebuilding of the nation itself, from within, and along democratic principles. Hack saw the fundamental difficulty attendant to this epiphany.

"The people hated us … In cities and villages alike, we moved families from their ancestral homes with the same disregard for their culture and religion as we'd shown the red man in America, and made them prisoners in 'strategic hamlets" about as free as concentration camps. Meanwhile we ruined their crops with our chemicals and their economy with our Yankee dollars, supported a chain of corrupt governments and a corrupt Viet military machine, and won hearts and minds by destroying villages to save them." Short of a miracle occurring, Hack finally concluded the war was irrevocably lost.

By late 1967 Hack wrote the NVA was experiencing great success in the Central Highlands and border areas.

Even though it never developed into a full-scale enemy attack, a month-long siege at a Marine outpost at Con Thien killed or wounded one thousand Marines. They had endured continuous NVA artillery shelling on their position until American B-52s rained 22,000 tons of bombs, persuading the Communists to slip away.

Gen. Westmoreland pronounced Con Thien "a crushing defeat" for the NVA. But as with most things he said about the war, Westy was wrong, Hack concluded.

A little more than a month later, the NVA had lured U.S. forces into the most rugged terrain in Vietnam using one of the oldest tricks in the guerilla handbook – a NVA "defector" – again choosing the time and place in which a decisive engagement would be fought.

The enemy had achieved a tenable tactical situation terrain battlefield, preparation and relative troop strength and so initiated action. American planes conducted 2,096 air strikes to achieve an alleged 1,644 enemy KIA while also expending 151,000 rounds of artillery – 92 rounds per enemy dead.

On top of that, we lost 344 U.S. troops; another 1,441 were wounded in action (WIA.)

Back in Washington, where Secretary of Defense Robert McNamara was beginning to project disillusionment with the war, Gen. Westmoreland told the National Press Club, "I am absolutely certain that whereas in 1965 the enemy was winning today he is certainly losing."

He proclaimed we were winning the battle of attrition that enemy losses were beyond his input capability.

Coming events would prove him wrong, although as Hack wrote "it would not be for nearly a score of years that the country would know that the enemy-strength figures had actually been manipulated to back up Westy's claims."

By early 1968, NVA troops numbering in excess of 40,000 surrounded Khe Sanh, an isolated Marine base supplied strictly by air and located near the Laos border.

In anticipation of an imminent attack, Westmoreland expanded Marine troop strength to 6,000. The attack never came.

The Marines did sit on the receiving end of two months of non-stop air assaults leading to 500 KIA, as our B-52s dispensed some 75,000 tons of bombs on the enemy.

Less than two weeks after the siege of Khe Sanh began, 75,000 Communist troops launched a surprise attack on more than 100 cities, towns and bases through South Vietnam almost simultaneously, under the cover of the Tet celebrations, as Hack and Slam had discussed one year before.

In spite of his understanding of the likelihood of such an event, even Hack was surprised by the size, violence and initial success it achieved.

"The Tet Offensive of 1968 gave the lie to almost everything stated publicly by General Westmoreland and his staff, such as the VC were on their knees, both in strength and morale, and would never be able to mount a sustained attack, or that 'pacification' was working; almost every city considered to be a secure area in South Vietnam was attacked during Tet of '68."

Less than a week into the fighting, it was reported the enemy had 14,997 KIA, what Hack called "an absurdly precise figure." A week after that, it had been rounded off to 31,000 enemy KIA. (American KIA were 920, with 4,560 WIA.)

Civilian casualties were enormous particularly after our forces geared up our war machine in counter-attack.

Hack wrote that the Americans did achieve a tactical victory in the Tet Offensive. It turned out, the people of South Vietnam were not ready to rally around the revolution.

"But while our firepower proved decisive on the ground and on the day, the strategic and psychological victory the Communist achieved during Tet – among the South Vietnamese people, the American public and the American fighting men – was incalculable."

The siege at Khe Sanh was ongoing throughout the Tet Offensive and the siege remained a point of obsession for both Westy and his commander, LBJ who believed the Tet Offensive was simply a feint to draw American troops away from the siege.

Hack monitored events from within the Pentagon and became incensed when he learned the Joint Chiefs of Staff were considering using nuclear weapons at Khe Sanh.

Hack knew our conventional air power would be sufficient to prevent the fall of the Marine base.

He wrote, "The recommendation to use the Bomb as a way to get us out of the terrible, stupid and totally avoidable trap we'd gotten ourselves into because few people had read the French report on Dien Bien Phu pissed me off so much that without thinking, I blurted out, "I'd take my son to Canada before I'd let him fight in this goddamn war!'"

Nuclear weapons were not used in Khe Sanh. Rat-ridden and shell-shattered, the base was subsequently abandoned by the Marines with no enemy response at all.

It was, as Hack said, the end for LBJ and Westmoreland, even though Westy did become Army Chief of Staff. He left behind in Vietnam 533,000 U.S. troops. Almost 25,000 American lives were lost during his four years as commander.

Hack was one of 16 officers asked to express their views in writing on problems facing the Army, then and in the immediate future. He let go with both barrels.

"The U.S. Army has badly botched the war. I have concluded, after exhaustive study, that we have lost. Here are the main tenets of my study.

We have not required the government of South Vietnam to establish reforms. It remains a corrupt, inefficient, graft-ridden collection of divided opportunists who have little interest in the people of their country.

"As a result of these factors, the people have no interest in their government and are either actively supporting the VC or completely indifferent to their programs. Without the active assistance of the people, an insurgent force cannot be defeated."

He noted various shortfalls.

"Failure to develop overall objectives and a plan of strategy to support these aims, which would bring the war to a successful conclusion.

"Failure to develop small unit tactics, which would support an overall campaign plan.

"Failure of our Army to understand the nature of guerilla warfare ... we don't have the initiative and are strictly on the defense – the enemy plays the tune and we dance ...

"We have sent a large force which is top-heavy with supporters and thin on fighters... The VC hide when confronted with a large force and fight only on their terms when victory either tactically or psychologically, can be assured."

Hackworth went on to say the tactical know-how of our commanders in the field was deplorable, that corporate manager-types dominated the ranks of officers that knew little about the "nuts and bolts" of their profession.

"Men who know how to win in battle do not get ahead in the military system that does not lend itself to fresh ideas, is intolerant to boat-rockers, too willing to suppress their feelings in order to accommodate the views of their superiors."

He received no feedback to his contribution to the study. Still on stateside Hack found the military-industrial complex "alive and kicking, growing stronger by the day." Industry dictated strategy to the military. In 1959, studies identified 721 retired military officers working in the top 88 defense industries; ten years later that number had grown to 2,072 officers of the rank of colonel or Navy captain and above were working for the 95 top military contractors.

Hack began saying ""no" to requests to return to Vietnam in various capacities. He even thought about resigning altogether.

"I was fed up with the system and the war but I still loved the Army. And besides, I didn't know what the hell I'd do in civilian life."

Next he accepted an opportunity to command a training battalion at Fort Lewis in Washington.

At about the same time, he mourned the deaths of soldiers he'd served with, the pain of loss cutting deep. After one such incident he lamented "senseless death in a senseless war."

It became clear to Hack that standards were lacking at the Army Training Center that he had visited early in his role as Chief of Individual Training and with the Schools Branch.

Among other things, he noticed few people outside the Training Committee were checking on the quality of training.

To gain insight into the experiences of conscripts at the base, he decided to don the fatigues of a recruit himself and infiltrate classes. With the blessing of his superior officer, he arranged to slip in and out of classes. "Despite the fact that I was about a million years older than they were, none of the trainees questioned this. As impossible as it seemed, I didn't get caught throughout the entire masquerade."

He referred to the training he received incognito as "criminal." He found that virtually everything these trainees got was wrong in terms of its applicability to the fight in Vietnam.

Other essential considerations were ignored. With mines and booby traps responsible for probably 50 percent of all U.S. casualties in Vietnam, he was struck that training in that area was miniscule. He wrote to one commanding officer, "Almost every U.S. full colonel in Vietnam has an air-conditioned trailer, but we don't have a training aid that could save legs and lives?"

Virtually no time was expended trying to explain to young soldiers the rational for our military intervention.

"Our recruits were getting little from their training to change their angry minds about the Army, the government."

Contributing to the problem, the average instructor had an even worse attitude than the trainees. They were "short-timers fresh out of Vietnam who hadn't wanted to go in the first place and had chips on their shoulders the size of a Soviet RPG-7 rocket launcher."

Hack realized that whatever quick fix or serious and lasting alteration to training he and his colleagues could affect would "never make a dent in what could only be considered a profound lack of concern for the basic requirements and welfare of the fighting man at the highest levels of the Army."

Fort Lewis, with its snowy winter weather, was an illogical place to prepare soldiers for fighting in jungles compared to Panama, Hawaii or the Philippines.

But it remained viable as, like all Army real estate, it provided jobs and income for the civilian constituents of senators and congressmen who were invariably running for reelection. Army camps were big business' politicians demanded they be kept open in exchange for their nod on continued military appropriations.

"The pussyfooting new breed of statesmen-generals didn't have the balls, the moral courage, to stand up and say that some things were more urgent, that it was insane to train jungle fighters in the snow. Instead, it was somehow more acceptable to allow badly prepared Willie Lump Lumps to die all over the battlefield, and go on answering the letters from brokenhearted parents asking 'Why?" that cascaded down on the desks through the offices of the very politicians whose ambitions partially held the answers."

Hackworth wrote he later realized those parents deserved more, much more, in reply than a few pat, randomly chosen paragraphs strung together on a page, or that the real explanation was that, other than criminal negligence, there was no explanation at all.

"And meanwhile, the training system just kept chugging along – impersonal, inept and yet terribly efficient – every nine weeks churning out young men with one of three frontline infantryman's MOSs (11B, C or D) stamped on their foreheads, and then channeling these kids into a sinister machine, the death disposal of Vietnam, which churned out body bags and little white crosses with equal facility."

Hack beheld the amoral essence of what was known as Project 100,000, a program that sought to conscript that number of young men who had failed, or would fail if put to the test, the armed services' physical or mental requirements.

Standards were lowered to next to nothing. Volunteers were seduced by recruiters' promises of training in skills to help them get along in the world outside the slums or backwaters, only to find themselves stumbling ill prepared through the jungles of Vietnam.

Ward Just wrote in **Military Men**, "These men proceed through the Army as they proceed through life, walking wounded in the center of a monstrous joke, forced to struggle with basic training as they are forced to struggle with everything else."

At Fort Lewis, Hack did his best to ensure those going to Vietnam got the best training he could help effect. At the same time, he did what he could to help those who didn't want to go stay out.

If a soldier said he was a conscientious objector (CO), Hack tried to help them get their stories straight. "I agree with you it's a bad war but that doesn't qualify you to be a C.O.," he'd say. "What religion are you?"

If they didn't have a religion, he advised them to get one. Hack found himself struck with the realization that had this occurred 10 years previously; he would have dealt with them with extreme prejudice. "Cowards every damn one of them," he heard himself thinking. "But it was a different world now, and a different war, a war that just months earlier I'd sworn I'd take my son to Canada before I'd let him fight in, a war without a villain – nationalists fighting for a better deal were not exactly Hitler or Tojo."

If a guy didn't want to fight, Hack knew there were plenty of others who did, young men who were programmed by fathers or family histories to think they wanted to, to prove their manhood or a point of honor and hang the cause.

Hack soon received orders to go back to Vietnam, again as a battalion commander. He was surprised how easily he accepted, "particularly given the intensity of the inner struggle that had been going on since my tour with Slam, which had me always wanting to go back to the gray even as all I wanted to do was quit and disappear before the anger of the senseless war blew up inside me…. Though I knew the war was a totally senseless exercise, I took it."

He wrote to Ward Just, "A 'pro' doesn't sit on the bench simply because he has played out his quota of time. He wants to get in there, mix it up and contribute towards moving the ball toward his goal line."

Bottom line, he felt our units in Vietnam should have the finest leaders possible.

In January 1969, Hack found the 4th Battalion, 39th Infantry to be in total disintegration, its morale "lower than whale shit."

He also noted what a mistake it was to listen to the generals from corporate HQ, who were briefed only in zero defect terms, and, so far from the cutting edge, expected nothing else. "It is among the biggest mistakes of the war; the politicians only listened to these generals and these generals to themselves. Few people asked the frontline soldiers, the only one who really knew.

"I suddenly realized it wouldn't be easy, this Delta war. It wasn't easy to tell the good guys from the bad guys anywhere in South Vietnam, but here in the Delta it was damn near impossible.

"I had to hand it to the Viet Cong. They were like little ants struggling with a crust of bread. They never gave up, and nothing wore them out."

One night he walked the berm around his base talking to the troops on guard duty in order to get to know his men, and get an up-to-date measure of overall proficiency, discipline and spirit of the battalion. One of the sniper sergeants stopped him and asked, "Why do you look so sad, sir? Have we had a low body count today?" Hack played along with him. "Yeah, six dichs. That's it, all day."

"Well, how about if I get you three more, sir?" he asked, and leaning against the sandbagged top of the berm, he aimed his powerful sniper rifle at three ARVN soldiers guarding a bridge about four hundred meters away. "That'll make it nine."

Hack knocked the barrel of the rifle up in the air. "Hold it, man," he said. "They're South Vietnamese."

"A gook's a gook," the sergeant replied, shrugging.

A gook's a gook, he said. Otherwise known in the 9th Division as the *mere gook rule*.

Hack knew why the solider felt as he did. He was not alone in his feelings. Most of the men hated the ARVN because day after day these Viet troops went out and never found the Viet Cong.

"Yet if we followed in their tracks, we had to fight it out every step of the way." They realized the ARVN units had reached a "you don't shoot us, we won't shoot you" accommodation with the enemy. If they saw a contact brewing, they just walked around it.

"My guys saw this, and when they saw the Medivac ships carrying away their buddies who'd been wounded or killed while ARNV sat back and let us fight their war, it bred tremendous resentment. The kind of resentment that made 'a gook a gook.'"

When a civilian bus was blown up by a VC mine, one ARVN soldier, instead of helping the docs patch up his countrymen, stole the bandages and MPs had to fire shots in the air to keep the unhurt civilians from robbing the wounded.

Hack allowed no Viet inside his quarters, regardless of rank. "I didn't trust a single one of them not to be a potential VC spy or collaborator."

Prisoners he interrogated routinely refused to divulge information even when threatened with death.

"Then I will be dead," one of them told him. "I expect to die anyway, fighting for my cause, the freedom of my country Vietnam."

Hack pleaded with him to cooperate.

"No, I believe in my cause," he said, and began pointing to his mangled leg and his many other raggedly healed wounds.

"I believe in it through all of these. I will never surrender. I will fight until I'm dead. If they ask me to defect, I will spit in their faces."

Hack realized that right, wrong, wise or simply gullible, they would prevail. "Unless we could duplicate their will and dedication, all the cannons, all the helicopters, all the high technology we could invent and employ, enough even to send men to the moon, would never beat them."

Hackworth found himself at Pleiku where he concluded the South Vietnamese at corps level did not particularly care about *Vietnamizing* the war, much less about our advice to that end.

"The main reason for this, as far as I could guess, was that they really didn't think the Americans were going to leave. Over the past four years the U.S. had fought the big unit war for the Vietnamese, and allowed them to sit back in a passive/defensive role (guarding towns, defending fire-support bases ... securing the people under the guise of pacification.)

"While we established bases, the Viets were allowed to grow fat and complacent and turn the war into a business venture. They helped the enemy recruit by acting out the role of occupiers – raping women, stealing livestock and rice – rather than protecting the people."

In battle, the South Vietnamese troops had low morale and little will to win. They were improperly trained, unmotivated and lacked commitment to success. At Ben Het when an outpost came under siege, they found themselves to be city boys in the Highlands facing the worst of all hardship duties.

"Their junior officers felt the same way." They stumbled through the deep bush into ambushes, always reacting to the enemy's moves, suffering heavy losses and 20-30 percent desertion rates. In the face of any tough opposition, they bugged out leaving U.S. air and artillery engineers supporting them to fend for them selves on the battlefield.

"This desertion under fire created an explosive situation between U.S. and ARVN units because of the high U.S. casualties that resulted," Hack wrote.

A battle at Ben Het was proclaimed a great victory for our side and proof that *Vietnamization* was working. ARVN forces did not prevail. Instead it was U.S. air power: tac air and B-52s, tons of bombs and napalm clobbering down and inflicting an estimated 3,000 enemy battle casualties that carried the day. At subsequent battles, the ARVN leadership showed no offensive spirit and only U.S. firepower proved decisive.

"It seemed almost incredible that at this critical time in the war the truth of ARVN's inadequacies was not being acknowledged, much less addressed," Hack wrote. "Despite the billions of dollars spent and the number of American lives lost on the Viet's behalf, it was as if nothing had changed since the early sixties when the silencing of … bearers of bad tidings … had sent a clear message to those who also recognized the truth but valued their careers more." Criticism of our ally was forbidden. Wave making and boat rocking were distinctly frowned upon, especially in the advisory effort.

Diplomacy was the key, a "be-polite-we're-guests-and-remember-it's-their-war" philosophy, which after 1966 "was patently untrue, but which, once adopted (and in the years since), had allowed South Vietnam to hustle the United States as adeptly as the smoothest carnival barker." Hack said it was a fundamental flaw in U.S. policy. While we paid the bills "and kept our toys and boys coming," we had little real control, and never would, a fact they knew better than we did, and a reason why they probably thought we'd never really pull out and go home.

Our always polite and diplomatic advisory effort never established procedures to prevent the South Vietnamese from buying and selling Army commissions, promotions or U.S. service-school assignments, or taking bribes and demanding payoffs, or stealing their troop's meal allowances or from being promoted to better jobs mere weeks after being found guilty of corruption.

"This was really just a matter of our arrogance," Hack wrote. "We assumed we understood the Viet mind and therefore didn't try to: the Viets, meanwhile, watched us carefully until they found out where we lived, and then they went right for it."

Hackworth found it inexplicable that existing policy made American advisors one to three grades lower in rank than their Vietnamese counterparts.

Letter to Ward Just: "Regarding ARVN ... I am convinced that they will never make it. The individual soldier has the potential to be great. But to be great he needs leadership and that is the rub. They Vietnamese just don't produce leaders. It is something in their sociological makeup. They acquire minimum creature comforts. To have these goodies they must wheel and wheel they do. Virtually everyone has a gimmick going for him ... designed to produce loot. Now producing loot leaves little time for fighting in a war. And after a fellow has his fair share of goodies who really wants to fight? I just do not think that the Viets can produce the type of leadership that is required.

"The fuckers are too corrupt, too lazy, too stratified (class wise), too indifferent, and too blasé to care. So we can continue to pour in the dollars and our nation's blood. But it will all go into a bottomless pit that will eat and eat and eat and then finally collapse."

Hack developed a keen eye. "You could always tell when a Viet had quit being a soldier and become a businessman by the fingernail on the little finger of his left hand, which he'd grow very long, and by the hair he'd start growing on his face, wispy strands that could hardly be called a beard but which said it all about where the guy was coming from."

At the end of April 1970 Hack learned that ARVN forces would enter Cambodia with the mission of finding and destroying Hanoi's Central Office for South Vietnam (COSVN.)

He thought it was unlikely that their Airborne or anyone else would be invading Cambodia without a declaration of war. Doing so would mean violating the sovereignty of a neutral nation, something he was sure America would never do. Soon he learned the operation was a go.

"The Cambodian exercise was the straw that broke the camel's back for me about the war in Vietnam and the direction America was heading," Hack wrote.

He felt it came five years too late during which time we lost the lion's share of our stud officers and the American people lost their stomach for the conflict. Also the way it was done violated the principles of the United States of America, the country Hack loved and soldiered for was built on.

He believed our incursion with no notice to its government from our ambassador to Cambodia, was not in his mind any different from the Japanese bombing of Pearl Harbor. In his estimation the exercise was an immoral, ill-thought-out venture, one that would prove to be both an expensive tactical donnybrook and an irreparable strategic defeat.

The assault began. There was token resistance as the enemy had abandoned the area the night before by vehicle, bicycle, or foot and headed west.

"The mission had been compromised, but it was little wonder; though most of the task force elements had had less than twenty-four hours of notice of the plan, the South

Vietnamese command structure was so heavily infiltrated with VC that news of the impending attack may as well have been broadcast over psyops loudspeakers."

There was little accountability …already stories were emerging that the Viet participants used their positions as license to indiscriminately steal, torture, and murder …

"The invasion into Cambodia had shown our Nazi side, there was no question about that. If we were Nazis, we were monsters, and who the hell wasn't a monster in this war? We were American democratic monsters fighting Communist monsters that didn't give a damn about the people in the first place.

"Cambodia broke my spirit, though I'm not sure I knew it at the time. "Unconsciously, I believe I made my decision to quit the U.S. Army then and there, and to leave America, because I couldn't cope with us becoming Nazis or killing students on college campuses simply because they wanted the country out of a bad war.

"The Cambodian exercise was a disaster. Five years too late in coming, with no ally support, with no destruction of large enemy formations, no victory of any description, just the galvanizing of people all over the world against our presence there."

Generals knew the NVA was using Cambodia as a sanctuary as early as 1966 and also knew that NRVN "was a spent force that would never win, and that it was not possible for us to do it for them given the political restraints. So what followed instead was deception built on deception, a lot of money, a lot of death, and to what end?"

In June Hack left the Airborne Division to take the job as senior advisor to the 44th Special Tactical Zone (STZ.) He encountered Colonel Hanh, his South Vietnamese counterpart and commander of the STZ.

Hack found Hanh "extremely fat, with an arrogant manner and no concern at all about the people he hurt or the hatred that burned in their eyes."

Back in the Delta for the first time in a year, Hack noticed tourists (visitors from Washington) were once again crowing "we've got them on the ropes" as they took the enemy's lack of aggressiveness as a sure sign of defeat. "Anyone who'd been in Vietnam for any decent length of time, however, or had any understanding at all of the nature of the war, knew that that was too simple of an analysis. The VC were not on the ropes. They'd just shifted down to a lower gear."

In Hahn Hack found "a corrupt, lazy bum, an unabashed warlord who got a percentage from every activity that went on in the Zone."

A Vietnamese in the general area could not open any business at all without Hanh's approval. Meanwhile, back at the war, under Hanh every major operation we had was compromised; the VC found out what we were doing faster than our subordinate units did. "I felt sure they were getting copies of our operations orders."

In 1970-71, Hack could see calculated deception going on, only now it was beginning at the highest headquarters, in the Oval Office.

Like Johnson before him, Nixon said he was not going to be the first President to lose a war; since he couldn't win it, he and Kissinger had created *Vietnamization,* so they could "honorably" walk away and in the meantime keep the restive American people at bay.

"This was a perfect situation for the war managers who had done Lyndon Johnson such a terrible disservice with the sanitized, zero-defect reports that had kept him in the dark as he wrestled with how to prosecute the war and had ultimately cost him the presidency.

"It was as if the system had come full circle: these same reports, which had been in large part responsible for escalating the war, were now eagerly sought after by the Nixon Administration as the ultimate smoke screen for their abandonment of the effort."

In the Zone, Major General John Cushman was Hack's closest superior. He struck Hack as being in the Westmoreland model – hard charging and ambitious, super straight and without one street-wise bone in his body, a cheerleader for the war effort.

And since he didn't understand the South Vietnamese or sense their total exhaustion with the war or their endemic corruption, through it all he was able to maintain his super optimistic views.

There was a price of admission to the American way that could justify self-sacrifice in war.

"But now I could see, through the Vietnam debacle, that while there was a price to be paid, it was only correct to pay it if the product – democracy – was sound. And it was not sound in the corrupt ranks of South Vietnam's government and military, nor had it ever been, nor would it ever be, regardless of how many of America's sons threw their lives into the pot. As a nation, we had to get out of there."

In January of 1971, an ABC journalist, Howard Tuckner, came to see Hack in the Zone. He'd read Ward Just's **Military Men**, and heard Hack was "The Colonel" mentioned in the book, a colonel with an unusual yet endearing need to speak his mind, his keen seasoned mind.

Hack knew that going on national television to tell the American people how badly we'd botched the war did not seem like a particularly smart thing to do.

Events on the ground began to wear him down. "We'd bullshitted ourselves, and the American people, long enough."

He was deeply influenced by the events at My Lai in which American soldiers massacred women and children. "Despite the determined effort of its commander Calley's battalion, brigade and division commanders to cover it up from the Army, and the Army's determined effort to cover it up from the press, what the facts revealed made the crime only too believable."

The events at My Lai reflected the horrific inadequacies in the training system and of senior leadership. My Lai became emblematic of a tragic bankruptcy of moral fiber in the Army's senior officer corps, a direct result of rampant careerism.

"But then, when the Army actually had the balls to stand in the door and convict Lt. William Calley for murder, to have Richard Nixon come along and for purely political ends interfere with military justice and essentially nullify the result was too much for me."

Seeing an officer he felt was inadequate on a short list to be eventual Chief of Staff concerned him. He felt that the Army had been lying to itself for so long about so much that it had totally lost perspective of reality. So he agreed to be interviewed on ABC-TV's "Issues and Answers."

"I truly believed that by going outside channels directly to the American people, I could make these guys think, and bring about change."

Hackworth appeared on "Issues and Answers" on a June Sunday morning in 1971. Tuckner began the interview citing Hack's lengthy resume before asking him to rate the quality of training of troops coming to Vietnam.

Hack said it had been totally inadequate. He referred to errors his men made as criminal.

"Great mistakes were made because of improper training, being not prepared for the war even though we had from 1953 to 1956 to prepare for the war." He cited the number of dead that they have killed among themselves, men that were shot by their comrades, and artillery that had fallen on them. He said poor training caused our casualties to rise at least 30 percent.

Asked if our generals did not really adjust to the tactics of this war, Hack said the average general that came to Vietnam did not have a good concept or appreciation of the nature of guerrilla warfare.

"In most cases because of their lack of even reading in depth about guerrilla warfare, they were not prepared for the war and they had to fall back on Korea and WW II and they used the thought process and the techniques that worked successfully there, moving in large formations, making battalion and brigade airmobile assaults on a small LZ and having everything tidy, artillery in position and fighting much as we did on the plains of Europe." Most commanders, he summarized, did not understand the name of the game.

Upper military management never learned from their mistakes nor developed a strategic realistic plan because he said they were too involved in systems analysis, in the normal bureaucracy of it all moving so much paper across their desks they could not see the forest for the trees. Conventional thinking led to horrible mistakes. In the Army he found "shallow dilettantes who run from pillar to post trying to punch their card and serving minimal time at company level." Too close to the heat of the furnace there, meaning you could get in trouble easily.

Most younger officers agreed with his views, he said, although most also were inclined to keep their opinions about the war to themselves because speaking out could be the end of their careers.

Asked if their silence meant that some who died could have been saved, Hack replied, "That is right, and that is why perhaps we who have not been vocal should be charged for just criminal neglect, because it is our obligation, it is our responsibility, not only to train our soldiers well, to lead our soldiers well …"

Tuckner pointed out that because he was considered one of the best infantry officers in the Army, Hackworth had been asked a number of times to go to the War College, which is preparation for becoming general one day. Hack said he had declined offers three times because, as an active participant on the battlefield, he didn't need to go to school to learn anything.

He said the constant need for body counts disrupted commanders in battle, causing them to lose momentum and, worse yet, weakening the moral fiber of the officer corps "because it has taught them to lie, to exaggerate because, again, it is a form of success."

Body counts beget hyper inflated numbers, irregularities of mammoth proportion and falsehood up the ying-yang; Visiting dignitaries were treated to razzle-dazzle briefings in which everything was said to be rosy.

"We are really nailing them and that is why we are winning this war. Just give us a few more troops, a few more resources and we will have them on the run. There's light at the end of the tunnel." Hack added, they didn't say the VC was holding the candle but he said the end was in sight.

Tuckner brought up Hack's report to Westmoreland in 1968 in which he asserted we had badly botched the war in Vietnam and from a tactical standpoint, lost it.

Three years later, he told the interviewer, his experiences only confirmed those comments. During that time, he had seen no changes, no viable reform.

"I felt that the corruption that exists in Vietnam, the graft, the failure to produce continues to exist. The Army we sent to Vietnam was not trained for the war, as it was top-heavy in administrators and logisticians and bloody thin on fighters."

Hack identified the nature of the beast in the military – to sanitize a report to look good. Situations were distorted.

"I think it is highly probable that all of these beautiful briefings and excellent reports were so production-line *Hollywood'zed* that by the time they got to the President and they got to the people who were making decisions, they didn't have the real facts; they didn't understand what was happening."

Hack said we failed to insist South Vietnam marshal well-trained soldiers, highly motivated similar to their Viet Cong enemies who were fighting for an ideal, something similar to Christianity, a cause, a crusade, not fighting to get a new Honda or a new watch or a portable radio or to have a nice home, but fighting for a cause.

"This has not been inculcated in the whole army of Vietnam."

Hack admitted he had become emotionally involved in Vietnam.

"One couldn't see the number of young studs die or be terribly wounded without becoming emotionally involved.

I just have seen the American nation spend so much of its wonderful, great young men in this country. I have seen our national wealth being drained away. I see the nation being split apart and almost being split asunder because of this war, and I am wondering to what end it is all going to lead to."

Within a week of the airing of the interview, Hack put in for retirement upon completion of his Zone tour. Even though his opinions had been previously published, he knew there was no way the Army would let him get away with his most public airing.

He was both relieved and devastated … by among other things the stark recognition that an orphaned kid from Santa Monica would make general.

And Meadows was the last …

In one of his final battles in the Delta, Hack lost one of his best men, a sergeant named Meadows, who died from his wounds.

"Regardless of the number of men I'd had die under my command – and Meadows was the last – it still got to me. And the pain was only eclipsed by the anger I felt, not just at Meadows' death but also at every American death. I knew that this war was not our own, that it had nothing to do with the security of America, and in which our sacrifices were totally unappreciated…"

An article Ward Just wrote for *The Washington Post* reported that between January and April 1971 54 Viet bases and outposts had been overrun – double the figure from the previous year.

Hack attributed the problem to bad leadership then realized what was really happening – the Viets were reverting back to the way things had been before the Americans came in 1965. "If we hadn't come then, South Vietnamese forces would have collapsed. Now, as our units were pulling out, that fate was about to greet our allies."

Hack wrote they were ready for the inevitable. Their faces were tired; spirits were heavy with the futility of it all.

Go Home, Colonel

"Just days before I was to leave the Zone for good, I visited a hamlet that had been clobbered the night before. The village chief and I sat down together to discuss what had happened, but the chief had something more on his mind. 'Many years ago, I lost all my sons,' he began. 'That was when the French fought here. Last night I lost my only grandson. I am the only man of my family who is still alive. Go home, *Dai Ta* (Colonel.) At least then we will live.'"

Hack recalled an associate who had predicted that when the Americans leave, there will be a coalition among the Vietnamese at the grass-roots level. "There won't be any idealism, there won't be any democracy," he had said. "But the people will have full bellies. The one thing both sides have going for them is they're both Vietnamese."

General Cushman gave Hack a max efficiency report. He said Hack's decision to retire "is a unfortunate loss to the Army. Col Hackworth is a brilliant officer, of impressive reputation as a combat unit commander, extraordinarily innovative, and with exceptional insight into the nature of insurgency. He is a natural leader of soldiers. He attracts outstanding people, especially those of his own "tiger" type. He is tremendously able in a troop situation. He is an excellent organizer, writes very well, and is very widely read in his profession. He has a magnetic, driving personality."

Hackworth ended up granting other interviews, believing they would not be published until after he was out of

Vietnam. He went on leave before returning to the country and found himself on the shit list of every upper echelon superior in the region or world.

"They were digging, looking for something wrong, something irregular, so they could throw the book at me, keep me in Vietnam, hold up my retirement, even court-martial me."

In intense interviews with military personnel, he was asked to give specifics for each of his allegations, including those concerning the body-count system encouraging false reporting, and the fact that the Vietnamese had been lousy in 1965 and there'd been little improvement since. (Fifteen years later these and other of my "allegations" would be accepted as among the basic facts of the Vietnam War, but this was no help at the time.)

"I knew I had to get the hell out of Vietnam."

He did, returning to Fort Lewis to sign out of the Army. Nick Proffitt a *Newsweek* correspondent was granted an interview with General Abrams, who wanted to talk about Hack. Abrams expressed interest in Hack's mood during his interview with Proffitt. After hearing what the reporter knew, the General said in a sad voice: "Colonel Hackworth is the best battalion commander I ever saw in the United States Army. We cannot afford to lose men of his caliber. If it continues, the damage to the Army will be irreparable."

In April of 1975 Hack watched with no satisfaction from his exile in Australia as his prediction of four years before came through, when the North Vietnamese flag was hosted to fly triumphantly over Saigon.

Hack was "filled with alarm" in 1981, the first year of the Reagan Administration, as the new President found himself enveloped by advisors who expressed belief in the concept of nuclear war between the U.S. and the Soviet Union being not only imaginable but "inevitable," who believed nuclear war would be a terrible mess but not unmanageable... "Like an amputation: traumatic, but not necessarily fatal."

Hack found himself stunned. "These men, most of them academics who had never been on a battlefield (and many of whom, it would later be discovered, had actively avoided service in Vietnam), who wouldn't have had the slightest idea about death, dying, destruction, and the wholesale suffering attendant on even conventional war, were talking about, conceivably, the end of life on earth as we know it, as if it were a back-lot baseball game."

To Hack, it seemed like Vietnam all over again, only the stakes were "infinitely higher and the key players understood the game even less."

From afar he sensed Reagan was merely trying to whip up fear and anti-Soviet hysteria to scare the American people into permitting a trillion-and-a-half-dollar expenditure to ensure "peace through strength."

Eventually he began to write *About Face*. It became a *New York Times* best-selling book that has largely informed *And Meadows Was the Last*. He said he tried to portray what he saw happening to the U.S. Army with his own eyes as it engaged in two un-winnable wars, themselves fought under the omnipresent umbrella of *the* un-winnable war – the Cold War.

He perceived both sides as being exhausted and broke from the standoff with neither side believing itself to be exempt from examining its past performances. "While the need for such scrutiny should be self-evident, historically the U.S. military as quickly and efficiently as possible sweeps under the rug the reality of its less sterling accomplishments, and there is little evidence to suggest there will be any change now."

Looking back on Korea, Hack observed, "The absence of a glorious victory was tantamount to defeat" – unthinkable in the wake of WW II. In the American psyche, the first seeds of self-doubt took root. America found itself unprepared. Remarkable failures in training, logistics, support and leadership undermined our effectiveness. The senior brass was so humiliated by their overall ineptitude … that the minute the war was over they hid the truth away, even from themselves. They learned nothing from the Korean experience, only to carry the same non-lessons into the next war to blow it all over again."

When the Vietnam War was over "the first instinct of the generals who managed it was to file it, like Korea, under O for Oblivion." Hack wrote, "Instead, over the last few years it has become clear that another tack has been taken. Now, the war managers are working overtime to *rewrite* the truth of what happened in that war." He suggested the Army was determined to conduct "a Psyops campaign, "an unwritten but vigorously maintained policy intended to enforce the belief that American arms accomplished their mission in Vietnam.

Hack wrote, "The catch cry of those rewriting American history in Vietnam is 'We won all the battles but we lost the war.' But as many of the 'war stories' in this book have proved, this is just not true – unless an entirely inappropriate, WW II measure for success is used.

"Of course our opponent in Vietnam could never have won the WW II-style pitched battles our forces employed. But what is not being addressed on the rewritten scorecard is that, with few exceptions, they didn't try."

Hack watched as the new chief executive spewed unwashed revisionism of the war he had so intimately helped orchestrate. "From the time, early in his presidency, that Ronald Reagan called Vietnam 'a noble war,' the whitewash has flowed fast from Army brushes to cover the more ignoble truth. This is a dangerous, dangerous trend, because it can only doom the Army, and the country, to repeat the mistakes of Vietnam down to the last death on the next battlefield…"

In subsequent military fiascos like our Iran and Grenada operations and very much like in Vietnam, little was learned from any of them because of what Hack called a zero-defect mentality that refuses to accept that errors can be (and were) made.

Hack discussed the notion of fighting Communism wherever the red flag waves around the world, calling it "an extremely vague objective, which can do nothing but leave our armed services floundering."

He quoted George Kennan, one of the authors of America's containment policy (which started the whole thing off) who had reappraised his position: "The lessons of Vietnam are few and plain: not to be hypnotized by the word communism, and not to mess in other people's civil wars where there is no substantial strategic interest at stake."

Hack concluded in the Epilogue to his story that the United States needed to look deeply into itself, to see what we have become.

"It seems to me that the values that would make someone a patriot – the values that compelled me to join the Army, and to believe that I had a vital role to play in the preservation of those values – have been bled out of America. The Cold War mantle of the free world's policeman (which, if not really a fact, was at least widely accepted as one for many, many years), though perhaps once a great source of pride to our nation, has proved to be a wellspring of arrogance, not unreasonably making us disliked even among many of our friends around the globe, and perhaps even sowing the seeds that have made greed the major growth industry in our land of opportunity."

He quoted Ernest Hemingway who warned in his introduction to **Men At War** in 1942 – "We must win it (WW II) never forgetting what we are fighting for, in order that while we are fighting fascism we don't slip into the ideals and ideas of fascism."

He observed America "strutting its stuff" on the world stage, spending billions and billions of our citizens' hard-earned money on military hardware "that can never be used" as industries close down in huge numbers, families go homeless, children unfed and we become the biggest debtor nation in the world.

America, he said, needs to choose its battles carefully and make sure its causes are right. It needs to reduce the military machine that breaks the back of the nation's economy and to rebuild our industrial plants.

Forty years earlier, a Captain Eggleston told then-18-year-old David Hackworth that he would make a great contribution to his country.

"I didn't know what he meant. Maybe he didn't either; maybe he just recognized a boy who believed and, a good leader that he was, wanted to give me something to aspire to."

Whatever his reasoning, Hackworth looked back on his career believing that whatever the Captain's reasoning, it worked.

"If I left the Army and America with anger in my heart, it was no doubt in large part because I did feel I'd given both my all, including speaking out when too many others were silent … Maybe that was my contribution. In any event all these years later the anger is gone, and in its place is the belief that I still have a contribution left to make. This book is a beginning."

Hack Post Book

Published in 1989, *About Face* elevated Hack into greater prominence. Not all Vietnam War veterans agreed with his summations, tone, self-aggrandizement and allegedly inflated resume.

Some pointed out he was not the most decorated soldier in the war, he did not receive the highest degrees of recognition and he defied military protocol in numerous ways during his fighting days.

I found it "grounding' in many ways to discover Hack's detractors' less-than-positive assessments on the internet. Their insights enabled me to see the whole person, beyond the highly idealized persona I've envisioned along the way.

As mentioned previously, he did earn eight Purple Hearts, 10 Silver Stars and was twice awarded the Distinguished Service Cross.

Given the controversial nature of the conclusion of his military career he was lucky to get out alive. He had just missed thousands of bullets and bombs, had taken on the machine he served, dared to speak truth to power and in doing so earned the wrath of the entire defense establishment, many assassins included.

Hack's men loved him, even as some of them wanted to shoot his head off at times. As a reader of his classic war book, I found him inspiring, candid about himself, brilliant in a literary sense and imminently thoughtful throughout his career.

Hack was known for his bravery, authenticity, integrity and perpetual smile. Ward Just, his 40-year friend, was struck by his "enthusiasm, magnetism, exuberance and invincible cheerfulness."

He done kicked my keister from Day One. Face to face with the power of his prose, I did indeed suffer a severe Hack Attack.

I do believe I would have been lucky to be his friend in his time. Because he did correspond with me during his days as a regular columnist on the *World Net Daily* website, I felt as if we were paddling in the same kayak down the river of life. I hoped as much of him would rub off on me as possible, grinning frequently at the deeper realization I could hardly manuveur in his shadow.

Not every person of his stature would take time to respond to a message from a reader, not to mention a limp-wristed '60s radical like me. His willingness to reach back out to a strange stranger revealed an aspect of his character I found endearing, enduring as well.

I was making all sorts of new friends on the then-young internet at the time; few engaged me on his level.

Weird as it might sound, I feel his presence all of the time now, much as I sense the proximity of relatives who are deceased but ever-present in my conscious and conscience. Hack gained permanent access to my brain as I wore out my already used paperback version of *About Face*. I bought into his story, regarding it as Gospel. I got to know him better than anyone else I met that year, any year for that matter.

I now keep a picture of Hackworth on the wall behind my computer terminal. In the shot, he is riding in a tractor with a dog at his side, a beautiful blue sky in the background puffy white clouds everywhere in a valley imposed against a major mountain range.

Hack is wearing a large-brimmed farmer's hat, not grinning nor frowning, just driving.

I imagine he is in either Australia or Colorado. I sense he has done his thing, spoken his piece, found happiness beyond the Army, processed Vietnam, discovered the lay of his new land.

Also on the wall are dramatic shots of San Francisco, waves breaking on a Pacific Ocean beach, a picture of a Chili Red Arowana and the cover shot from an old radical Bay Area weekly – *The Guardian* -- depicting a person hoisting a happy Asian child with the headline, "Vietnam Will Win."

After retiring from the Army, Hack became a farmer and later a restaurant owner/operator in Australia, where he was a prominent spokesperson for the Anti-Nuclear movement.

He returned to America upon publication of *About Face* and married Eihlys England, who became his literary and business partner until the time of his death in 2005. Together, they established the Soldiers for Truth Foundation (P.O.Box 54365, Irvine, CA 92619-4365.) From 1990 to 1996, Hack was contributing editor for defense issues for Newsweek magazine. He wrote several books, including **Hazardous Duty**, **Price of Honor** and **Steel My Soldier's Hearts**, in addition to the previously noted, **The Vietnam Primer**.

Hack succumbed to a form of cancer commonly experienced by Vietnam War veterans that were exposed to the defoliants called Agents orange and blue.

Before he died, he produced a number of profound quotes and observations that have been published and circulated, a few of which bear examination in this context.

Most vividly, he saw into the dark threat posed by Islamic religious extremist/fanatics also known as terrorists, whose goal is the same as the Axis fascists – the complete destruction of our way of life.

"Their plan is to return the entire world – not just the Middle East – to the days of the caliphate and either convert all of us so-called infidels into born-again Islamic believers or kill us," he wrote.

He observed "because our homeland and our very survival are once again at stake the American people can't afford to treat this new war like they did Vietnam."

Chapter Four
Letters From Vietnam

(The following section features letters from a soldier in Vietnam to his friend in the U.S. in 1969 and 1970.)

August 1

How is everything back in the world? I sure wish I was there. You know I have been away from home but never this far before and without a chance of making it home for another 344 days. Believe me I'm looking forward to getting home on 10 July '70. The first thing I'm going to do is get some round eye love and the second will be to put my luggage down. As you can tell I've got an address now so drop me a line and tell me about the riots, sex slaying in Ann Arbor and the latest in student protest and anti-war moratorium news. Actually, if it wasn't for the heat, the bad water (chlorine and/or bleach) and the fact that my weekly malaria pills give me the runs, this wouldn't be a bad place. You'd be surprised by what it's like here. I'm in a fairly secure area a couple of minute's walk from the South China Sea. There's not much danger while I'm on the ground at least until Tet (a huge combination of Christmas, New Years Eve, Memorial Day, the 4th of July, Labor Day and every Vietnamese person's birthday all rolled into one celebration). I guess things get pretty hairy at that time of the year. Other than that, the only problems stem from the fact that Charley doesn't like us flying around and tries to knock us out of the sky. Lately, it seems that he's been doing a pretty good job of it. I don't know any of the details because the people are a little hesitant to talk about the birds that don't come back. I plan to fly as much as possible in order to make the year go by fast. As a matter of fact, by the time I receive your reply I to this letter I should have my first Air Medal (100 hours of combat missions).

There are three people from my AIT (Advanced Individual Training) class at Fort Huachuca, Arizona here and everyone else is pretty friendly. I think my stay here will be enjoyable on balance and considering everything. There's an outdoor movie every night right in front of my hooch (a semi-permanent structure surrounded by 55 gallon drums filled with sand and topped by sand bags intended to protect us from incoming ordinance while laying on the cement floor or while in bed), and an Enlisted Men's club a few hundred feet from that. Drinks are real cheap. For $6 a month I have a hooch-maid (Vietnamese woman) who does everything (domestically) that I need done every day except Sunday to include washing and ironing my uniform fatigue, flight suits and civilian clothes everyday, shining jungle and flight boots, making my bed (laying in it too if I wanted, but I don't) and all the other things a servant can do for the great white savior of her homeland. I hope I don't fall victim to the jingoistic, racial hating of the enemy like so many of my fellow soldiers. These are good people who don't want this war and killing any more that we do.

I'll be in touch with you so drop me a line and let me know the latest news from back in the world. See you at Higgins Lake next year with my wife. You may have one by then too you never can tell.

August 23

Received your letter today explaining (in minute detail) your recent love bout. I'm always glad to hear that draft dodgers, malcontents, godless hippies and all around losers are having a good time back in the world. Seriously, I'm glad somebody is getting a little action. As for me the conquest count remains at zero. There's some of it around and of course it must be paid for but as of now I'm not too interested. It's a combination of reasons that causes me to refrain most prominent of which are my engagement to Sheryl and a healthy fear of getting an incurable disease, which means I would spend, the rest of my life on an island off the coast of Japan. Sounds like Army propaganda to me.

Would you like to read about the latest combat actions of yours truly? Once its all over and you're back on terra ferma its easy to write about. Last night (I fly missions almost every night) I detected, by means of a super secret device that I can't talk about, that we were locked on to by enemy radar. It had been three minutes by the time I found out (our super secret stuff is a little slow.) I told the pilot and he proceeded to do turns, rolls, banks and everything else he could think of literally going all over the sky. As soon as he started his maneuvers the tracers began coming up at us and we got the hell out of there ("hatted up" as we say) As soon as we were safe I called it in to local artillery and I'm glad to say that there is one 37mm radar-controlled anti-aircraft gun and crew that are no longer with us. I hope you don't mind me telling you my war stories. I can't tell Sheryl or my family and I have to tell someone. They don't have any idea that anything like this is happening to me. The only way they will find out is through the papers. I'm afraid that some of our recent mortar attacks have hit the press.

September 16

By now you've settled down to your middle-class, pro-establishment job. How do you like talking to clean-cut high school seniors? The open letter you received from me causes great concern at this end. Not so much for the personal inconvenience caused me but for the smell of decaying US Constitution that lingers in my nostrils. Whatever the case may be, I don't think we have anything to worry about. Innocence, even in The Army (I hope) is a defense. You mention a desire to send things to me. I would like to have some of your used books and that's all I want you to send. It's too risky to accept anything else in the mail at this time. You could do me a favor and try to get a fifth of whisky to my sister. She'll be 21 on Oct. 1 and I'd like you to arrange for someone to secretly place a wrapped bottle on my front porch with her name on it from me. Could you handle it? Thanks.

About the used books I mentioned, don't make them too deep or left wing. Remember, I'm just a poor dumb soldier unable to grasp the internal struggles of society. If you've got **Catch 22** that's first on my list. Life goes on as usual with me secure in the belief that I've got the best job in the Army. All I do is get my ass shot at for four hours a night and the other 20 are mine and all mine (usually spent in the beach---Wow!) We've been hit the last couple nights with B-40 rockets and mortars. Here's a note my hooch-maid left on my pillow saying she thinks communism is evil because it curtails the natural competitive impulse in man and that the Godless Viet Cong are the enemy of all Vietnamese and the free world. This is her belief to such an extent that she says she would gladly lay down her life for her world-view. What do you think of the political views of my hawk mind? I'll bet you thought that the

Vietnamese didn't give a damn, didn't you? Well, they don't. Does anyone care that people are dying over here? Is there anyone outside of the dead man's family who even takes notice?

We lost another plane yesterday. The pilot made it out but Technical Observer (my job) rode the plane into a mountain. I was supposed to be on that flight but traded at the last minute. As Elfago Bocca would say, one down and eight more cat lives to go. Heroics abound as I've been recommended for an Air Medal and have more hours in the air than any than any other observer in the company (thanks to the recent rotation back to world of two observers). As a result, my shit no longer stinks around here.

September 22

It's been over two months and the time is really going fast for me. Although it is nowhere nearly fast enough, I'm thankful time here isn't dragging the way basic training did. You're lucky that you won't be drafted and ever have to subject yourself to this bullshit. It's unbelievable the way the lifers continually fuck with you. It's regular chicken shit. We've got a whole company here whose men are subject to be killed and all they think about is haircuts and police calls picking up trash and cigarette butts. I would like to expose the incompetence and ineptitude I've found at all levels but no one would give a shit. The only ones who care have already been through the bullshit and know exactly what it's like. I have met only a few "leaders" of men who could hold a position of responsibility on the outside.

Please tell your colored friend, Mr. Stewart, not to give up his hope for equality and freedom any time soon because if the present trend toward racial equality continues at its current rate maybe his great- great-grandchildren will be looked on as almost equals in this fine free country somewhere near the year 2099. A lot of his fellows are here and they are treated very poorly. Since they don't have the same educational opportunities as white boys, colored boys are drafted in higher relative percentages and find their way over here much more frequently. Seriously, the USA is totally fucked-up on just about everything and no one cares. It's going to be up to you and me to straighten the place up. It's my opinion that the moneyed people are trying to maintain the status quo just like they always have throughout history. With this in mind it's easy to see how our air and water are being ruined with industrial waste. They won't miss the water until the well runs dry or is polluted beyond hope. Unless a person is directly affected by the injustice, he couldn't care less (other than useless impotent lip service). On this point take, for instance, this stupid "war" (I put war in quotation marks because that's what it's supposed to be called but in reality it's nothing of the kind). While on guard duty, you're not allowed to shoot anyone coming through the wire; you have to capture them. One time a month ago when we were hit with mortars a pilot spotted them and by regulation he had to call in and get permission to fire (although he was receiving fire himself.) Permission was denied and he was told to remain overhead and just keep an eye on them (still receiving fire.) He said he wasn't going to stay if he couldn't shoot back and he is now awaiting a court martial. Does this sound like a war?

If this asshole (red neck) from South Carolina gets on the Supreme Court I will probably lose whatever little hope I have for government initiated change. Your life as an educator sounds a little dull but then after being in The Army and living the life as a devil-may-care aviator nothing could excite me. In a way we're like the movies you see about WW I aviators. The juiceheads are constantly drunk and the grass-heads are always wrecked. The less you think about being here the better; everyone escapes in their own way.

There are about 500 people in the company of which there are about 25 pilots and 25 TOs (my job). It's easy to tell these 50 people from the other 450. We are the only one who face any danger. I only hope it doesn't have a lasting effect on me. I hate to be corny and say that living with death can mess up your personality but it's true. I have never been superstitious before but now I have a ritual I go through before every flight to relax me and make me confident that the mission coming up will be just like the last one, i.e. a safe RTB (Return To Base). If I'm hurried and don't have time to put on the whole show I feel very uneasy during the mission.

Oct. 2

Happy 24th Birthday tomorrow!

My how time flies. I just received your letter of the 25th and have now stopped laughing enough to attempt a reply. Your humor arrived at exactly the right time. For the last few days I've been gripped by a terrible sense of helplessness over events lately perpetrated against the lowly enlisted man (trash, scum, etc). After taking the matter into my own hands I have received some satisfaction by making an appointment to go see the Inspector General. It is a big move, which will surely put me on the lifer's shit list, but at least they'll know they can't push me around without some of the shit going back uphill.

I find lately that it is getting very hard to write letters. So hard in fact that I'm going to cut this one short. The reason is that we have a plane that's overdue and people are starting to get worried about it. I'm going out now to look for the plane and any survivors. (24 hours later) Haven't found them yet. They must certainly be dead; but we're going to go up again tomorrow. Every available plane went up (15) with the best pilots and observers aboard (including me.)

October 8

As always, glad to get your letter today. Happy birthday again. How does it feel to be 24? Just think you've got six more years before you can't be trusted anymore according to Abbie Hoffman.

Your sister Kay wrote me a letter telling me she took care of the birthday present for Barb. Please thank her and yourself for putting it all together. Also included were a nice letter and some interesting newspaper clippings. I wrote back and thanked her for both and thank you too. If you'll feel up to it and if I'm not dead and crippled I think we should travel the country in July and August of 1970. I'll have to spend a couple of weeks at home and then we can take a bag and a thumb and move out to some part of the country. I'd like to go west. You're probably wondering what Sheryl will say about this. To make a long story short Sheryl is no longer in the picture. I've decided not to marry her. I guess I'm not really ready and maybe she's not the one. I haven't told her but I have plans to do so soon. I feel kind of bad about it, but it's better to end it now than after we are married and with the possibility of children being involved. I know this was something I should have done in person but under these circumstances with me being here for a year she is much better off knowing now than having to worry about me and put her life on hold until next summer. Let me know what you think because I need some moral support.

I forgot to mention it earlier but I'm going to send you a tape with me singing happy birthday to you. It's a different type of singing (and tape) but I think you'll like it.

You say that I'm sounding like my old self again. I never did make a conscious swing to the right. At Ft. Huachuca I went overboard just to try and counteract other forces that had been working on you. If you'd been drafted you would have gone the C.O. route and when that failed you'd have gone the rest of the way and landed in jail for five years. My personal view is that in most instances the right is wrong. I don't believe in any type of violence or physical coercion. Strange sentiments coming from a guy who is just about to fly a combat mission where people will probably be killed. Change should be initiated through the government. If the activists spent as much time and energy on electing and lobbying legislators and congressmen rather than protesting in the streets, I feel that there would be more results than we are presently reaping. The ruling class of this nation has become a bunch of reactionaries running scared. The changes are eventually going to come but I hope it won't be because of barricades in the street; although judging from the apathy of the American voter that might well be the case. If this comes to pass I'll leave. I won't live in a country run or intimidated by a mob. Enough of this serious talk. If you let it bother you too much you'll be miserable all of the time. The important thing is to do our most for the movement while maintaining a sense of humor and not expecting to make too much of a dent in the establishment.

Who is the Ohio flame you're seeing at homecoming? It wouldn't be your old flame (and mine) Nita? I think I've always loved her but now that I'm free I think I'll openly love her (with your permission.) Seriously, how is she? I sure would like to get a letter from her or any other beautiful girl you might happen to know. On that happy note I think I'll sign off for now as I have a mission. I'm writing now at 7000 ft. en route home after a direct combat support mission over communist infested southeast Asia in defense of democracy and the American way of life— including the military industrial complex.

October 14

Wow. Let me tell you about my weekend. It was a great time and even if I were home I couldn't expect more fun. It all started Saturday night. I had a mission at 1830 but it was cancelled because of weather. There was an American stripper at the club so I broke a long precedence rule and went to the club and drank the devil's brew. She was great (probably because it's been a long time since I've seen a round-eyed woman.) I got real fucked up drunk and came back to the hooch and kept everyone up telling stories of my life. The next morning (Sunday) I was up bright and early and went down to the South China Sea for a couple of hours of sun and surf. After changing my clothes I woke up Kevin and we went to the nearby town of Tuy Hoa. It's about 15-20 miles away and we took a Vietnamese version of a yellow cab (a motorcycle with a trailer) -- total price, 50-cents. Having heard of the wonderful steam baths we tried one. For a carton of Salems ($1.50) you can stay in the mint-flavored steam as long as you want. Also included is one of the best massages I've ever had with women walking on my back and legs. I get them at the barbershop quite often but this was fantastic. When we got back there was a good-bye party for one of the guys. We had all chipped in $3 for the goodies. We had all the grilled hamburgers, salad, potato chips and beer we could eat and drink. Next, a few of us went down to the beach for a dusk swim and then finished off the night watching the movie at the Phu Heip Outdoor theatre drinking beer and listening to music. I had a mission to fly so I had to quit early. Well what do you think of my weekend? It seems that I've had nothing but fun since I broke my engagement. I'm sure we can have the same kind of unwholesome fun on our trip this summer if you can make it.

October 15

We could leave in August or September and plan on no longer than a year. I'll be able to take $2000-$2500. We can get over there for about $100 and go directly to Berlin and buy a VW micro bus and a couple sleeping bags and head in whatever direction the wind's blowing. We can take our time and see as much as is possible with the least amount of cash outlay. I'd also try and live at least partially off the economy. If you get time try and find out things from the government and from people who've made the trip. I'll do the same from here. Believe it or not we've got three or four people who have been around the world living right here.

October 17

Charley is starting a new offensive and it should be ready to go off about the time you get this letter. From our intelligence it looks like a major offensive throughout II Corps, with total control as its ultimate goal. He is found in strength all over but especially in the Dak Tao and Ben Het and the Dubai area. So strong in fact that we have recently lost three planes (6 men) and we are continually getting shot at. I was fired at yesterday while looking for one of the downed planes. My chances are still good but not as good as I would like them to be. I'll keep alert and try my best to make Europe with you. Enclosed is a picture of that famous Army aviator—what's-his-name—in full battle dress at 1500 ft. It makes you glad you're not a VC doesn't it? You can see a few dials and gauges in the background. Its all very hush, hush and secret. I have to have a Top Secret security clearance just to see them. If you can learn what to do with them you can come over here and take my place.

October 23

Today the reality of this place seemed to hit me pretty hard. I feel I have to share my thoughts with you. I'm becoming more concerned every day with what the American Way of Life is showing me. It's so unjust and unequal. Always before in my young life I've been able to have some effect on my environment. The reason, of course, is that I've never bumped heads before with anything as powerful as the absurd, self-justifying establishment at home. I have a very good life waiting for me in that establishment but I can't accept it. I'll go through all the motions and become accepted but I will openly work to defeat injustice. I have chosen a profession in which I feel I can have an effect upon the world around me and I plan to use this profession to bring what we do closer to what we're supposed to do. I can tell you this as though I'm giving my blood to you. If there is something I can't tell you I'll be surprised. I suppose we're as close as anyone. You've been my friend and I yours for quite some time now. How long has it been? Almost five years to the month. The two of us have been through a lot with each other. I've seen you grow up to the point at which you are today. These five years were probably the years of greatest change for both of us. I'm going into all of this just to tell you that you are truly my friend and your friendship is something I value highly. Somehow the two of us will make it out of this awkward stage. In the past two days I've received a letter from you, one from your mother, one from Mary Lu and one from Kay. If only Bob would write me I'd have one from everyone. I really appreciate your family writing me and it makes me feel very good. I received the books and am in the process of reading them. Catch 22 was my first choice. It's amazing how little everything changes. Thanks!

I would have liked to be one of those people on your living room floor. Was there any hanky-panky? For your sake I hope so. If I come home we'll have to go back to CMU for a homecoming. I guess we won't be able to make it in 1970 because of Europe but let's shoot for 1971. Regarding Viet Nam Moratorium Day (Oct. 15), we read a little of it in the *Stars and Stripes* but from what I read in your and Kay's letters we weren't told how big of a deal it was. I'm waiting for *Time* magazine now to find out the real scoop. We do read quite a bit about the Sgt. Maj. of the Army and the Provost Marshall though. It seems to me that if they tell us as much as they are it's really a big thing. There's nothing I like more than a scandal in the Army. First the Green Berets and now these two jokers. Also what's the deal with the red neck trying to get into the Supreme Court? Judging from his record, Griffin Bell won't let anyone on the court. He must be waiting for his turn. Very sorry to hear of the success of Operation Intercept at the Post Office. I'll do my part though to ease the load.

On a darker side I received my 3rd Air Medal a few days ago. Before I leave here I'll have set a record for the most hours in a Mohawk. If you don't mind me blowing my own horn I'll fill you in on my status over here. At present I'm the most experienced observer in the company. Most (well, about 50%) of the observers have been in Vietnam for more than one year which is twice as long as me. I've told you before that we have a pretty intelligent bunch. These old-timers signed up for three years (to avoid being a grunt) for what was given me as a draftee. I admit I was extremely lucky but I think I'd rather have 12 months of Viet Nam as opposed to 32 months of being stationed anywhere else no matter how good the duty. To get back to the point, in my two months plus of flying I've passed all of the other TOs in combat hours. I'm a regular hero now but the really good news is that none of the lifers fuck with me any more unless it's a last resort. Through this and law school (I guess) I've also gotten in good with the management (lifers) and am on a couple of committees representing the enlisted men. I'm Lenin to their Czar Nicholas.

With 7 months remaining and smoking grass occasionally the odds are that I'll be caught. The last person to get caught got the maximum—six months hard labor at LBJ, 6 months of extra duty and forfeitures of 2/3rds of his pay for 6 months. It's called 6, 6 and 2/3rds and I don't want it, but working with the pigs (while helping the enlisted men) and having as many hours as I do might be the difference between an Article 15 (company level punishment) and LBJ (Long Bhin Jail.) I hope I don't have to use it but it doesn't hurt to have this ace in the hole.

I'm very proud of the local vets in the Philippi area. They served with distinction in WW II. Now there was a good war and one none of us would mind fighting in. This is just plain bullshit, bullshit, bullshit, bullshit. There is no such thing as fighting oppression all over the globe and making the world safe for democracy or rather safe for our brand of capitalism. Give me a break! There never was a good war or a bad piece. It's only 25 years since WW II ended and we are already buying German and Japanese cars and products like there's no tomorrow. It's a comfort to know your local redneck WW II vets are still thinking of their country first and willing to take time out from their jobs—filling cars with gas, running the general stores, polishing seats in bars with their asses--to make sure the accursed Negro doesn't get too much and to beat up some college kids. When I come home I'll be able to speak with a little more authority and experience and when I make my new bar room friends I won't hesitate to tell them how fucking stupid they are. Even their beloved WW II was stupid if you look at all the information involved. For instance, why did we ignore Hitlers killing of the Jews for so long, why did Japan attack us and why didn't the president send a warning to Pearl Harbor when he knew of the attack at least 24 hours before hand. Or, there was a warning sent but it was by commercial telegraph and didn't arrive in time. Ever see a picture of the Arizona Memorial with all the men still buried beneath? Or, how could we expect Germany to act any differently toward us when we were supplying their opponents with 100% of their means to fight? The answer to these and many other questions will be coming your way in the next installment of Bullshit: The Letter That Tells It Like It Is.

Your point regarding the amount of information we receive about the World ("World" means back in the world or back home) and the amount you receive about this place is well taken. I imagine we're both kept in the dark. With your help I'll learn about the world and I'll fill you in on the status of things here if you'd like. Because of the nature of my work I'm briefed on every item of military importance in Vietnam for the day. This is secret material and not many people have access to it. Believe me there is not much of a war going on.

I've been awaiting your reply regarding my decision to stay single for a little while longer. A person can't ever be positive and without doubts in a matter like this and your reply will be welcome. I needed moral support and thank you for providing it. Your insight into the matter brought out my subconscious motive. You're right, for the first time in my life, I'll really be free. I can do anything I want to do. After this, all the pressure will be gone. Nothing will be hanging over my head, neither money, nor education, nor time, nor love (which I still have for her) will be forcing me to move on toward a goal.

I guess my letter regarding Europe hasn't caught up with you at the time of your last writing. Now I'm sure you know that I feel Europe for a year is #1. Even if you stay at A-B until 30 August it won't affect our plans. I'll get home around the middle of July and will have to spend some time at home for sure and it will be quite satisfactory if we leave in September. That way a lot of American tourists will have come home. Well, I can hardly move my hand anymore so I think I'll close. I'm not going to re-read this because I'm afraid it won't make any sense. All is well with me here, as I trust it is with you. Actually, I'll bet I'm happier and having a better time than most of the people you know. It really isn't that bad here.

Added to this letter:

For you Dave, the dreamer:

"The lunatic, the lover, and the poet are of imagination all compact."

"One sees more devils than vast hell can hold; That is, the madman. The lover, all is frantic, sees Helen's beauty in a bowl of Egypt."

"The poet's eye, in a fine frenzy rolling,
Doth glance from heaven to earth, from earth to heaven;
And as imagination bodes forth
The form of things unknown, the poet's pen
Turns them to shapes and gives to airy nothing
a local habitation and a name." [A Midsummer-Night's Dream]

After quoting Hamlet at length, he adds:

"This is a work for today's people and directing the issue at you and I, here is what I come up with—a perfect world we don't live in. Perfection can be obtained but only with total commitment. To be, or not to be, to fight, to care, to love or to give in, to exploit, to hate, that is the question.

Though things are unjust and wrong it might be better to suffer through it and not make waves because what will happen to us if we act could be worse than what we've got. Are we willing to prostitute ourselves in the status quo or roll up our sleeves and face the unknown?"

Shakespeare says that the unknown (as unacceptable actions in our society) make cowards of us all. But does it? Time will tell us. If the world continues to ruin itself in a Ford station wagon we'll know the cause is lost, but if the world becomes a better place it will be because of the work of 1-vote people, people who can talk to only 1 or 2 persons at a time. Change, for improvement, won't come from above. The air is difficult up there and is an addictive narcotic to those who breathe it. So addictive, in fact, that once you've breathed the air up there, the air that God breaths, you won't give it up without a struggle. Once this opiate (power) is in your blood you fight all that jeopardizes your position. Am I willing to stand up and jeopardize this position? Are you?

November 11

I don't really know where to begin. It's been a week or so since I've last written you and an awful lot has happened. I'll start with the two letters I received from you and save the best until last. It's good that you can enjoy your job. Actually that's about all you can really ask for. There are quite a few people here who just hate their jobs. As a matter of fact everyone I know here hates his job.

Your talk pertaining to the women and girls in your life sounds very objective. The scientific method is a tried and true theory but it seems to me as though something is lost in romance when you use it there. One thing to watch out for is love and marriage. Don't forget Europe is waiting and it won't be nearly as much fun to take a wife. I almost got trapped so don't let the same thing happen to you. You'll never know just how hard it was for me to break my engagement. I'm sure I could never have managed it if I hadn't been over here. Another reason why I'm lucky I'm over here. Not only do I have her feelings to feel guilty about but also those of our parents. Mine liked her quite a bit but more than that they were finally able to relax a little and quit worrying about what kind of trouble I was going to get into next. I must say, however, they've been extremely good about this. I think I can always count of the support of my parents and sisters unless I really go off the deep end. I thought I'd written to you in response to receiving your books but it appears that I hadn't. Thank you very much for the books. I've started reading Catch 22 but haven't gotten 100 pages.

I just don't know what the trouble is with me now—maybe I'm just homesick. Whatever it is it's lasted for almost a month. Hopefully it's just a temporary thing and I'll be back in good spirits soon. I think breaking up my engagement might be part of it.

What's all this talk about the Silent Majority and the vote of confidence the country is giving the president and his war policy? You may disagree but I'm all in favor of it. I'd like to see theflag flying from every porch and a red, white and blue armband on everyone's arm. I was in favor of the last peace demonstration (October 15) because whether right or wrong people were doing something about the war. I wish I could be there. Any demonstration is better, I feel, if it brings the country together. That's something our country badly needs. At least more people are getting involved and the more they get involved the more they learn about this war and the sooner it will be over. Another thing is if Hanoi sees that we've resisted to fight this war they might (it's doubtful but maybe ...) be a little more reasonable in Paris.

I volunteered to come up here to Plieku for a little change in scenery and a little excitement and to be with the 4th Infantry Division. I'll be here for just a couple of weeks while the regular guys here go on R & R. My job here is to remotely monitor the super secret systems on our birds so if we lose them I will have a record of what they picked up and can call it in the artillery or for air strikes. If you read the papers you'll notice this is where the action is. It started a couple days after I got here. I'm attached to the 4th Division Military Intelligence Detachment and am located about 20 mi. east of Cambodia on top of a mountain doing electronic communications work and being a part time grunt. There are only a few of us up here and our weapons are always loaded. I sleep with a pistol under my bed and a grenade on my desk. I was grounded toward the end of last month by the Flight Surgeon so that was also partly why I came up here. I had exceeded the number of hours I was allowed to fly and the Flight Surgeon checked me over and said I needed a rest. I guess I was a little jumpy. I can assure you that being up here hasn't helped my nerves. Let me tell you about this place. Uncle Ho claimed he was going to have Thanksgiving dinner up here and if he hadn't died he would just might have had it here. There are three of us who live in this 6-room hooch. We each have a bedroom plus kitchen, workroom (we never work so there's no need for it) and a TV room (also doubles as a guest room). We have our icebox filled with fresh meat, eggs, real milk, soda, beer and anything else you people back home have sent us.

There is no one to tell us what to do and the only officers on the hill can't even come inside—it's a restricted area. What do you think of that? The only people in this whole country who have life any better are politicians and 2-star generals and above. On this happy note I'll close for tonight. Do not forget Europe.

Nov. 30

I hope you didn't get fired and if you did you should have picked a better reason. The flag isn't the symbol of the establishment or of Washington but of the country and Constitution—neither of which deserves your scorn or trite protest. A little careful thought should make this apparent to you. The Constitution neither started nor continues this war but rather it gives us a means for ending it LEGALLY which is more than I can say for the policies you seem to be advocating. All the things you think you're fighting wouldn't be worth one damn piece of shit without that Constitution (i.e., flag) Anarchy is not the answer and that seems exactly what you advocate. Dissent should be allowed and even encouraged but the desecration of the flag in the name of protest and dissent amounts to little more than anarchy. Are your representatives in Washington and Lansing and Birmingham aware of how you feel? If the answer is "no" than all your righteous protestations of truth are the worthless utterances of a rabble rouser and a demagogue. I hope I've misunderstood you but I'd rather find that you've seen through your position and maybe see my point. That Constitution that you so easily ridicule happens to outline the best form of government yet devised. The men who operate under the

Constitution may be at fault (and probably are.) But not the Constitution itself.

Dec. 7

Remember Pearl Harbor
Once again I'll attempt something which is almost impossible for me to do—write a letter. I surely hope I can snap out of it when this is all over. If not, I'm going to be in bad shape trying to cope with the world. There isn't much to report. I'm still alive and well although my chances were lessened with this new offensive. It's bigger than Tet 1968 and is about to explode in our faces. If you'll read the papers you will find Ben Phrng mentioned. That area is in our responsibility and as a result I'm flying down there quite a bit.
Catch-22 was great. Everything seemed so real to me as if I could see similar things happening right here. Yossarian is my hero now. Soon I'll be getting a medal and I'm toying with the idea of getting that smoked too just like Yossarian. Heller affected me so much that I even talk like Yossarian—saying things that sound ridiculous unless you know the inside story and only I know the inside story to have it make sense. Please go into detail in your next letter in reference to my father's conversation with you. I am wondering exactly what they think about my ending the engagement and the trip to Europe. Also interested in meaning behind father's response to "hallucinatory." I'll be signing off for now. Take care of everything back in the world.

Dec. 25

I'm coming off a 2-week, daily flying binge (maybe 3, can't remember) and thought I'd write to you and let you know I'm still alive and well. For the last month this place has been a real circus or zoo depending how you look at it. S&S (M&M in the book) is up and running. "No one minds because everyone owns a share." This is a very profitable venture and it's expanding to the other areas. S&S now has daily truck runs to supply the local black market. Everything in the black market is done on a double your money rule of thumb. However much money we spend on the goods taken to town will be pure profit. If we buy $10 worth of cigarettes we'll sell them for $20. There are still two middlemen between the end consumer and me. I'll eliminate one of them and increase my profits by at least 100%. No one can laugh at 200% return on your money in one day. Because of connections and the old social chairman experience, I've (rather S&S) now have a party catering service, which is showing a very nice, profit as well. The money collected is usually $100-$125 for the party. This is turned over to me along with a truck and driver. When it's all over everyone is satisfied and I take home 15%. This isn't a very good return on my time but I enjoy the work and at any time it could explode into a real nice business. As you can tell, Catch 22 and its characters had quite an effect on me. Yo-Yo is still my hero. Anyway S&S keeps me out of trouble. On top of all this I'm now a section leader for 15 men and going up for battalion soldier of the month in January. That will be the joke of the year in The Army. As a result of all this, I am seriously worried about my sanity. My close friends have become aware of the condition and have been mentioning it to me. I just hope it goes away as soon as Vietnam does, but if not I'm going to be in trouble. I'm afraid there are just too many things going on. On top of everything I've told you that's happening I've been flying every night for some 30 days. God-dammit—after re-reading this letter I must seem like a real mess but it isn't really that bad (or at least I hope not.) I'll write more but have to go fly now!

Tet has begun and we're all anxiously awaiting Charlie's arrival. We've got a few surprises but for all intents and purposes I feel that if he wanted to spend tonight in my bed he could probably do it. I'm just keeping my fingers crossed. If I can get by the first or second mortar my chances of making it are pretty good. When they start coming they come every three or four seconds and if you're not flat on the ground or under something you're in trouble. I've got 600 hours (six air medals) and when I reach 1,000 I'll quit that and probably run the officer's club. I could have done this before but would rather fly but anything over 1,000 is definitely pushing your luck. I'm very glad to hear via letter that you're beginning to sound a little more optimistic about yourself and the world. Life's too short not to enjoy every minute to the fullest. Eat, drink and be merry for tomorrow we may die. How about that for rah-rah WW II stuff (and Roman gladiators)? Thank you for taking care of Christmas presents for my parents. I appreciate it greatly. I wonder if I could ask another favor of you. I've got a TEAC A-20 cassette deck and would like some Joan Baez cassettes. I will be sure to return the holder to you with a little something in it. I don't know when I'll write again but if it's a while don't give up on me. It's almost impossible for me to write anymore. I'm going to Bangkok or Tokyo on Feb. 14 and plan on having a seven-day orgy of fun and sightseeing. I'm keeping a diary of my last six months here starting Jan. 10 and as I finish each steno pad I'll send it to you. You may find them interesting and maybe a little unbelievable but I swear it's all true. Save the installments, as I want to show my son someday what war is really like. Europe is calling. I'm still game, are you? It should be one of the greatest experiences of our lives if we handle it right and have the proper frame of mind.

Feb. 28

As usual it's been a long time since I've written you and again as usual I'm a different person. I took my 7-day R&R in Japan but unilaterally extended my stay for a few days because I was having such a good time. I broke all the rules but what are they going to do to me? Send me to Viet Nam? I had originally wanted to go to Bangkok but The Army as usual fucked up and sent me to Japan. After I'd spent a couple of days in Japan I not only forgave The Army but also wanted to write a letter to the draft board and thank them. Everything The Army had done to me in the past 15 months was all worth the 10 days in Japan. I'm returning again in May on another R&R and am thinking seriously about going back after I finish The Army in July. I would like to know your opinion on this change of plans. What I would like to do now would be to come to Ft. Lewis, Washington to E.T.S. from The Army and at that time I'll still be in The Army for 24 hours. With luck I'll hop a plane going back to Vietnam and get off in Japan for free. I'll have a job waiting for me once I get to Japan. The pay will be about $400.00 a month and this is a lot of money in the Japanese economy. About the same as $750-1000 in the U.S. I could get the same job for you if you're interested. We will be English conversation instructors with no requirement other than the ability to read, write and speak English. My plans after that are a bit hazy but I would like to work for three or four months and then fly to Australia and bum around there for awhile and back to Japan for a couple more months and then to Europe, via Korea, Taiwan, Manila, Bangkok, India, Pakistan, Israel and finally Rome. How does that sound to you? If you go to Japan you certainly won't be sorry. It's the most wonderful place I've ever been in my life. The people are great and the girls are beautiful—I mean beautiful!!! I have quite a few friends in a small town in southern Japan, one of which just might be the girl of my dreams. I'll know more about that later though. Please contact a few airline companies and find the prices for the plan I just set down for you. If possible, I'd like to buy a one-way ticket from Tokyo to Rome with as many of the stops I outlined above as possible. If it could be arranged I'd like to spend about a week or two in each of these capitals. Also contact the C.I.A. and see if they will give me (us?) any money for keeping my (our?) eyes open and reporting when we get back. Now I'll briefly tell you about my trip to Japan. We spent 2 days and a night in Saigon seeing the sights and enjoying the ambience. There were 170 of us on the plane and 167 of them signed up for guided tours in either Tokyo or Atomi. Yours truly and two friends from the 225th, being such sophisticated and experienced world travelers, decided to go it on our own being fed up with being told what to do and when to do it since joining The Army. As a result we ended up in the middle of the largest city in the world without a word of Japanese in our vocabulary and no place to spend the night. Somehow we managed to find a vacancy (entrance exam weekend at Tokyo U.) and lived it up in Tokyo; again seeing the sights and enjoying the touristy things this great city had to offer. The next morning we left via bullet train (160/mph) to a small town south of Tokyo named Numazu where we spent the next week. These people are great. They all like Americans (only because they don't know them.) We were probably the only three Americans in the whole town and in most cases the only Americans they had ever talked to or seen. They treated us like visiting royalty and just couldn't do enough for us. The kids were the most fun and would come up to us just to touch the hair on our arms and our white skin. A surprisingly large number speak a little English. While most G.I.'s go on R&R in a pretty horny condition we were not in such a situation, each having Vietnamese girlfriends. As a result we could think past our balls and really see the country and its people rather than the inside of a bedroom. I managed to meet a beautiful girl who I spent a lot of time with and who became my girlfriend. She, like most Japanese girls, was pretty conservative. They're way open and honest about sex but don't just jump into it preferring to go slow. When I return I'm guaranteed a good time in every respect. My girl, Masico, was a model in Tokyo and had recently returned to Numazu to help out in the family restaurant. They especially go for body hair. They just can't seem to keep their eyes and hands off it. Although the weather was cold I tried to wear short sleeves as much as possible. I could go on and on but it will all be covered in the next episode of my diary.

It was awfully hard to come back to this place and I can hardly stand it anymore but there are still four months remaining. I've been put in for Spec. 5 but today the pigs found two bottles of whiskey in my stuff so I think I'll just get busted but I don't really care. I wonder what I would find in their stuff if I got the chance to look. There is still a chance that nothing will happen but I doubt it. After all I'm only 24-years old and John Barleycorn can mess up my mind unless I'm a lifer dog.

P.S. There is a good chance that my children and wife will be Made In Japan.

March 28

Just received a letter from you. As my time is slowly slipping away I'm wondering if you would like to take advantage of any financial bargains made available to me over here. I can get anything in electronics, sweaters, cameras and any number of other areas for one-half the cost in the U.S. A camera will be a must in our travels. Just let me know what you want and I'll send the details.

April 6

I've got a SitRep (situation report) for you. I'll try to tell you everything that is going on in my mind and what the various alternatives are. First of all I've got only 90 days left in The Army. By the time you read this that number will be closer to 60. When that time comes one of two things will happen. First, I will hopefully end up in Japan. In that instance I have a job (one for you, too) and will spend 6-8 months here in the Far East then on to the Middle East, Europe and finally home late in 1971. The second alternative would be discharged in Ft. Lewis, Washington between June 10 and July 10. My sister will be in California and I understand that you will be there, too, so I'll fly down and spend a little time then I'll go home. This journey will take about a month. I plan to spend a month at home then on to Europe and possibly the

Middle and Far East if you're willing. While in Europe I would like to hitchhike and camp out as much as possible and try to find work. Also I want to go behind the Iron Curtain. If we play our cards right here we might be able to get some C.I.A. money. This phase will be up to you and your Washington contacts. If you could manage it we would really be on easy street. There is a fairly strong possibility that you might be coming home alone. If I find some place that I halfway like I might just stay there. I'm afraid that if I come home I'd start throwing bombs. As a matter of fact I'm sure that one look at DEAD LAKE ERIE will put me in a fit that only violence can soothe. I've had it, Dave. The pigs are running the world and nothing legal can stop them. I see no alternative but to advocate extra-legal methods to save our country. This last statement presupposes the fact that it's worth saving and I'm not sure the supposition is correct. Are you? There are a few countries in which I could continue where I left off. For instance, Australia, England, New Zealand and South Africa. I'll have to start law school all over again anyway so it might as well be in Australia. I've heard from a great number of people that Australia is as close to heaven on earth as any place can be. The girls are beautiful and very willing. The upward mobility is three to four times that of the U.S. All of this spells happiness to me. Dave, let me know where your thoughts are on these subjects. Also please take advantage of my P.X. privileges: all cameras and electronic equipment at half-price.

April 17

Got your letter yesterday and it was a pleasant change of pace having you write in response to my letters. You being on the road and unable to get mail makes it difficult for us to make plans. How often will you be going back to West Virginia? Or have you other plans to receive your mail? Glad the diaries got to you. Through them you can get a real good idea of what life over here is like for me. As you can see 90% of the time I'm enjoying myself. I tried to be honest and personal with them and maybe someday I can write another **Catch-22.** You say I haven't changed but you're wrong. The me that came over here is gone, never to reappear. For instance, the odyssey we're about to begin wouldn't have been very likely in my pre-Vietnam days. If I were to explain the transition in a word it would be "perspective." Things appear to me now in a different perspective. Before I never had time for anything but school. I just had to be a lawyer and do it as soon as possible. I came very close to being the youngest lawyer in Michigan because I was accepted after only 3 years of college. Now, free from that obsession, I have the entire world and everything that's in it open to me. This is not to say I'm free from obsessions but rather I've just traded my old one for a better new one. My goal now is to lead the most exciting and interesting life possible—in short to do EVERYTHING. Are you game? (I think you are—we work on the same frequencies!) I enjoyed very much the tape I received yesterday. Everyone I care about in the good ole' U.S.A. was represented. I'm not usually a mushy person but I was truly touched hearing those voices. For the hours that tape was playing I was home. I wrote down some of the things you mentioned in the tape and I'll now say something in response. Of primary interest is The Odyssey so I'll discuss that first and then take in the order the other items of interest mentioned by you. I can see no time limit. Our trip could be as short as a week or as long a lifetime. I have a completely open mind and look at myself (poetically) as a leaf casting its fate to the wind. Your willingness to come to Japan was a tremendous relief to me. I wanted to spend some time there but this is going to be a partnership deal and if you weren't going to be there I wouldn't go. I will seek employment as an English conversation instructor making the equivalent to $800-$1000/mo. The job entails nothing more than talking and reading to our Japanese students and correcting their grammar, pronunciation and syntax. A great many of these students will be eligible females to whom even an ugly Westerner is beautiful. Sex is looked upon differently over here in Asia and it is very likely that we will spend just a few nights sleeping alone. I will have spent two or three months in Japan by the time you get there so you can rest assured that we will be fairly well set up—also a similar job for you can be arranged quite easily. Using Japan as a base of operations we could hit all the high spots of the East, then on to the Middle East and finally Europe. The Japanese deal is not a for-sure thing as The Army is involved and they could fuck up in any number of ways. If they do I'll wait in the world for you to finish your contractual obligation (a good idea—burnt bridges should be avoided). We'll head for Europe as soon as possible. I really want to come back to this part of the globe and show you the Eastern culture. I'd be willing to bet that even your most generous opinions of The East will be an understatement. Money-wise I'll have between $3000-$4000 depending on how things go over here. I've got about $2,500 VN but no way to convert it to dollars. Time will tell but I'll possibly end up using it as wallpaper. How much will you have? Was your wisdom teeth extraction a painful situation? I've had three removed over here—two on the same day and flew that afternoon. I brought a paper cup on the mission to spit blood into. Us soldier guys are real tough. Talking into a tape recorder is a very different process, isn't it? I have a great deal of difficulty with it but the rewards are high. Why don't you get one and when we leave give it to your parents and converse with them in that manner? There is a fairly strong possibility that I may get out of the service in the middle of June instead of July. I'm hoping this will the case but like so many other things I'm just going to sit tight and wait. Somehow you got the impression that I've quit flying. This is not the case. I set a goal of 1,000 hours and still have about 200 to go. As far as drinking in the officer's club I don't know where you got that idea. I wouldn't drink with the pigs on a bet. You say you want to go to Europe for the non-American culture there. I'm afraid that in many ways it will be very similar especially in comparison to how non-American Asia is. If I had a choice between Europe and Asia I think I'd choose the latter. Your mother wrote me on the back on one of your letters that she wanted some information about the clothes I was collecting for needy Vietnamese children. I don't know how she heard but I asked my mother to send me some clothes that Barb and Lorrie had out-grown and that I was going to give them to the chaplain. Actually the clothes were intended for the women of my adapted city---Lo Ba and dear Lang specifically but I couldn't say that. My mother has since informed me that she's sending little kid clothes. These damn do-gooders really can mess things up. All I wanted was to make my girlfriend happy and now I'm going to end up clothing the whole village. You mentioned seeing "M.A.S.H.' I read the book. It's not a **Catch-22** but very good and along the same lines. Also very believable. In a way it's too bad you aren't going to be in The Army. Aside from the obvious bad points there is a lot to be learned. Now that my time is almost up (and baring death or jail) I'm almost glad it happened. I truly believe I'm a better person for it in many ways. I am also a much worse person, e.g., alcoholic, junkie, pimp, black marketeer, degenerate and a serial exaggerator as this sentence can attest. These are all parts of life. Again speaking of movies, I saw Alan Bates in "The Fixer" the other night. It was a damn good flick and moved me a great deal. If you haven't seen it please try. It's a study of determination and guts—something that wouldn't hurt any of us. Your letter refers to a beautiful 60-degree day. It may be beautiful and sunny for you but I'd be freezing my nuts off. The temperature here is never less than twice that during the day and the humidity hovers around 90%. It's very similar to a steam bath and that's no joke. It dropped down to 80 the other night and I was cold with two blankets.

Just received another letter from you and although the stationary was quite different the contents weren't, I'm sorry to say. Dave, you're making a very big mistake in feeling sorry for yourself. Be assured, I'm writing this with compassion, empathy and as your friend. None of us can or are doing exactly what we want. Maybe you're bored to death and I can see why but don't get down on everything. Start shooting smack and you'll feel a lot better. Seriously, Dave, cheer up, we'll be having enough fun in a few months to make up for all boredom you're suffering right now. When you walk do you look at the ground in front of you or up at the horizon? Think about it as it might make some sense. Understand that Bob is a man now. I'll send him a letter of congrats. I've always had the impression that he's got a good, sound head on his shoulders—maybe more mature than his years which is something neither of us can claim. I've lost about 30 lbs. since you've last seen me and have big bushy stash. You probably won't recognize me and just walk past without saying a word. You remember Kevin from your stop in Ft Huachuca. He's a great guy and was my best friend over here. We were together most of every day for 9 months. I'm sure you will like Kevin when you get to know him. Please try to contact him. I've got a lot more to say but I'll mail this so you can have something to think about and to answer.

April 28

There is no sense in telling you about my exploits of late as you'll soon be reading them in Vol. IV. Glad you're still hot for Japan and the East. But hold on until we know for sure. Will you be ready to go from Seattle? If so, I will just get word to you from Japan (fingers crossed) and meet your plane. I almost bought my lunch the other day. I'm lucky, very lucky, to be alive. I got put in for a medal. What do you think of that? I'll probably end up with 15 of them. Do you still want to travel knowing I'm a war-monger?

May 5

Sorry for the delay in writing. It seems that I have another war on my hands and it's taking a lot of my time. If I could get my hands on Nixon I'd show him how we feel over here about this Cambodian business. They couldn't kill me in Vietnam after trying for 9 months so I doubt if they can do it inCambodia during the next two and half months. I say this very easily but, Dave, I am scared. I don't want to die. I want to live. Things are getting pretty bad. People, human beings, friends are leaving here on a mission and not coming back. I don't think this kind of talk will do either of us any good but I do think you should know how I feel. If it does happen I'll see you in hell.

As you can see from the preceding page, we all get down in the dumps once in a while. Luckily it doesn't get to me very often and I'm still fairly happy—much happier than anyone else I know here. My nickname and call sign is Ice Cube. I'll tell you later how I got it.

Now let's get down to business. I understand that you'll finish up at A-B on 15 May. From there you'll go back to Michigan for a while. I hope to be home between June 15-July 15. Time is getting short for me. I want out of this very badly. I have the feeling of a person deep under water and racing to the top but not knowing if I can hold my breath long enough to make it. Send me your Michigan phone number and you might get a call in a month or so. Please approach me with caution, as there is very little difference between an animal and me. You know how we trained and experienced killers are. Seriously, I do anticipate some problems adjusting back to civilization. I'm tired, bone tired. I need my mother. That may sound odd coming from a 24-year-old but it's true.

17 June

This will be our last chance to communicate before I come home. These are the facts, as I understand them: You're now in British Columbia (is there any possibility you won't receive this letter in time?) I'll be in Ft. Lewis, Washington on or before 16 July. You're going to spend the rest of the summer out west and return in late August or early September and head for Europe shortly after your arrival in Michigan.

I'd like you to come down to Ft. Lewis on the 16th. I have no idea of whether you can or want to come down but I will assume you will be there (with two beautiful, liberated, bra-less chicks?)

I have a plan. There must be a downtown Holiday Inn in Seattle. If so and if you get this letter in time, make reservations for us.

Home Again

And so this vivid stream of correspondence is concluded. The writer of these letters returned from Vietnam, permanently altered, one might assume.

Whatever terrible changes had taken over his psyche began to lessen in the weeks and months that followed. Friends offered him the support he needed to slip back into his real identity.

Soon after he parked his Army duds in his parents' upstairs closet, he resumed his prior hell-bent approach to modernity.

I'd hitchhiked down to meet my returning soldier/friend from the seaside compound of driftwood and rock I'd built on the coastal shore west of Tofino, British Columbia, on magnificent Vancouver Island. For more than a month I'd resided among other disaffected mostly Canadian young people who sought solace in this tranquil habitat.

Days on the beach had been spent detoxifying from the war, detaching from the acrimonious political divide at home, reading, scamming visiting tourists for food and local transportation, studying seagulls and writing songs. This was the closest to Vietnam I would get, geographically, but the furthest away I could be between my ears; my detachment from the anti-war struggle brought emotional relief, helped me transition to Next.

Letters reached me General Delivery at the Tofino post office. When I knew the time to depart was upon me, I assembled my belongings, caught a ferry boat ride to the mainland and began seeking rides south. Somewhere along the line, I spent the night in my sleeping bag alongside a busy highway. What was commonplace at that time seems unimaginable to the older person typing these words this morning.

At the U.S. border above Washington state, I found myself riding with a kind couple who'd picked me up hours before. As the customs agent questioned us, I identified myself as a guest rider in their car; he asked me to get out of the car and follow him inside to an examing room. There he emptied my knapsack of its various components of sleeping bag, cooking utensils, bags of food and books.

"You like to read don't you," he asked in a friendly voice. I did. "You really like health foods don't you?" he asked hoisting a two-pound bag of raisins into the light. I did.

At one point I told the gentleman I was heading to Seattle to meet a friend who was returning from the war in Vietnam, which was true but which would have been a great bullshit line had I been trying to deceive him. I'll never know if that comment helped enable me to exit the exam room with my belongings back in my knapsack.

However that worked out, I'll always appreciate the fact the man did not empty out that bag of raisins. Had he done that I might still be in prison in Canada for within the bag was an even smaller bag of dried ganja flower tops.

I made it to Seattle, at least I think I did. The fatigue I was experiencing was more than painful; I hadn't slept in a real bed for months and two long days of hitchhiking found me exhausted beyond exhaustion, well into perma-slouch.

We finally convened, apparently at the designated hotel although it is hard to recall. I do remember my friend was gaunt, lethargic, distant and mightily disoriented. He said he wanted to go out bar-hopping. I hated to disappoint him but my capacity for staying awake was non-existent. I went to bed and he went out on the town by himself. And got promptly rolled by street thugs. It was a bad start to our long-anticipated reunion.

We were coming from different experiences; he had been to war and I had been to beach, where I spent my days trying to grasp the syntax of Timothy Leary and playing guitar. I composed songs as he became decomposed in the welter of war to which our generation had been so aptly consigned. We had met according to long established planning that destined an eventual trip together to Europe, something we had agreed to do five years earlier as college student fraternity brothers.

We understood a deal is a deal but this deal seemed very illogical to me although I didn't have the heart or the courage to announce. I found myself inclined to adhere to our plan although my heart would have led me in another direction had it not been for the sacred spirit of the original agreement.

Our initial plan was to hitchhike back to Michigan together, stopping along the way to visit soldier-friends he had made in Vietnam. With this in mind, we stood together on an urban roadside the next morning, plotting our course. He studied an address book he kept, searching for familiar names he might identify then tie them to a hometown that might be along our proposed course of travel.

Less than two minutes went by. He flipped through pages in the address book and began to cross out names he came upon; as he quietly realized, those friends had been killed in action. It didn't take a whole lot more of this pre-planning to convince us to scrap our travel strategy. Five decades later I still sense the sorrow he felt at that moment, the utter despair evoked by the tragic discovery. I can't even think about it now without having to wipe my eyes and resettle my nerves.

He made it back from the war. But war followed him, haunted him always, perhaps never more than this moment by the roadside where the implicit sadness of our long military sojurn pierced through both of our hearts.

We made it back to Michigan, separately by different means. I think he took a flight to Florida before heading north. I hitchhiked across country by myself, making it as far as the Ann Arbor area in a few days where I accepted a brief four-day job offered me by a driver who picked me up in Indiana; he was helping organize a large scale rock concert. I agreed to become its director of sanitations a short-term gig that never appeared on any of my subsequent resumes.

My friend and I eventually flew off together for three months in Europe. We figured we could live over there on about $100 a month which was an entirely false notion, more like shere delusion particularly for two college graduates. The adventures we shared were alternately enjoyable and despairing, depending on the day and the person you talked to. We stumbled around several countries together, teaming up with another couple of young Americans from New York we'd met on a train trip while waiting for the used Mercedes we bought to be repaired.

By late fall we came back, he to Michigan to start law school again, me to Tucson where I made a half-assed effort to break into the music business while also attending graduate school and driving a truck for a construction company.

About a year later, I came back to Michigan to be in his wedding party. The night before the day of his fated betrothal, the two of us, his Dad and the other groovy groomsmen devoured several six-packs of beer and burned through a copious amount of Vietnamese pot he'd saved from the large stash he shipped home with his war belongings. The highlight of the night was his Dad's willingness to not only indulge our madness but also to participate nominally yet respectfully. May God smile upon his magnificence.

My friend became a dazzling professional in his chosen field; the law, an advocate of sensible government, a husband a father, later, a grandfather and consistently joyous soul.

He spent the rest of his life with a riveting sparkle in his eyes, projecting an unmistakably sincere appreciation for life. He retained a razor-sharp intelligent edge and a boundless capacity for making and keeping friends. His letters survived in their original context.

Today they remain in his possession -- testament to what life was really like for a cerebral draftee, a highly commendable solider, a blue chip American boy committed to the cause but cynical to the bone, young but uncommonly world-wise.

The passage of time would surely have its inevitable effect, some gradual diminishment of the residual accumulation of memories, telling encounters, regular brushes with death, mortality all imposed upon the uncertainty of war.

Some 45 years later, while fighting with the VA for disability benefits, this former soldier wrote the following about the only tangible thing left from his experience in Viet Nam:

To Whom It May Concern

I was drafted into the Army on November 14, 1968 at the age of 23 and honorably discharged in July 16, 1970 at the age of 25.

After Basic Training and during my 5 months in Advanced Individual Training and 12 months in Viet Nam I was an aviator flying in the right seat of an OV-1 Mohawk twin turbo propeller powered fixed wing airplane.

During my time in Viet Nam I was frequently in the immediate proximity of small arms fire, in the close proximity of artillery (105 mm and 155 mm) fire. I spent many hours in open door helicopters. During none of this exposure was I able to use ear protection devised due to the exigencies of the moment.

I flew well over 250 separate four hour plus missions in the OV-1. The noise of the airplane engines was very loud during each mission. This was also the case during the set up and take down time before and after each mission despute wearing communication headphones.

My ears were damaged by all of the above but I think the most damage came from monitoring and communicating on at least 4 different radios as well as an intercom between the pilot and me during these missions. All of these radios were turned to maximum volume during each mission in order to hear the radio traffic over the roar of the engines and to communicate over them.

Adding my training time and my on-the-ground time with my combat time in the OV-1, I probably have over 2500 hours of being in close proximity (within 2 and 3 meters, respectively) of the two 1800 horsepower jet turbo engines.

I could tell my hearing was diminished when I returned home. Many, many family members and friends commented on having to repeat things for me. Shortly before my discharge I asked to have my ears examined by army doctors. This examination took place shortly after my discharge in Ann Arbor MI. I was told at that time I had no hearing loss.

My hearing has continued to decline to the point where, starting about 20 years ago, I began testing various hearing aids but I was never comfortable with them in my ear. I have now come to the point where, despite the discomfort, I have no choice but to wear hearing aids just to participate in normal conversations or listen to the television at volume levels not painful to others. I am also unable to watch movies in theaters or television programming without subtitles.

During the 45 years since my discharge I have not been exposed to loud or uncomfortable noises. Because of my poor hearing I never attended rock concerts or played recorded music; loud or otherwise, I have no interest in guns, hunting or fireworks (probably because of my Viet Nam experience) and I prefer to use the air conditioner in my car rather than drive with the windows down. Thus, I don't see how my post Viet Nam life could contribute to my hearing loss. No one in my close or extended family has ever complained of hearing loss or worn hearing aids.

Sincerely,

Chapter Five
Recollections/Reflections

The Vietnam War has broken our hearts. It prolonged something we started to do to ourselves at Hiroshima; it's simply a continuation of that: an awareness of how ruthless we are. And it's taken away the illusion that we have some control over our Government. Vietnam made it clear that the ordinary citizen had no way to approach his Government... the Government wasn't going to respond, no matter what the citizen did... It simply is not interested.

Kurt Vonnegut

This final section is comprised of different perspectives on the war. Readers will discover a mix of viewpoints, all posited after the war by a variety of voices, some regarded as subject experts others average citizens.

Dozens of papers and positions follow, in their original context.

Curious-minded readers will discover varying perspectives and interpretations. Material is presented "as-is." I add as few embellishments, summaries or comments as self restraint allows.

Keep in mind the voices of the sources that follow share in common genuine commitment to understanding our war in Vietnam.

I believe that one hour spent digesting this small mass of material has the potential to further encourage a malleable mind to expand, shift around a bit ponder points of view previously unconsidered, disregarded, disdained, underestimated or missed altogether.

I hope it does.

A Vietnam Timeline

French involvement concluded in 1954 with the fall of Dienbienphu. An armistice that divided Vietnam was signed in Geneva.

In 1955, the U.S. took charge of reorganizing training of South Vietnamese Army. After winning a referendum, Ngo Dinh Diem declared South Vietnam a republic and himself president.

From 1956 to 61, U.S. aid and U.S. advisers increased yearly.

In 1962, a U.S. Military Assistance Command was set up in South Vietnam.

The first Buddhist monk, Quang Duc, immolated himself in the first of a number of protests against persecution by South Vietnam.

Later that year, a coup overthrew Diem; Diem and his brother were killed.

William Westmoreland became commander of U.S. forces in Vietnam in 1964.

The Gulf of Tonkin incident occurred in early August; Congress passed a resolution committing U.S. forces a few days later.

It was later concluded that Johnson used a North Vietnamese gunboat attack on two U.S. destroyers to ram through the resolution even as U.S. military goals were never established.

In 1965, U.S. forces at Plieku were attacked. President Lyndon Johnson ordered round-the-clock bombing of North Vietnam and the first U.S. combat unit in Indochina landed in Danang.

B-52s bombed North Vietnam for the first time in 1966 and a year later the same air ships arrived at U.S. bases in Thailand.

Also in 1967, Nguyen Thieu and Nguyen Cao Ky were elected president and vice president of South Vietnam.

In Washington D.C., more than 50,000 people participated in an anti-war rally.

In 1968, the first Tet Offensive shook American confidence, the My Lai massacre shocked the world and Johnson announced he would not run for re-election and declared a unilateral bombing halt. Peace talks began in Paris.

Violent protests pitting 10,000 protestors against many times more Chicago police officers juxtaposed against the televised Democratic Party Convention seized public attention, drawing visceral attention to the lingering controversy of the war.

In 1969, the first American troop withdrawals commenced as then-President Nixon began conducting meetings with his South Vietnamese counterpart and Secretary of State Kissinger conducted secret meetings with North Vietnam's Le Duc Tho.

In Washington D.C. a reported 250,000 of us marched against the war. (*The Washington Post* doubled that number to 500,000 in its next-day coverage.)

Nixon announced his controversial Cambodian "incursion" in 1970, the same year five students were killed in protests at Kent State University. The next year, the U.S. invaded Laos and *The New York Times* began publishing The Pentagon Papers.

In 1972, North Vietnam launched a spring offensive and America engaged in the first bombing of Hanoi and Haiphong since 1969.

The Paris Peace talks sputtered, peace was both at hand and not at hand, according to Henry Kissinger.

In 1973, a peace agreement was signed in Paris, Kissinger went to Hanoi, and POWs were released. Kissinger and Le Duc Tho were awarded Nobel Peace Prizes (Le Duc Tho refused.)

President Gerald Ford offered clemency for draft evaders and deserters in 1974, the same year the House voted down military aid for South Vietnam. In 1975, Ford asked Congress for $300 million for military aid to South Vietnam and $222 for Cambodia. (Congress never authorized it.)

In March, a North Vietnamese offensive began and President Thieu decided to abandon most of Central Highlands; the imperial Capitol of Hue was abandoned without battle and the North Vietnamese occupied Danang. Congress refused more military and humanitarian aid that spring as things in Saigon devolved into chaos.

In April, Cambodia failed and Phnom Penh was evacuated. Days later Thieu resigned, accusing the U.S. of breaking promises.

On the night of April 21, the President delivered a long and at times tearful resignation speech in which he excoriated the U.S. as "unfair … inhumane … irresponsible. "You ran away and left us to do the job that you could not do," he as quoted as saying in a *Time magazine* article that appeared in 1995.

Tran Can Huong was appointed president on April 21; On April 28 he resigned, the same day four rockets hit the Capitol, followed by a bigger series of explosions.

Five captured F-5 and A-37 jets, flown by South Vietnamese pilots who had defected to the North, carried out the raid.

An evacuation of Saigon was ordered, ending on April 30; South Vietnam surrendered unconditionally.

By the Numbers

58,022+ Americans killed

303,704 Americans wounded

2-3 million Vietnamese soldiers and civilians killed

2 million Cambodians and Laotians killed

300,000 Vietnamese still missing in action (1989)

$140 billion spent by U.S. (other estimates cite $5-6 billion)

Vietnam landmass slightly larger than the states of North Carolina, South Carolina and Virginia combined

9.2 million Americans served during the war

2.7 million Americans served there (this number varies by source)

2,500 listed as missing in Vietnam; 3.4 million in Southeast Asia theater

2,338 American Missing in Action (MIA)

303,704 number of American wounded in action

Vietnam Veterans comprise 9.7-percent of their generation

Peak troop strength -- 543,482 Americans in Vietnam— April 30, 1969

Some 735,000 Vietnamese, Cambodian, Laotian and Hmong refugees entered the United States; about 40 percent of them settled in California. Surveys indicate at least 50 percent of the Southeast Asian refugees received some form of cash assistance other than food stamps. Following the fall of Saigon in 1975, 1.4 million people fled the victorious communist forces in Vietnam, Cambodia and Laos.

120,000 Vietnamese and 20,000 Americans evacuated Vietnam in the last month of the war. Almost exactly one hour after the last American helicopter hauled people off our Embassy roof, NVA Gen. Tran Van Tra ordered his columns to move into the city from five different positions. South Vietnamese soldiers fled the country in droves, throwing away everything that could identify them as soldiers as they tried to melt into the general population. There was more to come: for Vietnamese, the re-education camps, the flight of boat people, the gradual softening of a harsh communist regime.

For Americans, "the new sensation of total, undisguised defeat."

Facts compiled by the Vietnam Veterans Leadership Program of Houston, Texas

Common fiction indicates over 9 million Americans served in Vietnam. According to this compilation of facts, 9,087,000 military personnel served on active duty during the Vietnam era – August 1964 to May 1975.

This figure includes service personnel who were stationed in the United States.

The number of personnel who were on active duty during direct U.S. involvement in the War was 8,744,000.

Those who served in the Southeast Asian Theater – Vietnam, Laos, Cambodia, Thailand and sailors in adjacent South China Sea waters – numbered 3,403,100 including 514,300 offshore naval personnel.

Serving within the borders of South Vietnam were 2,594,000 personnel. Another 50,000 personnel served between 1960 and 1964, during which time, 246 of them were killed as a result of hostile action.

Of those who served in South Vietnam, between 1 and 1.6 million (40-60%) either fought in combat, provided close combat support or were at least fairly regularly exposed to enemy attack.

Of those stationed in Vietnam, only about 20% actually served in the first echelon combat arms (infantry, armor, artillery, etc.) where they regularly pursed and engaged the enemy on the ground.

About 83.5% of the 7,484 women who served were nurses; eight of them died. Women comprise 2.1% (197,513) of Vietnam-era veterans.

Casualties included 47,258 from hostile death; 10,446 non-hostile death – total 57,704. Another 303,704 were reported wounded – 153,329 of them requiring hospitalization. Severely disabled numbered 75,000 – 23,214 of them 100% disabled. Those missing in action and not accounted for at the end of the War were 2,528.

Draftees far outnumbered enlisted men in Vietnam. They formed a disproportionate share of the Army's combat arms enlisted personnel yet only 25% (848,500) of total forces in the country were draftees, who accounted for 27% (15,404) of combat deaths in Vietnam.

Statistics compiled by this veterans group give doubt to the fictitious notion that Blacks fought and died in extraordinarily high proportions relative to the rest of the population.

Less than 10% of Vietnam era forces were Black. In fact, 88.4% of the men who actually served in Vietnam were Caucasian and they comprised 86.3% of the men killed as a result of hostile action.

The numbers also belie the notion that America sent mostly its poor to fight in Vietnam. Men from lower middle class or working class backgrounds comprised 76% of those sent to Vietnam. Three-fourths had family incomes above the poverty level; 50% of these men were from middle-income backgrounds. About 80% of men who served in Vietnam had a high school education or better when they entered service. They were said to be the best-educated Army America had ever fielded.

82% of veterans who saw heavy combat strongly believe the war was lost because of lack of political will; 75% of the American public agree.

Vietnam (2000)

Population – 77,311,210

Per capita income -- $1,700

Chief religions – Buddhist, Taoist and Roman Catholic

Health – Life expectancy: 65% for men, 70% for women

One stunning statistic gives the lie to the impression that less-laudable circumstances defined the discharge of many veterans of a controversial war; 97"% of Vietnam-era Veterans were honorable discharges.

The average age of the Vietnam War GI was 19 compared to 26 for WW II. Two-thirds of the men killed in Vietnam were 21 years or younger when they died.

Books on Vietnam

Visitors to any flea market book booth will attest to the ubiquity of Vietnam War-era books, covering the conflict from as many different points of view as any curious minded semi-literate poseur could presume.

A student of the subject could -- and probably already has -- occupy a lifetime reading about this subject as the ever-expanding body of work shows no sign of abating, not in the lifetimes of those impacted by the seriousness of the era and the firm hold it held on our senses.

I compiled the following partial list of books on Vietnam, including ones mentioned by Hackworth and others recommended by friends:

A Bright Shining Lie: John Paul Vann and America in Vietnam --Neil Sheehan.

We Were Soldiers Once ... And Young. La Drang – the Battle That Changed the War in Vietnam -- Harold R. Moore and Joseph L. Galloway.

The Killing Zone: My Life in the Vietnam War -- Frederick Downs, Jr.

The Price of Honor --David Hackworth

Soldiering On In a Lost War -- William Shurkurti

The Things They Carried --Tim O'Brien

On Strategy – Harry Summers, Jr.

Stolen Valor -- B.G. Burkett

Street Without Joy --Bernard Fall

Modern Warfare – Col. Roger Trinquier

The Battle of Dien Bien Phu – Jules Roy

In Pharaoh's Army – Tobias Wolff

Born on The Fourth of July – Ron Kovic

Vietnam: A History -- Stanley Karnow

To What End – Ward Just

Military Men – Ward Just

Hazardous Duty – David Hackworth

Price of Honor – David Hackworth

Steel My Soldier's Hearts – David Hackworth

My Father My Son – Elmo Zumwalt

Seen Through the Eyes of Others

This section ambles along with pieces from David Hackworth, culled from the internet in the years following publication of *About Face*.

Stolen Valor: Setting Vietnam record straight
By Col. David Hackworth
(Published on WorldNetDaily.com 10/07/98)

The Vietnam War just won't go away. Daily it kills vets who fought there. Daily it kills Vietnamese who live there. Daily it haunts those warriors who survived the battlefield but still live with the nightmare of America's most divisive war.

Of all the wars our country has fought, Vietnam was perhaps the toughest for the grunt; the most reported, but the least understood. It was the only war where our heroes who did the bleeding were never honored. There were no parades. No "Welcome Home." No "Job Well Done."

When it ended, it was quickly buried. The Pentagon swept it under the rug. Colleges refused to teach it. Many vets even denied they were ever there. Collectively, society wanted to forget it.

But still it wouldn't go away.

Hollywood produced its Rambo version, the media followed with theirs, and the rumor mills churned out still more sleaze. The vets never countered these massive misrepresentations. Their voice was silenced by their shame at being accused of losing the war – a first for America – and the stigma that bar war engendered.

Myth eventually replaced truth.

The fiction became that the "baby killers" of Vietnam were unstable losers, drug fiends, suicidal creeps, murderers, pathological time bombs, animals unfit for society.

They were branded like cattle. Too often at the top of a negative story – a crime, a murder, a violent act – would be "Vietnam Veteran …" For thirty years, reporters produced thousands of distortions. Big hitters like CBS's Dan Rather, for example, who received a prestigious media award for a story about a nuts Seal in Vietnam who later turned out to be a rear echelon weenie rather than a member of that elite unit.

Time magazine reported a vet shot a pregnant woman while in Vietnam, except the impostor had never served in Vietnam. *The Boston Globe* told the story of a vet who was in the slammer for murder because of a heroin addiction he picked up in Vietnam. The story won him an early release until it was revealed he'd never served in Vietnam.

These lies from and about wannabes and total frauds are just three of countless stories designed to degrade those that fought there. Many in the press accepted these cons and exaggerations without doing their homework because too many reporters bought into the propaganda that Vietnam vets were bums. And when caught along with CBS, *Time* and *The Boston Globe*, their false stories were seldom retracted and the record was seldom set straight. Why apologize? For decades it's been open season on the men who served our country so faithfully and so bravely in Vietnam – the ones who didn't follow the example of over 14 million of their contemporaries who shirked in Canada, shirked in college or shirked in the National Guard.

Few have stood tall to the press and said, "Wait a minute. You got it wrong." Vietnam vets didn't have many public defenders.

Now Vietnam vet B.G. Burkett, a Texas businessman, has taken on that role. For 10 years, at a huge personal cost, he dug through the National Archives and filed hundreds of requests for military documents under the Freedom of Information Act. Finally, he gathered enough for his self-published book, **Stolen Valor**, and launched a vigorous counterattack that has "uncovered a massive distortion of history."

In his own words, his research revealed "killers who have fooled the most astute prosecutors and gotten away with murder, phony heroes who have become the object of

313

award-winning documentaries on national television and liars and fabricators who have flooded major publishing houses with false tales of heroism which have become best-selling biographies."

Former Navy Secretary James Webb called Burkett's work "one of the most courageous books of the decade." In **Stolen Valor**, Burkett tells the story of more than 1,700 people who tried to steal the valor of others or to disgrace the service of those who did their duty in Vietnam by distortion and lies.

Few regular bookstores stock it. Most are as afraid of a lawsuit as the publishers were. But Bronze Star recipient Joe Galloway, a distinguished combat correspondent, says Burkett's book exposes more fraud than the Justice Department. You can get it by calling 1-800-253-6789.

Defending America: The Turning Point
By Col. David Hackworth
(Published on WorldNetDaily.com 07/29/98)

Too many of the press have for too long had an open hunting season against our warriors both when they fought in Vietnam and when they came home, and seemingly all who've served our nation since that terrible war ended. James Webb explained the press' persistent hostility towards the military in a recent article: "It has deep roots in the elites among the old antiwar left, whose members not only avoided service but openly derided those who went to Vietnam as either stupid or evil."

Back in the '60s and '70s when our warriors fought in the most difficult and divisive war in our nation's history, the press worked overtime to paint them as murderers, druggies and warped misfits. They were caricatured as psychos who spent their time fragging leaders, burning villages and napalming women and children.

Our Vietnam Forces could do no right. Even when they beat the tar out of the North Vietnamese Army during the Tet Offensive of 1968, the press preached gloom and doom. On that occasion, Walter Cronkite, no less, announced from Saigon, "We have lost the war."

The reportage was mainly about the horror, the horror the horror. The nation only heard the dark, the evil, and the "Apocalypse Now" side of Vietnam. And few reporters empathized enough with the grunt to report on how to them the war was only about staying alive and keeping their buddies alive. Their gallantry, their brotherhood, their sacrifice and the thousands of daily unselfish acts of courage were seldom noted.

When the vets returned home, few fought back. They silently wiped off the spit, blocked out the curses and charges of "baby killers" and wore the cheap shots fired off by the media elite and a good number of the 75,000 doctorates cranked out during the Vietnam War. Many of these are the same draft dodgers now sadly running both our media and academic America, infecting the current generation with their anti-Vietnam, anti-military, anti-America poison.

Even after our heroes returned home, few reporters and teachers let facts get in their way when they could trash a Vietnam vet. They made up fairy tales such as: Vietnam vets were into suicides by the tens of thousands; they'd swollen the ranks of the homeless; and loser Vietnam vets have committed a disproportionate number of crimes and bad deeds from the Vietnam War to now.

I believe that guilt for not serving, not doing the right thing by answering the call of their country is the reason the press and the academies have cut the vets no slack. If fighting in Vietnam was bad and those who fought there were sickish, then they could continue to justify having dodged the war. They could assuage their guilt, still look in the mirror and tell their kids, "I didn't go because it was an immoral war."

CNN/USA president Richard Kaplan, the guy largely responsible for CNN's phony story, well fits that profile. And he's famous for his derisive statements about the war and how he escaped by hiding in an academic bunker.

But now the average age of our Vietnam vets is 50. They're no longer the 19-year-olds who three decades ago were moving targets in the middle of the killing fields – now they're among the top lawyers, doctors, CEOs, foremen and master craftsmen who make up a big percentage of the guys running America. At last they have the clout to hold their denouncers accountable.

Their first shot to this end will be an awesome lawsuit aimed at CNN and *Time* magazine and the key players responsible for Time-Warner's big lie. The second volley may well be a demand in Congress to investigate CNN's nerve gas story frame by fraudulent frame.

Then perhaps the media will no longer bad-mouth our vets or our serving soldiers without just cause and airtight evidence. And then maybe our valiant warriors from a war fought long ago will finally have exorcised the ghost of Vietnam.

Writer's Note

I disagree with Hackworth's opinions about those of us who opted for college in lieu of submitting to be drafted. College was always the objective where I was from. Everyone went to college, as certain as they went to the bathroom.

The pursuit of any destination other than higher education was without precedent. I believe my high school graduating class of 240 produced only one plumber who quickly became a real estate magnate.

Whether you went to the best university or to some previously unheard of and obscure community college with no academic standards for admission, you matriculated somewhere, somehow, whatever it took.

Even before the Vietnam War's demands for ever-more conscripts revved-up the Draft to body-gobbling numbers, anything short of pursuing a college degree was outside the lexicon in our upper-middle class suburb.

I think Hack comes down a bit unrealistically on people like me in this regard. His harsh opinion ignores <u>the larger truth</u> we learned during the war, that being, all of us came at this from a different direction, a different place in time. We learned to respect and understand one another, not to pass judgment as judgment was way too subjective for our emerging sensibilities.

Heck, Hack knew that.

I don't remember feeling any dishonor jumping from one college to another never quite unpacking my suitcase. Although certainly the measures I took to remain matriculated were extreme.

Hackworth's tone and vivid contempt for the millions of us who attended college in the 1960s is somewhat at odds with the views expressed in *About Face*. I find it remarkable to encounter this contradiction even as my larger inclination is to cut the man as much "Hack Slack" as we both need.

My respect for him, his thinking his perspectives is larger than whatever umbrage I take from his remarks.

Clearly the man knew what he was talking about.

In Vietnam he stared into the illogic of it all, the pure horror, corruption, greed, self-aggrandizement, cowardice, arrogance, extreme stupidity. He depicted his revulsion in his book with sheer force. His recollections affirmed my abiding opposition to that war, all wars really.

The Vietnam Syndrome
By Christopher Hitchens
(Published on *vanityfair.com* 07/27/06)
In the 1960s, the United States blanketed the Mekong River delta with Agent Orange, a chemical defoliant more devastating than napalm. Thirty years after the end of the Vietnam War, the poisoned legacy lives on in the children whose deformities it is said to have caused.
To be writing these words is, for me, to undergo the severest test of my core belief – that sentences can be more powerful than pictures. A writer can hope to do what a photographer cannot: convey how things smelled and sounded as well as how things looked. I seriously doubt my ability to perform this task on this occasion. Unless you see the landscape or ecocide, or meet the eyes of its victims, you will quite simply have no idea. I am content, just for once – and especially since it is the work of the brave and tough and undeterminable James Nachtwey. The tradition of giving pretty names to ugly things is as old as warfare. In Vietnam, between 1961 and 1971, the high command of the United States decided that, since tree cover was apparently protecting a guerilla struggle, a useful first step might be to "defoliate" those same trees. Famous corporations such as Dow and Monsanto were given the task of attacking and withering the natural order of a country. The resulting chemical weaponry was euphemistically graded by color. Agent Pink, Agent

Green, Agent Purple, Agent Blue, Agent White and –
spoken often in whispers – Agent Orange. This shady
gang, or gang of shades, all deferred to its ruthless chief,
who proudly bore the color of hectic madness. The key
constituent of Agent Orange is dioxin: a horrifying
chemical that makes total war not just on vegetation but
also on the roots and essences of life itself. The orange, in
other words, was clockwork from the start. If you wonder
what the dioxin effect can look like, recall the ravaged
features of Viktor Yushchenko – ironically, the leader of
the Orange Revolution.

The full inventory of this historic atrocity is still being
compiled; it's no exaggeration to say that about 12 million
gallons of lethal toxin, in Agent form alone, were sprayed
on Vietnam, on the Vietnamese, and on the American
forces who were fighting in the same jungles. A prime use
of the chemical was in the delta of the Mekong River,
where the Swift Boats were vulnerable to attack from the
luxuriant undergrowth at the water's edge. Very well, said
Admiral Elmo Zumwalt Jr, we shall kill off this ambush-
enabling greenery by poisoning it from the skies. Zumwalt
believes his own son, Elmo III, who was also serving in
the delta, died from the effects of Agent Orange, leaving
behind him a son with grave learning disabilities. The
resulting three-generation memoir of the Zumwalt family –
My Father, My Son (1986) written by the first and second
Elmos about themselves and about the grandchild – is one
of the most stoic and affecting family portraits in
American history.

You have to go to Vietnam, though, to see such fallout first
hand. I had naively assumed that it would be relatively
easy to speak to knowledgeable physicians and scientists,
if only because a state that is still Communist (if only in

name) would be eager to justify itself by the crimes of American imperialism. The contrary proved to be the case, and for two main reasons. The government is too poor to pay much compensation to victims, and prefers anyway to stress the heroic rather than the humiliating aspects of the war. And traditional Vietnamese culture has a tendency to frown on malformed children, whose existence is often attributed to the sins of a past life. Furthermore, Vietnamese in general set some store in pride and self-reliance, and do not like soliciting pity.

I am quite proud of what I did when I came to appreciate, in every sense of the word, these obstacles. The first time I ever gave blood was to a "Medical Aid for Vietnam" clinic, in 1967. That was also the moment when I discovered that I have a very rare blood type. So, decades later, seeing a small ad in a paper in Ho Chi Minh City (invariably called Saigon in local conversation) that asked for blood donations for Agent Orange victims, I reported to the relevant address. I don't think they get too many wheezing and perspiring Anglos at this joint, let alone Anglos with such exclusive corpuscles; at any rate I was fussed over a great deal while two units were drawn off, was given a sustaining bowl of beef noodles and some sweet tea, and was then offered a tour of the facilities. This privilege, after a while, I came almost to regret. In an earlier age the compassionate term for irredeemably deformed people was *lusus naturae*: "a sport of nature," or, if you prefer a more callous translation, a joke. It was bad enough, in that spare hospital, to meet the successful half of a Siamese-twin separation. This was a more or less functional human child, with some cognition and about half the usual compliment of limbs and organs. But upstairs was the surplus half, which, I defy you not to have thought if you had been there, would have been more mercifully thrown away. It wasn't sufficient that this unsuccessful remnant had no real brain and was a thing of stumps and sutures. ("No ass!" murmured my stunned translator in that good-bad English that stays in your mind.) Extra torments had been thrown in. The little creature was not lying torpid and still. It was jerking and writhing in blinded, crippled, permanent epilepsy, tethered by one stump to the bedpost and given no release from endless, pointless, twitching misery. What nature indulges in such sport? What creator designs it?

A Vietnam-era lesson in telling the truth
By Pete McCloskey
(Published in *The San Francisco Chronicle* 05/08/04)
In March 1971 I had just returned from a 12-day visit to Vietnam and Laos. The Nixon administration was then denying reports of the bombing of Laos and Cambodia. On Dec. 31, 1970, Congress had just repealed the 1964 Gulf of Tonkin Resolution, which had authorized President Johnson to "meet aggression with aggression in Southeast Asia," essentially against the Viet Cong and North Vietnamese in Vietnam. We had started to remove our troops from Vietnam. There was no longer even a semblance of legal justification to bomb in Laos or Cambodia.
While in Vietnam and Laos during March 1971, I had taken sworn affidavits from a number of pilots. They stated they had been bombing targets in Laos and Cambodia, many with the coordinates of specific rural villages, some being in Laos' famous Plain of Jars, a considerable distance from the Ho Chi Minh Trail, which had once been a legitimate bombing target.

Upon returning home, I testified before two Senate committees. I related the stories of the bombings of which I had been told. Various high-ranking administration spokesmen who stated unequivocally that the United States was not bombing in Laos immediately denied my statements.

A few days later, it was announced that we were indeed bombing in Laos, but that for security reasons, this knowledge had been withheld from the civilian secretaries of the Air Force, Navy and Army. At the direct order from the White House to the Joint Chiefs of Staff, false coordinates were reported to the secretaries for the daily and nightly bombing runs over Laos and Cambodia. The justification, then as now, was that national security required that the bombing raids not be disclosed to the American people.

Why Iraq Will End as Vietnam Did
By Martin Van Creveld
(Published on lewrockewell.com 11/19/04)
As Shakespeare once wrote, they have their exits and their entries. Between about 1975 and 1990, following the US defeat in Vietnam, military history was extremely popular among the US Armed Forces. After 1991, largely as a result of what many people considered the "stellar" performance of those Forces against Saddam Hussein, it went out of fashion; after all, if we were able to do *that* well there was not much point in studying the mistakes our predecessors made. Now that comparisons between Iraq and Vietnam are becoming very fashionable, indeed, history is rushing back at us. Here I wish to address the differences and the similarities between the two wars by

describing Vietnam as one man, Moshe Dayan, experienced it.

After extensive interviews with leading American government and military leaders, Dayan summed up his impressions. Almost all the Americans he had met were pleasant enough. None, however, could tell him how they were going to win the War. Most could not even give a convincing reason why the US had to be in Vietnam in the first place; at least one said that, had President Johnson had been presented with a way to get out, he would have jumped on it and withdrawn his troops. What really infuriated them was any attempt to question their motives. As far as they were concerned their cause was noble and just. The fact that the Communist States did what they could to support the Viet Cong and North Vietnam was bad but understandable. They were, however, puzzled by the attitude of their European allies. Those Europeans supposedly shared America's liberal-democratic values. Still many of them were strongly critical. At a loss to explain the problem, the Americans attributed it to cowardice, envy, and the resentment that arose from Europe's own recent failure in waging "Imperialist" war. He thought that, in ignoring Europeans, the Americans were making a big mistake.

One of their problems was the need to get their names mentioned by the media so as to advance their careers. This, Dayan thought, did not turn them into better persons, or, what was more important, better commanders. He admired the American rank and file, particularly the Marines and the Green Berets. He was even more impressed by the tremendous military-industrial muscle that enabled 1,700 helicopters to be deployed in a single theater of war.

While in America to advise on the war, Israeli retired general Moshe Dayan met Walt Rostow. As deputy head of the National Security Council, Rostow was first American to admit that the US objective was not just to help South Vietnam but also to set up a permanent military political presence in South East Asia so as to counterbalance the growing power of China.

General Maxwell Taylor admitted that in spite of the heavy casualties being inflicted on the VC – estimated at 1,000 a week – the latter's operations kept growing more extensive and more dangerous.

Robert McNamara had doubts but was convinced the War was not hurting the US economy. Dayan's skepticism was more firmly rooted.

Leaving Washington on his way to Vietnam Dayan concluded none of the Americans he had met could tell him how they were going to win the War. Most could not even give a convincing reason why the US had to be in Vietnam in the first place. What really infuriated them was any attempt to question their motives. As far as they were concerned their cause was noble and just.

Dayan got to Vietnam, and met a Vietnamese professor of nuclear physics to whom he was referred by an Israeli friend. He was told the Viet Cong were much stronger than the Americans knew or wanted to know.

Sources in France had told him the battle for the hearts and minds would not work, given that the Vietnamese had their own cultural traditions and that "Californization" was the last thing they wanted.

He knew from his own experience how hard it was to make a long-established culture change its ways. Clearly doing so in the midst of a war, when every achievement was under constant threat from Viet Cong terrorists, was much harder still.

Among the problems he discovered was the Americans need to get their names mentioned by the media so as to advance their careers. It was 1966. Soldiers were also being rotated in and out of the country too fast to learn its ways and become really effective in doing their work. Nothing could make up for the lack of accurate and timely tactical intelligence. Partly its absence was due to cultural obstacles; wherever he went, translators were very much in demand and, of course, said exactly what they pleased.

He left with the impression that the Americans were winning everything – except the war.

Our problem he thought was intelligence – the inability to distinguish the enemy from either the physical surroundings or the civilian population.

Most of the blows they delivered – including no fewer than six million tons of bombs dropped – hit empty air. All they did was make the enemy disperse and merge into the civilian population, thus making it even harder to find him. Worst of all, the lack of accurate intelligence meant the Americans kept hitting noncombatants by mistake. They thus drove huge segments of the population straight into arms of the Viet Cong. Nothing is more conducive to hatred than the sight of relatives and friends being killed. The campaign for hearts and minds did not work. Above all, the idea that the Vietnamese people wanted to become Americanized was an illusion. All that the vast majority really wanted was to be left alone and be able to get on with their lives.

Martin Van Creveld is a professor of history at the Hebrew University in Jerusalem. He quoted Dayan as saying "any comparison to the two armies ... was astonishing. On the one hand there was the American Army, complete with helicopters, an air force, armor, electronic communications, artillery and mind-boggling riches; so said nothing of ammunition, fuel, spare parts, and equipment of all kinds. On the other there were the North Vietnamese troops who had been walking on foot for four months, carrying some artillery rounds on their backs and using a tiny spoon to eat a little ground rice from a tin plate."

For Van Creveld that, of course, was the problem. "In private life, an adult who keeps beating down on a five year old – even such a one as originally attacked him with a knife – will be perceived as committing a crime therefore he will lose the support of bystanders and end up by being arrested, tried and convicted. In international life, an armed force that keeps beating down on a weaker opponent will be seen as committing a series of crimes; therefore it will end up by losing the support of its allies, its own people, and its own troops. Depending on the quality of the forces – whether they are draftees or professionals, the effectiveness of the propaganda machine, the nature of the political process, and so on – things may happen quickly or take a long time to mature. However, the outcome is always the same. He (or she) who does not understand this does not understand anything about war; or, indeed, human nature.

"In other words, he who fights against the weak ... and loses loses. He who fights against the weak and wins also loses. To kill an opponent who is much weaker than yourself is unnecessary and therefore cruel; to let that opponent kill you is unnecessary and therefore foolish. As Vietnam and countless other cases prove, no armed force however rich, however powerful, however advanced and however well motivated is immune to this dilemma. The end result is always disintegration and defeat."

Iraq is not Vietnam
Posted on the Internet 11/30/04.
(My notes: From the perspective of 11 years later, many of these interpretations do not exactly meet the test of longitudinal examination. That would be a lot to expect. Even the views that ring inconsistent with eventuality reflect the 2004 mindset and draw important comparison to the multiple mistakes America made in Vietnam.)
Unlike Vietnam:
Our allies are treating the local populace well and are fighting effectively.
Our troops are not torturing anyone or committing atrocities anywhere.
Our allies are committed to democracy, and are capable and experienced in carrying it out.
We are backing strong, independent leaders, rather than quislings and puppets whose power base rests with our military forces and economic support.
We are beloved by the people we are saving.
Our president and his cabinet officers are leveling with the nation about the costs of victory and likelihood of defeat.
We have the support of the international community.
It is particularly popular in the region where the war is being fought, and among the alleged audience abroad we seek to impress with our wisdom and resolve.
Our actions are not inspiring anyone to take up arms against us and thereby increase the level of threat we face.
Dissenters within the government, particularly those with expertise in the history and culture of the people we seek

to govern, are being heard with care and respect for their views.

This is also true for experts in academia and with direct experience in these nations.

Our wise leaders have a clear idea of the cultures into which we have inserted ourselves.

We are not asking the poorest and least well connected between dying and us to do the fighting.

Our troops are well trained for their well-defined mission, (a particularly hefty congratulations goes to Colin Powell for so effectively preventing the same kind of abuse of grunts he witnessed in Vietnam.)

Our civilian leaders are taking seriously warnings and advice of more experienced military leaders.

Those who point out problems with the present course are not being sullied as "counsels of despair and defeat" and giving "aid and comfort to the enemy."

We have the whole thing planned out.

This is a war against an enemy that had the will and capacity to threaten our lives at home.

More Points of View

The destabilization of Southeast Asia was in fact the result of Western colonialism and intervention in the region by France and then (with all the best intentions) by the U.S., leading to the First and Second Indochina Wars.

Cambodia's leader, Prince Sihanouk, who had warned that the U.S. could not win in Vietnam, was ousted in a 1970 coup that had American approval and perhaps covert support. A month later, the U.S. invaded Cambodia to clean out North Vietnamese guerilla bases – an incursion that sparked protests on American campuses, including

Kent State University, where four students died after being fired on by the National Guard.

Camille Paglia

From 1965 through 1971, the U.S. Air Force and U.S. Navy dropped more than two million tons of bombs on the Ho Chi Minh Trail in Laos. Despite the intensity of the bombing the supply efforts of the North Vietnamese continued almost uninterrupted down the trail.
Further, the bombing actually proved counterproductive to the American cause. Vast areas of Laos were destroyed, turning the Laotian people against the Americans.

Marty Brazil

Academic Interest Surges
More than 300 university-level courses on various aspects of the Vietnam era were offered in the 1986 academic year; in 1980 there were almost none The courses at colleges around the country cover everything from actual action in Southeast Asia to student demonstrations at home and the drives for civil rights and women's rights, according to the Project on the Vietnam Generation, a private organization whose project office was opened in donated office space at the American Museum of American History.
The project began as a clearing house for inquiries from teachers, students and Vietnam veterans who want to join in what has gradually become a sorting out of conflicting perceptions of the war – to some an experience of national shame, to others a difficult duty, honorably done. Project founder John Wheeler described it as a review of "the dynamism and idealism of the generation that bore the brunt of the wary, in Vietnam and at home – the 60 million people who, in round figures, are 32 to 49 years old in

1986, and of whom 10 million were in uniform during Vietnam, 3 million actually went there and 58,000 died there."

Vietnam War: A Study in U.S. Crimes
By Robert Jensen
(Jensen makes the case America won the Vietnam War.)
U.S. policymakers have secured a huge propaganda victory in shaping perceptions about that war, and paradoxically, one of the propaganda achievements has been convincing people we lost," he wrote in an op-edit piece. A journalism professor at the University of Texas-Austin, Jensen suggested the reason for the "seemingly strange strategy" is simple: Putting forward the idea that we lost obscures both the real reason we fought the war and diverts attention from U.S. crimes during the war.

His words challenge black-and-white thinkers to gaze within the realm of open-ended possibility.

"Despite the claims of U.S. leaders, we did not fight in Vietnam to establish democracy. Instead, we fought in Vietnam to derail democracy."

Jensen's narrative begins with the Vietnamese defeat of French colonialism in 1954. He points out the U.S. and its client regime in South Vietnam blocked elections.

He cites Dwight Eisenhower's memoirs, in which he says the President explained, "Honestly in free elections, the socialist government of Ho Chi Minh would have won by an overwhelming margin." He wrote the central goal of U.S. policymakers in Vietnam was to make sure that an independent socialist course of development did not succeed.

Jensen said U.S. leaders relied on Cold War rhetoric about the communist monolith "but really feared that a virus of such independent development could infect the rest of Asia, perhaps even becoming a model for all the Third World.

Jensen framed the issue: What might happen if all nations emerging from colonialism believed they had a right to decide their own futures, outside the U.S. orbit?"

He said it is much easier to obscure these U.S. war aims if talk leads to how we lost the war, leading to the fall of a South Vietnamese democracy "that never existed." Of similar ease, he suggested, is to obscure the brutality of the U.S/. war.

One other benefit: "So long as we believe we lost the war, the question can be asked: If we had fought harder, could we have won?"

Reminding readers that many among us still argue we could have prevailed in Viet Nam had we not been required "to fight with one arm tied behind our back." Yet, with only one hand, we managed to drop 6.5 million tons of bombs, 11.2 million gallons of Agent Orange to destroy crops and ground cover and 400,000 tons of napalm on the people of Southeast Asia.

He said it is easier to ignore saturation bombing of civilian areas if people can convince themselves that we were "restrained gentlemen" during the war.

"By telling the story that we lost the war, the U.S. can continue to evade the truth about its foreign policy. While it is true that we did not achieve total conquest of South Vietnam, 25 years later the nature of the U.S. victory is clear. Vietnam, still recovering from the massive destruction caused by the U.S. attack, is forced to accept – by economic pressure, not bombs – its place in the international economic order run out of Washington and New York."

Jensen concluded: "The Vietnamese people survived U.S. aggression as an independent people. The question is, will they survive their victory?"

Vietnam Then and Now
Wall Street Journal Review and Outlook
By James Webb
Vietnam was John F. Kennedy's war: The key decision in terms of the U.S. commitment was the coup against President Ngo Dinh Diem. After we had overthrown an ally and allowed him to be killed, we couldn't walk away. Certainly Lyndon Johnson couldn't when he became President three weeks later. In a sense, the war was the price the nation paid for lack of Presidential character. Vietnam was a losing battle in a hugely successful campaign. As many have noted, America's effort in Vietnam bought time for the rest of the region. While Vietnam, Cambodia and North Korea wallowed in the backwardness of their Communist triumphs, the rest of Asia today enjoys a prosperity and security purchased in no small part by the American boys who fought and died in Vietnam.

With Vietnam, America chose the wrong place, blundered badly and abandoned an ally to a fate it didn't deserve. But surely America's willingness to fight somewhere some time was instrumental in bringing about the better world we see today.

A quiet but intense debate has raged over our involvement, with the forum largely controlled by the media and academia, two of the most staunchly antiwar communities during the conflict (a third being Hollywood) All of these groups have a large stake in having the war remembered as both unnecessary and un-winnable.

Simplistic, cartoonish mythologies accompany both the communist and antiwar versions of the war, no doubt bringing solace to those who were on the right side of its outcome. It is easier to understand why our former enemies persist in such notions than it is to comprehend why so many of our own best and brightest still cling to the illusion that allowing – or in some cases assisting – a Stalinist takeover in South Vietnam was an honorable enterprise. … What is not natural is that our own commentators, now provided with so much evidence to measure results, should abet the rewriting of history. These errors of omission and commission have prevailed so long that they have permeated public thought. In order to justify the war as more of an inevitable reunification of the country than a communist takeover, scant mention is made of other nationalist parties inside Vietnam that the communists systematically eliminated beginning in the first days after WW II. The continuing focus on American and other 'atrocities' blurs the reality that assassinations were an essential part of the communist insurgency. According to the late Bernard Fall, communist terrorists killed an average of 11 government officials daily during the early 1960s – the equivalent in this country of an Oklahoma city bombing every day, for years. In a form of deliberate amnesia, commentators rarely mention that such policy-driven assassinations continue throughout the war, with thousands being executed in the City of Hue alone during the brief communist occupation of the 1968 Tet offensive.

Webb's essential article entitled "*History Proves Vietnam Victors Wrong,*" appeared in the Wall Street Journal on April 28, 2000.

He continued, "In order to demean attempts to nurture a democracy in the south even as a war was being fought, the South Vietnamese are continually portrayed as corrupt puppets of the U.S. Communist leaders, meanwhile, are elevated to the now-familiar caricature of the selfless noble savage. Communist soldiers – who fought well but lost repeatedly – are reverentially referred to as wily guerrilla fighters who continually bested the inept, over equipped forces of the U.S. and South Vietnam. These misrepresentations persist despite Hanoi's admission that more than 1.4 million of its soldiers died in the war, as opposed to 58,000 Americans and 245,000 South Vietnamese.

The American military is portrayed as an army of unwilling draftees with an overrepresentation of minorities. In reality, two-thirds of those who served – and 73% of those who died – were volunteers. With respect to minorities, African-Americans comprised 13.1% of the age group, 12.6% of the military and 12.2 of the casualties. In terms of attitude, the most comprehensive survey of those who fought in Vietnam (Harris, 1980) indicated that 91% of those who served were "glad they served their country," 74% enjoyed their time in the military,"" and 89% agreed with the statement that "our troops were asked to fight in a war which our political leaders in Washington would not let them win."'

The American antiwar movement, whose former members dominate the present administration as well as many of the media and academic filters through which the debate must pass, is benignly portrayed as a reactive force that mobilized only in response to a failed American strategy. In truth, many of its core leaders were dedicated to revolutionary change in America even before the Vietnam

War started. Many of them … continued to coordinate directly with Hanoi after the American military pullout in 1973.

Most retrospectives spend little time on what happened after Tet, with the implication that the war was lost by then. In reality, the Tet offensive was a massive military and political defeat for the communists, who had wrongly expected the South Vietnamese people to rise up and support the offensive. In addition, President Nixon's *"Vietnamization"* program that began in late 1969 enjoyed great success. Military critics of the war such as Col David Hackworth, who had four years on the ground in Vietnam, still maintain that if South Vietnam had survived a few more years, the young leaders who had come of age on the battlefield under American tutelage would have been unbeatable.

While it is correct to say that the American people wearied of an ineffective national strategy as the war dragged on, they never ceased in their support for South Vietnam's war effort. As late as September 1972, a Harris survey indicated overwhelming support for continued bombing of North Vietnam (55% to 32%) and for mining North Vietnamese harbors (64% to 22%.) By a margin of 74% to 11%, those polled agreed, "it is important that South Vietnam not fall into the control of the communists." Present-day commentators largely ignore the 1973 Paris Peace Accords, which earned both the American and North Vietnamese negotiators the Nobel Peace Prize. If we were to treat these accords as a binding international agreement between two still-existing governments, Hanoi would be held accountable for having taken South Vietnam by "other than peaceful means," and for failing to uphold its promise of internally supervised free elections.

"The humiliating end result of the communists' final offensive in early 1975 is usually placed on the shoulders of a supposedly incompetent South Vietnamese military. Little mention is made of the impact our "Watergate Congress" had on both its inception and success.

That body had been elected in November 1974, only months after Nixon's resignation. It was dominated by antiwar Democrats who in one their first actions voted down a supplemental appropriation for the beleaguered south Vietnamese that would have provided with another $800 million in military aid. Webb described that as "a horrendous blow" to a country that had trusted its American supporters, an indication Washington was abandoning them, even as the Soviet Union and China, among others, continued their support for our adversaries. Regarding the aftermath of Saigon's fall, Webb attributed it to "a gruesome" holocaust in Cambodia, two million Vietnamese being forced to flee their country and a Diaspora inside Vietnam, with a million South Vietnamese sent to re-education camps, the establishment of an apartheid system put into place to punish those who had been loyal to the U.S.

Webb acknowledged recent decades witnessed a gradual warming of relations between the U.S. and Vietnam. He argued history owes something to those who went to Vietnam, and to the judgment of those who believed the endeavor was worthwhile. "We can still debate whether the war was worth its cost, but the evidence of the past 25 years clearly upholds the validity of our intentions."

Was the U.S. wrong in Vietnam, immoral and stupid? Webb suggests the young men who marched off to the jungles for years of unrelenting blood and terror had possibly done the right thing. To advance that notion is to "confront the great Gordian knot of the Vietnam era itself," he wrote. Getting all of that straight, he said, was essential to facing the future relationship of the two countries. Webb wrote a new relationship can only be built upon honest foundations, with the full participation of those who believed in the validity of our war effort, and of the Vietnamese community in America. "Honesty must cut both ways," he said, meaning those who fought the communists must be able to admit that North Vietnamese and Viet Cong soldiers truly believed they were fighting for Vietnam's independence from foreign domination. Concurrently, Vietnam's rulers must be able to admit that the Americans and South Vietnamese who opposed their effort truly believed they were fighting for freedom.

Stanley Karnow, author of **Vietnam: A History**, wrote an article on April 28, 2000 for Knight Ridder newspapers to mark the 25th anniversary of the end of the Vietnam War. Following are excerpts:
Vietnam still haunts Americans. The longest war – and first defeat – in the nation's history ranks as a tragedy of epic proportions for the United States as well as for Vietnam.
At least three million Vietnamese soldiers and civilians on both sides, roughly 10% of the population, died in the relentless bombing raids that devastated their land.
The recollection of Vietnam remains embedded in their psyche as the epitome of a cataclysm they are reluctant to repeat, an unorthodox war without clearly defined objectives or an exit strategy;
Mistrust in our country surged as huge discrepancies appeared between the declarations of progress regularly circulated by official spokesmen in Saigon and

Washington failed to jibe with the constantly spiraling casualties in Southeast Asia, begetting "a credibility gap" of mounting proportion.

Later, the skepticism was validated when Robert McNamara confessed he and colleagues had been "terribly wrong" to propel the United States into the Vietnam quagmire.

Alas, naïve Americans "swallowed such facile concepts" as the domino theory, an ominous prediction that fizzled, Karnow wrote. Nearly everyone also bought another particular piece of garbage peddled by propagandists – that the people of Vietnam did not relate to death the same way the people of Peoria do, as if Asians were less attached to this life as opposed to the ostensible next one.

The genesis of Vietnam dated back to the 1940s, when independence movements began springing up against prior colonialist domination. Our Vietnam disaster evolved out of what Karnow called "bungles, misperceptions and squandered opportunities." In a country we hardly understood we found ourselves squared-off against what turned out to be a brilliant, zealous, inspirational, transcendent and, it turns out, entirely immortal adversary, revolutionary leader Ho Chi Minh, who had organized a band of guerillas, the Viet Minh. With the help of the scholar Vo Nguyen Giap, both idealists were determined to oust France, which had ruled Vietnam since the late 19th Century.

Ho put everything in perspective in 1946 when he warned a French functionary, "If we go to war, we will lose 10 men for every one you lose, but ultimately we will win." The French, and subsequently the Americans, ignored his prescient pronouncement. Nor did either of us understand the Vietnamese, who were less than primitive and had borrowed the essence of their civilization from the Chinese, which had occupied the land for millenniums. Even as some felt Ho could be co-opted, President Truman "blindly accepted" the French argument that Ho was subservient to Moscow and thus took the first step of propelling the U.S. into Southeast Asia by granting funds to the French to finance their effort to retrieve their possession.

Karnow wrote that Truman was rattled by Mao Tse-tung's conquest of China and North Korea's invasion of South Korea. Also, as most understand, he was under pressure to act tough to assuage conservative Republicans who assailed him as being soft on communism.

Historians weigh-in fairly collectively on what happened next. The Viet Minh defeated the French in 1954 in the battle of Dien Bien Phu. An international conference convened, rendering a decision to split Vietnam into two zones, ceding the north to the communists and the south to a government headed by Ngo Dinh Diem, at least until elections could be held to determine which faction would control the unified country.

With U.S. approval, Ngo reneged on the exercise before the disappointed communists triggered a rebellion against him.

Karnow had found Ngo to be "a peculiar choice" for the position. He was a textbook autocrat, cloistered in his palace, insisting on obedience to his decrees, a rambling cigarette-smoking autocrat who spoke in "singsong" French, elaborating endlessly on artifacts in his midst, a devout Catholic whose favoring of members of his own faith antagonized the Buddhist hierarchy. The intrigue didn't stop there.

Ngo also managed to alienate the Saigon upper crust, which he shunned as decadent. Well shoot, everything convened, leading to his murder, and that of his brother, at the hands of his own senior officers who blamed the expanding Vietcong threat on his practice of interfering with them.

In 2016 people remain hungry for insight on what it was that led the U.S. into war in Vietnam. Those of us now 70 and older, forever young-types who were so directly impacted by our government's insistence that our generation honor our obligation to go off and put out lives on the line for that effort, simply want to know the answers, without embellishment.

How DID this mess go down? Does anyone agree on any agreed-upon explanation?

Clearly, the best we can do is study the opinions of those who assert to know, weigh the logic of their views as we assess it. In that sense, I think any of us would be crazy to ignore Karnow's overview. In 1959, while visiting Saigon for *Time* magazine, Karnow reported on the deaths of two U.S. military advisors who had been killed at Bien Joa, a South Vietnamese army camp about 25 miles northeast of the city. They were Maj. Dale Buis and Master Sgt. Chester Ovnand – the two names that would head the chronological list of nearly 60,000 young Americans indelibly etched into the Wall -- the Vietnam Veterans Memorial in Washington.

Karnow had no idea at the time he had witnessed the opening salvo of a conflict that would drag on for 16 years, tormenting and dividing the United States "almost as grievously as the Civil War."

In this regard, Karnow asserts Henry Cabot Lodge, the U.S. ambassador in Saigon, encouraged them, with

Kennedy's approval, in the coup d'etat – but they did not, as has been alleged, anticipate the assassination.

Whatever the case, the episode was pivotal. Increasingly the conflict became America's to wage. Along came Lyndon Johnson, who Karnow described as being obsessed with his Great Society. LBJ inherited Vietnam as the conspirators "scrambled for the spoils."

Johnson sent the first U.S. combat detachments to Vietnam in early 1965 using as his authority the Tonkin Gulf Resolution that Congress had approved with little dissent. By late 1967, the number of Americans serving there approached half a million.

Commander William Westmoreland was convinced his superior sophisticated technology would overwhelm the communists. His barometer of success became the eventually debunked body counts. Karnow said Westmoreland's optimism was "an illusion." He found himself confronted by resilient adversaries who were prepared to make extraordinary sacrifices to attain victory. He was said to be baffled by their stamina and perseverance. After nearly a decade, support for the war began to dwindle at home even as LBJ reaffirmed to the nation that all was well. The Tet Offensive on Jan 31, 1968 punctured Johnson's rosy rhetoric, even as the enemy failed to spark uprisings throughout the south and took huge casualties. Glued to their TV sets, Americans were appalled by what they saw.

The public began to believe our massive expenditure of resources, both human and material, were not yielding positive results. Our death toll in the war was rising; campus protests were springing up across the land, exhausting Johnson who in March 1968 announced his intention to retire.

Along came Richard Nixon, who had concluded the war was depleting the nation's resources, leading to his pursuit of an ambiguous objective – "peace with honor."

Nixon and his aide Henry Kissinger devised an approach to extract the U.S. from the mess without staining our reputation. His plan was to withdraw our troops while stiffening the South Vietnamese troops to fight more effectively. Karnow says, "they fumbled."

As David Hackworth would acknowledge, while many of the South Vietnamese troops were courageous, they could not operate under incompetent, corrupted officers who owed their promotions to their links to South Vietnams' President Nguyen Van Thieu.

His patience growing thin, Nixon ordered an incursion into adjacent Cambodia so smash enemy sanctuaries, igniting a new domestic upheaval that included the Kent State shootings in May 1970, leaving Nixon "beleaguered, frustrated and furious." Nixon went so far as to order partisan thugs Howard Hunt, Gordon Liddy and other twisted patriots to monitor his antiwar opponents, a gambit that would contribute to the Watergate scandal, which emerged from a break-in at a Washington area office and apartment complex that had direct ties to the pursuit of possible Daniel Ellsberg vulnerabilities.

In 1973 a ceasefire was signed between the United States and North Vietnam, against the wishes of Thieu. Two years later, North Vietnam and the Viet Cong coordinated attacks on South Vietnam. By 1976, Vietnam was reunified as the Socialist Republic of Vietnam; Saigon was renamed Ho Chi Minh City. In July of 1995, Vietnam and the U.S. normalized diplomatic relations.

In San Francisco, Vietnam War veteran and author of **In Pharaoh's Army** Tobias Wolff was not surprised by the fall of Saigon or of Vietnam itself, "Because the war had already been lost by the time I got there in the spring of 1967," he wrote in *Time magazine*.

"The suspicion that this was so came upon me not as a thought but as a deepening unease at the way we treated the Vietnamese and the way they treated one another." Everywhere he went, he saw Americans "raining contempt" on Vietnamese." It was obvious to him that we couldn't win the war by simple force of arms, "that the real battle was for the trust and loyalty of the common man." Yet we slapped people around, trashed villages, shouted curses from our jeeps defining ourselves as the enemy and thereby handed more power and legitimacy to the people we had to beat."

Wolff found the South Vietnamese soldiers to be even worse than we were. "Their army suffered from a corruption so pervasive and timeworn that it had become institutionalized; officers didn't get paid enough money to live on because it was assumed they'd make up for the rest by graft. Their soldiers went into the field, not to fight but to oppress." Even before 1967, he found the South Vietnamese had suffered "a catastrophic moral collapse. Same with the army.

The Tet offensive in 1968 "brought to a boil" all the bitterness our soldiers felt toward the Vietnamese people, unable to believe how such a massive operation could have been carried out without their knowledge and complicity. "After the first shock passed, we opened the gates of hell on that country, and we didn't spend much time making distinctions between enemies and friends…. In this way we taught the people – and taught ourselves, once and for all – that we didn't love them and wouldn't protect them, and that we were prepared to kill them all to save ourselves."

Wolff wrote that deep fissures remain within the generation affected by the war. "Whether you went or not, that war put a crack in you because of the impossibility of finding an untainted response to it. If you protested the war, you couldn't help worrying about the bafflement and pain you were causing those in danger, and their families. How did you make peace with the fact that, however unintentionally, you were encouraging a hard, often murderous enemy who was doing his best to kill boys you'd grown up with. If you went, you had to notice that the government we were trying to save wasn't worth saving, and the people were generally uninterested in our brand of help. In time you might even come to see them as the enemy. Where did that leave you?"

Lessons Learned/Unlearned

McGeorge Bundy, National Security Advisor to Presidents Kennedy and Johnson: "Determine ahead of time the importance of a foreign endeavor."

Clark Clifford, Defense secretary in Johnson Administration. "U.S. should not commit troops unless national security is threatened."

J. William Fulbright, Senate Foreign Relations Committee Chairman in Johnson and Nixon administration. "America's macho policy toward the Soviet Union and Nicaragua says the U.S. has not learned anything from Vietnam.

Eugene McCarthy, U.S. Senator from Minnesota challenged LBJ in 1968, ran unsuccessfully for president in 1972 and 1976, "Lesson of Vietnam is to not let military planners make foreign policy."

Robert McNamara, Defense Secretary in Kennedy and Johnson administrations. Refused to discuss Vietnam publicly until subpoenaed in Westmoreland-CBS libel suit. Said that by 1965 of 1966, he did not believe war could be won. *Time* magazine in April 1995 reported that McNamara belatedly confessed his handling of the Vietnam War had been "terribly wrong." McNamara's book, **In Retrospect** has a chapter on lessons learned in the war. If America had learned lessons, he said he would not have written the book. In interviews at the time of its publication in 1995, he pointed to the dangers of underestimating nationalism, or faulty evaluations, of asking the military to achieve more than weapons can deliver.

Dean Rusk, Secretary of State in Kennedy and Johnson administrations. Says American involvement in Vietnam showed Soviets that U.S. wouldn't back down on commitments. But says he underestimated resolve of North Vietnamese and overestimated patience of Americans with war.

Maxwell Taylor was the U.S. ambassador to Vietnam. In retrospect, he said U.S, should have officially declared war and also should have barred television cameras.

Ho Chi Minh 1946: "Kill 10 of our men and we will kill one of yours. In the end, it is you who will tire."

John F. Kennedy 1963: "In the final analysis it is their war. We can help them ... but they have to win it, the people of Vietnam."

Members of the military argue that they were asked to do the impossible: fight a limited war in a strange land against native guerillas.

Harry Summers was one prominent voice speaking in their behalf. He was an infantry officer who became a teacher at U.S Army War College.

He asserts the North Vietnamese followed the principles of war almost to the letter, but the Americans violated every one of them.

He traced the military's mistakes to its role in the post-nuclear age, argued military leaders should have forced civilian leaders to clearly define their military objectives. Instead he says goals were shifted as the domestic political situation changed.

Troops spent too much time skirmishing with Viet Cong guerillas, he said. Trying to pacify villages to win hearts and minds was also a bad idea in his opinion.

Instead, the military should have been pursuing "traditional objectives" such as engaging large enemy large enemy units, capturing territory and cutting off enemy lines.

"One of the things that Vietnam brought home to us is the un-quantifiable dimension of war: The effect of will and determination. Because, by any quantifiable measurement the U.S. should have won the war the day we got into it." Instead, he said, it was U.S. determination that flagged. Over the years, that will to fight was tested in Lebanon and Nicaraguan jungles against rebels.

"Anything that looks like it may be a slippery slope into something like Vietnam is avoided, even though Congress is more gung-ho for defensive and anti-Soviet policies than they were, say 10 years ago," wrote Brookings Institution scholar Richard Betts in 1985. "The public wants to be strong, but they don't want to get involved in questionable bloody messy wars that could lead to an indecisive result like Vietnam."

Is it time for the United States to confess that the Vietnam War was a major mistake?
(The Philadelphia Inquirer Review & Opinion section, April 28, 1985)
"I've thought so since 1973," says Pete Zastrow, one of four national coordinators of Vietnam Veterans Against the War. "Of course it's time. We were fighting the wrong people in the wrong place at the wrong time."
Jack Stevens, Michigan State Commander of the Veterans of Foreign Wars disagrees. "The Vietnamese asked us for help, and a lot of us thought that if we didn't stop Communists they would go all the way."
Mary Stout, a former Army nurse who was president of the Vietnam Veterans of America: "It comes to a personal issue whether we can deal with our country being wrong, and ourselves being right. I feel I did what my country asked me to do, but whether we should have been there to begin with, that's a personal issue that everyone has to answer. Many Vietnam veterans will acknowledge the importance of the anti-war movement in drawing attention to what was going on, to stop the killing. But it's painful because the anti-war activists targeted the returning vets."
Ron Kovic, author of **Born on the Fourth of July**: "The most positive aspect of the movement was that they said the war was wrong. It was hurting our country and the people of Vietnam. The movement saved lives. Those that protested against the war were courageous. "
Time magazine presented the following perspectives in one of its anniversary of the end of the war issues:

The war was not even about Vietnam. It was a protracted battle of the Cold War, fought to block the extension of communist power in Asia. "The remarkable thing about the American involvement in Vietnam is that was not remarkable then." The war reflected a mainstream consensus that if South Vietnam fell to communism, then other dominos like Thailand, Malaysia and Indonesia could be next.

Former Secretary of State John Foster Dulles was determined to keep the French from returning their holdings over to Ho Chi Minh. His successors believed that they were following the lessons of WW II when they committed American troops to fight in Vietnam.

By challenging Chinese and Soviet aggression in Vietnam, they hoped to head off WW III. The war was afflicted with contradictions because it was fought in the midst of a cold war.

"On the one hand, American leaders assumed they had to fight: but at the same time, the U.S. had to fight within tight, self-set limits, fearful that using too much force would prompt Chinese intervention."

Johnson committed 500,000 troops but was unwilling to invade North Vietnam, blockade its coasts or bomb close to its border with China.

In his memoirs, McGeorge Bundy wrote that America's plan was to "grind up the other guy's army until he would presumably not take it anymore, and then we would get a political settlement. I thought North Vietnam would reach a point when it would be unwilling to continue making those terrible sacrifices" and negotiate a settlement.

As the magazine reported, that point never arrived.

The U.S was on the strategic defensive for the entire war. The Americans were not allowed to march north to face the enemy while the North kept the initiative, choosing when to attach and when to lie low and rebuild its strength. More than one million North Vietnamese troops were killed until the U.S. negotiated its own withdrawal in 1973. In his book, McNamara recalled, "We thought there was considerable evidence China intended to extend its hegemony across Southeast Asia and perhaps beyond. I'm not at all sure now."

Walt Rostow, special assistant to Johnson: "This was a war about balance of power in all of Southeast Asia. We lost the battle in Vietnam, but we won the war in Southeast Asia."

The crucial question becomes: did the Vietnam War, tragic as it was, provide the time and security from the communist threat for Asia to develop its present independence and booming free-market prosperity?

Let future historians wrestle with that question.

Notes From a Reporter's Notebook

Tom Finarelli of Hanover Township, Pennsylvania served during the war. "No question, I'd go again, because I believe in the American way," he told this reporter in 1985 at the time of the 10-year anniversary of the end of the war. "But I wouldn't want my kids or anyone else's kids to have to go through that. You're talking nightmares. I don't think people really know how we lived over there. It was a living hell, a crazy conflict. It wasn't like a real war because the people we were trying to help hated us. I'm talking the South Vietnamese themselves."

Jim Roxby, a veteran from the Wilkes-Barre, PA area, said Vietnam was an experience from which he would never recover. "I got my butt kicked because of some stupid asshole back here in the States making money off the war and wasting lives," he told me. "For me, the war won't end, not unless the great wrong is rectified and made right. It was all a big lie. If we'd killed as many Viet Cong as we said we did China would be empty today. I feel betrayed by the American public. They've turned a deaf ear to us, even while we're still dropping dead at as quick a rate as we did over there.'

(I met Tom and Jim while working as a newspaper reporter on a series of articles published on the occasion of the 10-year anniversary of the fall of Saigon. Jim and I became friends, drinking buddies, puffin' pals and close confidants. In Vietnam, he served on a large truck that carried tanks of lethal defoliant, Agent Orange. He told me that he and his buddies would spray one another with the chemical, just for fun. His arms were mangled, distorted, hugely out of proportion. He said he could predict on coming storms just from the way his body felt. This brave soul did all he could to remain, upbeat and guard his pervasive cynicism. (Jim Roxby eventually died from his wartime exposures.)

Campaigns Break Truce That Let America Move Beyond Vietnam
By *Detroit News* columnist Nolan Finley
Americans called a truce on the issue of Vietnam 30 years ago, agreeing to patch that ragged tear and move on.
The resolution was informal and gradual. Like the war itself, the domestic struggle drifted to an end without a defeat or victory. The combatants wearied of the fight, got on with their post-war lives and shrugged off any lingering hard feelings.

Eventually, as the reasons for waging the war became more universally discredited, the choices individuals made became more accepted.

Some went, many didn't. The principle that there was no dishonor in either decision was validated in 1992 with the election of Bill Clinton. Clinton pursued the national pastime of draft avoidance with as much vigor as any young man of his generation, and yet voters awarded him the presidency.

But now, in the midst of another war that is bitterly dividing the country, the Vietnam truce is being broken for political gain.

Those who never faced the wrenching choices of Vietnam are busy heaping scorn on those who did. The collective investigative might of the American media is focused on determining who pulled strings, who forged documents, who ducked their duty, who lied about where they were and what they did.

We are as stuck in the 1960s as a tired, classic rock station. If you were young in that era, particular if you were a young man who had your future mapped by a number drawn from a fishbowl, it's hard to muster any self-righteousness, any sense of outrage about the Vietnam War record of either George W. Bush or John Kerry.

Because you know how things worked then. Plenty of guys worked every angle to first avoid service but failing that to stay out of the jungle. Marriage, college, conscience, caffeine, sexual ambiguity -- anything that might get the draft board to look elsewhere for a recruit.

Some, like Bush, chose the National Guard or enlisted before the draft notice came in hopes of getting a more favorable placement in Germany, South Korea or stateside.

Others did go to Vietnam and, like Kerry, came home to virulently oppose the war, a choice condemned as harmful to those still fighting.

There is no high ground to claim. There was too much confusion then, too much moral chaos.

The only way we got beyond it was to forget, if not forgive.

But the presidential campaigns won't allow the approach that worked so well for three decades to continue.

Kerry chose to base his bid on his Vietnam heroism, leaving audiences like the one at the Detroit Economic Club last week with a military salute, as if he'd spent his career as a general rather than lackluster junior senator.

Bush backers responded with a vicious attack to tarnish Kerry's medals and opened the door for the president's enemies to muck about in his own murky military files.

America won't be better for this. Touching old hurts is rarely a good idea and is particularly dangerous at a time when there's again so much hatred between the political camps.

Iraq is the war that matters today. Both these men have records in the Iraq War that can be measured. Perhaps that's why they'd prefer to re-fight Vietnam.

Random Newspaper Pieces/Letters to Editor
Clarkston Reminder – 1989
Karen A. Bostwick wrote the editors to comment on an article, *"A battle of words on Vietnam, Korea."*
"As a woman who grew up in the Vietnam era and as one involved in veteran's issues, I cannot believe a seemingly intelligent man would easily reveal his biased opinion against Vietnam veterans, especially through name calling

and such absurd general statements as made in the writer's remarks.

"First of all, to summarize "their greatest problem was the Vietnamese jungle," is, if an attempt to explain the complex situation of the entire war, a truly absurd statement. A great many things were involved in the war, the government, and our society at the time. And to remark further that "you can't be goofing off or intoxicated on drugs or alcohol" does an even greater disservice to those young men who, with honor, integrity, did their utmost to serve with the best of their ability.

Karen wrote, "Sixty-six-percent of those who served in Vietnam volunteered for the service. I, for one, do not believe they did so as "an easy way to make money and a big joke." Perhaps they did know what to expect. But I doubt those like the writer who served in Korea did either. For him to resort to name calling fellow veterans and state he was "sick and tired of Vietnam vets playing on the sympathy of the general public" should be considered a general affront to anyone involved in the concerns of veterans today. Respect, consideration and benefits are guaranteed to veterans by the government of this country to any and all who served honorably.

Karen wrote she hoped the Korea vet would agree that war does not work for humanity.

She expressed hope all veterans will continue to speak out, talk about their wars, not put them in the past and forget about them.

"They might continue to 'cry' for the wars and injustices of humanity and work towards improving life for all this planet. It is a continuing process to work out good and bad and right and wrong. Maybe we can work it all out and live as one. But unfair judgments an name calling of 'their war' and 'our war' just won't help anything.

Karen lauded Vietnam vets for organizing "to help change things for the world for the better."

Kim Kozlowski, writing in *The Detroit News* on April 30, 2000 – 25 years after the fall of Saigon.

"Everyone has their own personal Vietnam. It wasn't just the men and women who traipsed through the Vietnamese jungles, rifles strapped on their shoulders, fear racing through their minds. Nor was it just the loved ones left behind. Vietnam touched the lives of everyone who lived through the period of history that transformed our society into one that is a little less innocent and a lot more cynical.'

Detroit News writer Jodi Cohen:

There were those who fought a war trying to stop the war. They rallied for peace, dodged the draft and inspired the songwriters of their generation.

When Saigon fell, anti-war activist Tom Weisskopf did not feel joy or want to say, "I told you so."

Instead he viewed it as the final sad chapter in a war that Americans had no business fighting. "My feeling was one of sadness for 10 years of tremendous loss of lives and wasted energy and money," he told *Detroit News* writer Jodi Cohen.

"It should have been obvious from the beginning that it would have ended like this." Weisskopf became an economics professor at The University of Michigan. During the war, as a student at Harvard University, he organized draft resisters, participated in anti-war demonstrations and wrote articles on the subject. He was arrested four times when police tried to break up protests. He said the handwriting was on the wall, long before the fall of Saigon.

"It was just a question of when it would happen. To me, the most significant time was 1968-1970, when the anti-war movement really had its biggest impact in restraining the U.S. and beginning to turn things around."

He depicted the era historically unique. "The biggest thing was a sense of being part of a much larger movement that could have an impact on public affairs. There was a real electricity in the air and a sense that a great many people were sharing a vision and understanding. That was something really terrific, really impressive really memorable. It's something I don't know if we will ever see again."

The Civil War.
The Great Depression.
The Vietnam War.
To former Army Secretary John Marsh, those are the three great events – great turning points – in American history.

"We were embarrassed and we wanted to get away from it," said Sydney Schanberg who covered the war for *The New York Times* from 1970-75. "But we didn't know how. We weren't used to losing. We ran away from those we said we cared about, and made villains of soldiers."

The names of Vietnam's victims etched into the Memorial, said Pulitzer Prize-winning historian Stanley Karnow, "Bear witness to the end of America's absolute confidence in its moral exclusivity, its military invincibility, its manifest destiny."

The war was a big cataclysm in transforming the idealism of the Kennedy years into bitterness, Stuart Rochester told *Gannett News Service* writer John Omicinski.
"It's a good question whether we ever again will experience the illusion of being able to change things."

President Gerald Ford's biographer, James Cannon – "I'm not sure the American public will ever support a war if they have to watch it on TV. War is just too dreadful."
In an interview with *The Detroit News* in 2000, Ford suggested America became enmeshed in the Vietnam War not to contain communism but to placate France whose troops were thrown out of Southeast Asia in 1954.
Ford recalled going to Saigon in 1953 and being assured by the French they would win the war with communism and nationalist forces led by Ho Chi Minh.
"Well, they got their fanny kicked out. I can't help but feel to sort of help the French image following their defeat we mad the first gestures in Vietnam as an effort to salvage something where they failed."

Bob Kerrey, War Hero
By John McCain
(Published in *The Wall Street Journal*)
For a long time many Americans thought the Vietnam War was a bad war. The citizen soldiers who defeated the fascists in Europe and the Pacific were ennobled by their service in a good war. Vietnam veterans fighting communists were not.

In a good war mistakes are seldom made. No one lies. Breakdowns in discipline that lead to atrocities never occur. The righteousness of the cause sanctifies the experience of all who fought in it. In a bad war everyone lies. Innocents are slaughtered. Villages are destroyed to save them. Combatants are corrupted. Casualties in a good war are martyrs. In a bad war they are the wages of sin. But the notion, as a veteran of any war can attest, is simplistic and completely wrong.

All wars occasion much heroism and nobility, but they all have their corruptions, which is what makes war a thing worth avoiding if possible. I hated my enemies even before they held me captive because hate sustained me in my devotion to their complete destruction and helped me overcome the virtuous human impulse to recoiled in disgust from what had to be done by my hands. I dropped many bombs in Vietnam, and wish I could say that they only destroyed military targets. But surely non-combatants were among the casualties.

The combatant, who may be a righteous, God-fearing, lovely human being, must become inhumane day after day if he is to do what his country has asked him to do. The injunction to love all as we would be loved is the first casualty of war, any war. Wars are that awful, and anyone who tells you otherwise is a fool or a fraud.

That does not mean that we should forget our humanity. Our experience does not absolve us of our moral obligations, but they can be very hard to keep, given the extraordinarily difficult and conflicting expectations imposed on us: to kill and be good.

Good men, heroes, make mistakes. Sometimes those mistakes have the most terrible consequences imaginable. We should not be spared criticism for them, but it is unlikely that the judgments made by others will be as severe as our own regret.

My friend, Bob Kerrey, made a mistake in Vietnam. He was sent into a free-fire zone to kill for his country, and he helped kill the wrong people. Those who now judge him must follow the dictates of their conscience. But unless you too have been to war, please be careful not to form your judgment of him on your understanding of what constitutes a war hero. They are not the Hollywood copy you might expect.

Bob received a Bronze Star for his action that night. He would be the first to agree that his conduct, no matter how unintentional, did not merit commendation. But one month later, his conduct on another night won him the decoration our country bestows on only her greatest heroes. And were you to read the citation that accompanied his Medal of Honor, you would know beyond a doubt he earned it.

When he came home from Vietnam, like many others, Bob Kerrey tried to bury his dead. He did not want to remember, much less talk about, a lot of his experiences, especially his mistakes.

But there are ghosts you cannot bury, like our shame over those occasions when circumstances conspired with our own weakness to make an awful experience worse. If the fact that he recovered his humanity, that he felt remorse that he sacrificed even more for his country does not strike some as adequate compensation for his mistake, it is enough for his salvation, and a harder task than most can imagine. That's a war hero, folks, a sinner redeemed by his sacrifice for a cause greater than his self-interest. That's Bob Kerrey, my friend and hero.

The Consequence of War

By James Webb

(Published in *The Wall Street Journal* April 27, 2001)

The Vietnamese government is happy to trot out witnesses from the supposed atrocity conducted by Bob Kerrey's Navy SEALs at Thanh Phong. It is doubtful that they would be so cooperative if questions were asked about Communist killings in places such as My Loc.

In April 1969, the Marine rifle company to which I was assigned was operating the An Hoa Basin of Vietnam, west and south of Danang. In addition to our routine of long-range combat patrols and defensive positions along a vital and heavily contested road, it was decided that we would provide security for a "town meeting" hosted by the South Vietnamese government's district chief, who had been criticized for living in the distant and more secure confines of Danang. Over the space of a few days, visits were made to nearby hamlets, where 30 delegates were chosen to attend the meeting. After that, the district chief and his senior aide were brought in on the morning convoy."

And so began James Webb's account of this effort, which was quickly interrupted by a Vietcong attack that left nearly two dozen participants either dead or horribly wounded. Webb recalled encountering one victim, a woman sitting motionless against a wall, he face stunned and her dark eyes piercing, "untouched except for a small, square hole in her forehead."

By the next day, the incident was over, "a little piece of history in the long and ugly journey of a combat tour." Webb wrote that in reflecting on this episode, he realized civilians have a terrible time in any war zone. In a guerilla war, the support or control of the local population, rather than the conquest of territory, is the ultimate objective.

"Civilians become enmeshed in the actual fighting, inseparable from it."

The smallest dynamics reveal the complicated nature of trying to assess such moments. Civilians fight among themselves for political dominance of a local area, Webb wrote. They form an infrastructure and subtly support one side or the other when it moves through their village. As battles engulf their environment, they endure great suffering. Emotions overcome logic. Troops snap. Villagers of My Loc were killed by the Vietcong for having met with a South Vietnamese government official, giving legitimacy to his authority.

Had an American authorized a similar slaughter, he would have been court-martialed. "This distinction was basic to our policy in Vietnam," Webb wrote, adding that the question of how history will judge our involvement in Vietnam remains in play, with a big part of that issue being to continue to demean the American sacrifices in that war. His comments came in response to the dissection of American mishaps, also known as atrocities and massacres. These reappraisals occurred in direct response to reports Bob Kerrey was involved in war scenarios that may have involved less-than valorous conduct.

"Aggressive reporters have played 'gotcha' with every Kerrey statement," he proclaimed. Webb pointed out that such parsing brings back anger for many who went through extensive combat in Vietnam. Their concern derives from memories "not of the war but of the condescending arrogance directed at them upon their return, principally by people in their own age group who had risked nothing and yet microscopically judged every action of those who had risked nothing and often lost a great deal."

Webb sought to establish perspective. Combat in guerilla war, he wrote, requires constant moral judgments amid constant pressure, zero sleep, no second chances. "Were we perfect? No. Were we worse than Americans in other wars, or our enemies in this one? Hardly."

Letter to Editor, *The Wall Street Journal*
From John C. Webb, Westerville, Ohio
James Webb raises some good points in his article on the history of Vietnam ("History Proves Vietnam Victors Wrong") but he succumbs to some selective amnesia of his own when he faults Hanoi for "failing to uphold its promise of internationally supervised free elections" in the 1973 Paris Peace Accords. He should recall that it was the South Vietnamese government, with the support of the U.S. that refused to participate in the internationally supervised free elections scheduled for 1956 by the 1954 Geneva Peace Accords.
President Eisenhower admitted in his memoirs: "I have never talked or corresponded with a person knowledgeable in Indochina affairs who did not agree that had elections been held as of the time of the fighting, possibly 80% of the population would have voted for the Communist Ho Chi Minh as its leader rather than Chief of State Bao Dai (**Mandate for Change: 1953-1856**, Doubleday, 1963, page 372.)
The release of The Pentagon Papers confirmed U.S. support for Ngo Dihh Diem was designed to prevent a Communist victory that was likely in Vietnam-wide elections after Diem replaced Bao Dai.

Neil Sheehan is author of the acclaimed work, **A Bright Shining Lie: John Paul Vann and America in Vietnam**,

(Random House) an award-winning biography by a reporter who had covered Vietnam in the rice paddies and at The Pentagon.

Sheehan cited an era of "boundless self-confidence" that led us to war.

The biographer met his subject, a 38-year-old lieutenant colonel John Paul Vann in 1962. Sheehan had become a United Press International correspondent in Saigon, his first job out of the U.S. Army.

Sheehan arrived as a patriot but like others realized the South Vietnamese and their American patrons were losing the war, contrary to the official U.S. version of events. In the battlefield, reporters encountered Vann, a courageous warrior with a penchant for the truth. Sheehan said, "He'd say, 'The war is too important to bullshit about. You've got to tell the truth."

Under another newspaper's employment, Sheehan found himself in the mid-'60s back in the theater of war, frightened and concerned.

"The country that we were supposed to be saving, we suddenly began to bomb, blast and burn apart," he said. "And this people we were supposed to be helping, we started to victimize. The corridors of the province hospitals would be stacked with civilian war-wounded, and the Americans weren't interested."

Revised and updated in 2006, Gwynne Dyer's book, **Future:Tense (The Coming World Order)** focused primarily on America's war in Iraq. In that context, the author frequently alluded to our Vietnam experience, establishing parallels, consitencies and larger instructions. He placed into context the plans and conduct of American political military and foreign policy, as established by our elites, as occurring around the assumption the world is unchanged, that it is as it has been for centuries – a permanent military theatre of conflict in which large dominant countries contend forever for what Dyer called "superiority."

Rather than deferring to international institutions and anointing as preferable a spirit of cooperation between the great powers – perceived by Neo Cons as transient and unreliable guarantees of safety – he said power to them is the only permanent reality.

Dyer questioned their strategic acumen, saying they had "a grossly inflated notion" of the effectiveness of American military power, "and an astounding ignorance about how the rest of the world would respond to an American offer-you-cannot-refuse of benevolent hegemony."

He recalled Nixon being elected in late 1968 on a promise to end the Vietnam War, accompanied by a promise that he would do so without the appearance of a humiliating defeat for American military power.

Nixon's quest for "that elusive objective" took almost five years, during which he and Kissinger "bombed North Vietnam flat" and engineered the invasion of Cambodia, incurring two-thirds of all of the American casualties suffered in Vietnam – all just to create a 'decent interval' between the American withdrawal and the subsequent collapse, so that American military power and political prestige did not suffer a public defeat.

Dyer expressed concern that "a smiliar pattern of behaviour will prevail in Iraq,"

Born in Newfoundland, enlightened in the Canadian military and academia, the author's detailed historical take on America's incursion into Iraq and the entire Middle

East is both fascinating and chilling as it relates to the world "going forward."

His sense of what the rest of the twenty-first century holds for all of us is worthy of consideration and serious contemplation.

Our most important shared national undertaking will be to come to terms with the fact the good-old U.S.A. is basically one more country on the block.

Big and powerful? Yes.

Indispensible? Maybe not.

Dominant in military power? Probably.

Only problem is, he asserts, our power can only be used against pip-squeaks, that war with any serious opponent would create so many casualties that the U.S. public would not countenance the arrangement.

Dyer suggests how well or badly America copes with the change in our perceived dominance of all world order will be determined in the next 50 years. Seeing ourselves as the cradle of democracy and also "the head office" of the perfect economic system, free-market capitalism, are cited as "illusions.'

Letting go of them will be painful, he writes, adding "There are powerful interests in Washington and elsewhere that will fight hard to keep them alive. The may not win, but if they do, Iraq will just be the first stage in a very rough ride."

Epilogue

In wrapping up this journey into the past, I've tried to construct a treatise for my sons and others from their generation, a warning of sorts to them.

I did not set out to craft a conclusive account of the war. Instead, I sought to speak directly to my sons, knowing they would factor in my biases as they pondered my appraisal of the matter.

As a young man I saw the American War in Vietnam as pure fabrication, a gigantic gesture of deceit bestowed by our government on young men of my age group. We were asked to go off to fight, kill and die for what amounted to sheer subterfuge, a falsehood of galactic significance. Seriously singed by it, my impetus now is to inform those who follow that government can and will mislead their citizenry, to whatever end.

Therefore my message to my sons and others is some measure of skepticism should accompany the digestion of all stated policies. Especially when your own life is on the line.

For me, Vietnam was flat-out excruciation an acutely painful and prolonged event that came down on me like it did on everyone else my age – like a ton of bricks.

Because we were coming of age as our government divined this matter as ours, we accepted it, gained definition from how we each navigated our responsibility to comply implicitly branding ourselves from that time on. Those who survived the war, at home or 7,000-miles from here in The Mekong Delta, have experienced full lives in the intervening decades. We've enjoyed the freedom some ostensibly fought for, gained a better understanding of the war that shaped our lives. Along the way I imagine many of us also determined to make good on the promises we made to ourselves along the way.

My deal to myself was to channel the Vietnam angst that welled-up deeply in me into some measure of possible redemption, a story perhaps, a method I could utilize to convey lessons learned to my most heartfelt sources – Garrett and Fraser.

I share a story lacking in valor, heroism or distinction -- a rather inglorious account of cowardice in the guise of protest, packaged in a plain brown wrapper. I know they can handle the ignobility.

In examining the minor role I played in our war in Vietnam I've had to confront the decisions I made at the time against the backdrop of the appreciation I've gained for the larger sacrifices of others from my generation. Big picture, I was small potatoes.

Compared to multiple burdens imposed upon the men in the platoon depicted in Tim O'Brien's classic novel, **The Things They Carried**, what I did as the long Vietnam War wore on was the equivalent of shooting baskets by myself on a playground in the Hollywood Hills.

As inconsequential as my life was at the time compared to the experiences of soldiers that served in the war, I also recognize the potential of my story to serve as a useful mosaic from within which to derive greater understanding of a troubled era.

I've laid it out because it is "a" story from the Vietnam War years, one man's gaze into what most now regard as an enormous national tragedy.

In this context, I believe anyone's story is equally valid and worthy of consideration to the extent it offers an honest human perspective to larger events.

Fifty-years after the conclusion of our involvement in Vietnam, "my story" now conveys as a deeply felt sense of obligation to honor our veterans, all who served.

Way older now, recently enriched, I am compelled to draw attention to those who made epic sacrifices; the millions of Vietnamese people we killed; the hundreds of thousands of us who took our opposition to the war to the streets, put our career ascent on hold in order to prioritize our actions to do what we could to change its trajectory, help convince those running the show to draw back from what we had come to believe was an unworthy crusade.

All parties deserve time in the sun.

Credits

Several empathetic individuals contributed their skill and intellect to helping me overcome a lifelong affliction with failing to get to the point.

Having heard a large concortium of editors over the decades accuse me of dancing around the outer edge of topics rather than diving right in, I wasn't surprised to have to endure similar assaults on my craftsmanship as I shopped this work to erudite friends willing to indulge the bilge.

A few of them in particular deserve specific atta-boys and atta-girls.

Demonstrating a magic touch, Laurin Gracy-Parker rescued the Preface from the realm of pure gobble-dee-gook, causing my words to actually flow when in their original iteration they were more inclined to coalesce around the dispensary.

Then, Professor Richard Rosenbaum took on Chapter One, draining several red ink pens in a one-month overhaul of this writer's messy melange of reckless rhetoric, imbecilic inference and rampantly inchoate bluster.

Without their input I would still be staring at this content on my computer screen rather than finalizing it tonight. Only they know what I know – they cleaned up many a mendacity, saved a treatise visited wonderment upon it.

Bonafide bookworms Fred Bailey, Bob Arnold, John Marshall, Vince Rakestraw, Mike Smith, Rocky Saxbe and Jodi Switalski embraced early segments, responded with encouraging words, offered to help finance pending carpel tunnel surgery. Even if they hadn't liked what they saw I probably would have kept writing; as it was, their positive feedback lifted my wings, made them flap at least a couple of times.

Final thanks extend to the late-David Hackworth for being the baddest stud in the Delta, and for confirming what I always suspected to be "the truth" about The American War in Vietnam, if such truth even exists.

Above and beyond his amazing example, I gained the ultimate inspiration to park my ass in a chair for a year and write this book from the incredible sacrifices of the American soldiers who served in this most controversial of all wars, who fought an ambiguous enemy with incalculable courage.

David Trout Pomeroy
Waterford, Michigan 2016

About The Writer

David Trout Pomeroy was born in Detroit in 1945. He attended public schools in suburban Birmingham and earned a bachelor's degree in political science from Alderson-Broaddus University. After working as an advanceman on a U.S. Senate campaign he embraced the war protest movement with zeal.

For many years, he resided in Arizona and California until the cleansing impact of the American Bicentennial in 1976 washed away the final residue of his dissent, rendering him a centrist taking up permanent residence in Michigan.

He became a newspaper reporter, columnist, author and creative director in the automotive training industry before his retirement.

He is married to Bonita Pomeroy. They are parents of grown sons, Garrett and Fraser II and have two grandchildren. They reside in Waterford.

www.ingramcontent.com/pod-product-compliance
Lightning Source LLC
Chambersburg PA
CBHW061956280526
45787CB00005B/1887